SACRED LIGHT
SPIRIT EAGLE

My Visionary Life and Near Death Experience

To Emma —
Enjoy my book!

by

CRISTAEL ANN BENGTSON

Cover Photograph: Glorieta Mesa by Arnold Woodworth

Author's Photo by Mary Rose Wright

ISBN: 1477475311

ISBN 13: 9781477475317

Library of Congress Control Number: 2012908921
CreateSpace, North Charleston, SC

To my son Arnold
Your support gave me the courage to
turn myself into a writer.

So should you view all the fleeting world
A star at dawning, a bubble on a stream
A flash of lightning in a summer cloud
A flickering candle, a phantom, and a dream

THE DIAMOND SUTRA

CHAPTER 1

It was a warm and sunny California morning, and I was down in bed with a case of the flu. But this was like no flu bug I'd ever had before. Fever burned in me, white hot, turning the touch of bedsheets into torment. Agonizing muscle spasms tore through me, arching my back as I kept crying out with pain. I kept on trying to dive down deep into my subconscious mind, down into an inner refuge where all my pain would go away.

A great blackness began to rise up all around me like a midnight tide, until I was submerged in an ocean of darkness. I found myself rising up out of my body, floating up into a vast dark place, into a world that was no world, into a place that had no where, no when. There was only the blackness of the void. Not like outer space, with its limitless stars and galaxies, but an absolute darkness where there was nothing at all.

I began moving through that endless blackness, and I cried out into the silence, Where am I? Where is this place? Please tell me where I am! I wanted to cry, but I could not shed a single tear. I looked all around me, and then I looked down, and my head began to spin as I realized I was seated cross-legged on nothing at all. I squeezed my eyes shut so I wouldn't have to look at the endless black emptiness below me.

Then I saw a full color, three-dimensional picture of myself, seated on a flying carpet. Startled, I opened my eyes. And there I was, just like Aladdin, zipping along on a real flying carpet that had woven stripes of red and blue and purple and yellow and green and gold. I began to feel a flow of peace, and excitement started bubbling up inside me. I had the feeling that I was exploring a great unknown.

I sensed my mother's presence, just behind my right shoulder, and I felt rather than heard her voice. "Wouldn't you like to come up here? We would like so much for you to come up here and be with us."

This is odd, I thought. What is Mother doing here? I turned my head and looked all around, but there was nothing there. No mother. No distant horizon, no stars, no markers of any kind. Just black on black.

I kept on staring into the blackness, and I began to discern hundreds, and then thousands, of still and silent human figures. They glowed a dim blue-gray against the blackness, and all of them were seated with their legs pulled up against their chests. Bald blue heads with insane and chilling fixed eyes stared straight ahead. One head turned, and I looked straight into the depths of a dead eye. That eye came to life as a glare of venomous hate glanced through me.

And I saw a flash from my past, back when I was a student at the University of New Mexico. It was the sixties, and drugs were raging throughout the educational system with the ferocity of a forest fire.

I was walking through the Student Union Building, heading toward the side door when I saw a group of young hippies seated on the stairs that led up to the SUB offices. They were all dressed in tie-dyed t-shirts. The girls all had long hair, some braided, some simply hanging down their backs, and the young man sitting in the center of the group had on jeans and a flat-top, brown suede hat with a wide brim.

All of them looked at me with drugged hostility as I went by them. The dark eyes of the young man stared at me with an unblinking hatred that seared through the air of the hallway as I walked out the door.

And now I watched as those emaciated, blue-headed, frozen souls flowed on by me, moving in absolute silence, fading into a far off darkness.

Just as those menacing figures disappeared off in the distance, my carpet of many colors slowed and came to a halt. I found myself looking up at an immense wrought-iron work of art, shaped like a morning glory. There were huge black petals all around a cavernous opening that was bigger than the Super Dome. Bigger than the great pyramids of Egypt. Bigger than just about anything on Earth.

My magic carpet floated closer and closer, moving into the very center of that immense black flower. I felt infinitely small as I went gliding through that opening, on into a huge cavern where a thick, black velvet darkness brushed against me.

And then I was inside a vast cathedral that had all the lights turned off. The hush was solemn, the immensity breathtaking. I went floating through the silence that breathed all around me. What is this place? I silently asked. Please, somebody tell me where I am!

I was in no pain. The logical part of me took note of that, and I began to analyze. This was no fantasy, no dream. I was wide awake, fully aware, searching with my faculties of sight and hearing, trying hard to sense whatever was going on around me. Every energy wave that made up the totality of me, the whole of myself, was on high alert. But if this was not a dream or a fantasy, then where was I?

I looked down at myself, and I saw that I had become a sphere, a glowing mist of blue and white and gold. I had no arms, no legs, no trunk, no solid body, no colorful, magical flying carpet. And no terra firma anywhere in sight.

Should this alarm me? I asked myself. But it didn't seem to make any difference, so I floated on.

Once more I sensed my mother hovering just in back of what should have been my right shoulder. "Honey, would you like to stay up here with us?" Mother's voice was heartfelt, pleading with me. "We would love to have you come up here and be with us."

I felt a flash of annoyance. This was just a case of the flu. I'd had the flu before, and I'd always gotten over it. So why should this time be any different?

Way off in the distance, I saw a pinpoint of light coming toward me. What's that, I asked myself. Am I seeing something real? Or is this, after all, a dream of some kind?

The tiny dot of light kept getting bigger and bigger, until I could see that it was rectangular in shape. It looked like an envelope of light opening up, or like an opening door tipped over on its side. And right in the center of that rectangular Light, I saw a glowing sphere.

The Light door faded as the brilliant sphere came closer to me, growing larger and larger. I shook my nonexistent head in wonder as the Light came to a stop, right in front of me. And I thought to myself, Everything up here is so bloody big!

I stared up at that blue-white sphere, and I began to see radiant patterns. They looked like long, fuzzy, golden caterpillars flowing over the surface of the Light. Layered on and around and within those golden thought-pulses were star-like webs of pure thought branching out from each central golden concept.

I felt myself blinking as I tried to focus my nonexistent eyes to make sense out of those dancing patterns. In absurd disappointment I thought, am I nearsighted, even when I'm out of my body? For I was now fully aware that this was no dream.

I could hear Mother's voice. "Honey, wouldn't you like to stay up here with us? Please, please, come up and be with us."

I sensed a great fear emanating from my mother, a fear of my being down there on Earth, of the terrible dangers that were coming. But this was 1998. It was the Clinton years, and the whole world was enjoying a breathing space of peace. No nation was at war with another nation. I silently asked, where is the danger.

"Please, please…" came Mother's fading voice.

But I could not answer. I could not move. Even my sense of breathing was suspended as I gazed into the depths of the Light coming toward me, moving ever closer until it enveloped me. And I was surrounded by ripples and cascades of Light, rising and falling all around me, like immense waves in the middle of a huge ocean. Held and sheltered within that mighty flow of Light, I was a tiny girl-child, newborn. I reached out with my glowing hand, and I touched the Light. Underneath my hand the swell of a mother's breast took shape as I was swept away by powerful currents of Light.

Ahead of me, the Light parted, a great curtain opening to reveal panoramic vistas of buildings and parks and trees and flowers and beauty and so many things I could not comprehend or understand.

"Where am I?"

To my surprise my question was answered. But not in words. Instead, my mind began to wrestle with pure thought-concepts that resonated around me, carrying ideas and thought-forms that I could not fully translate into mere words.

"Now you are at the moment of beholding the Imperial Heaven, the heart of God, the great Master Awareness that overflows to create all that is."

And I found myself in the midst of large and imposing structures. I looked around in wonder as I walked on paths that were bordered with flowers. Their vivid colors glowed from within, and their gentle scent filled the air.

Then I found myself standing in a great hall. In the center of the hall was a light that shone down from above, illuminating an immense golden crystal. Answering golden rays radiated out from the golden crystal's deep core. Each measured step that I took on the parquet floor made a gentle chiming sound that resonated through my body and mind.

I paused and took a deep breath, and then I walked into coruscating rays of Light that shimmered all around me like showers of golden sparks.

I stood before the golden crystal, and I put my hands on it, feeling vibrations in my hands and arms that resonated through my body. I moved my hands over a few of the infinite numbers of brilliant facets, all of them radiating fountains of Light that rose and fell in endless liquid motions.

I touched my forehead to the great golden crystal. And I found myself within the crystal, looking at glowing facets all around me. I could see scenes from my babyhood, clear on up to the present. Stunned into wonder, I was still and silent, a simple observer as I watched all that was happening around me.

I saw and felt my parents' early love for each other and for me. I felt my mother's yearning to have another baby, a yearning that tore at her as she went on into her forties and fifties.

I saw huge gaps and ragged tears in the fabric of my life plan that had been so carefully worked out before the birth of my earthly body. I knew they were the frustrations and the blocks of all that I had wanted to do with my life. I saw, one after the next, all of my thoughts and all of my visions.

I looked down at my cupped hands, and I saw a multicolored jewel of ruby and gold and white and sparkles of colors. I looked deeply into the jewel and saw my Grandmother Wilson. She was painting in oils, while I was slap-dashing various colors of paints on my canvas, trying to paint pictures of horses.

"Your grandmother had a special love for you," said the gentle voice of the Light. "She loved all her grandchildren, yet she always felt you were special. From the time you were born, your grandmother knew you had gifts, and she told your mother so. She loved teaching you to sew, to do embroidery, and to paint."

The Light continued, "Meditate often on these jewels."

Then the jewels and the crystals and the City of the Imperial God-Throne were all gone, and I was back in the blackness, floating in front of that great shining Light sphere. I asked the Light, "What is the meaning of what I've just seen?"

A sudden flash of realization flipped over in what would have been the area of my stomach if I had been in my body instead of being such a tiny spherical collection of awarenesses and thoughts. And I realized what all this was about. I knew what was happening to me.

"This is it!" I said to myself. "Right here, right now, I could die."

I shook my nonexistent head. "Wait a minute," I said. "This can't be right. I've just finished updating my lists of life goals. I've broken down my yearly goals into twelve monthly sets of objectives, and I'm right in the middle of setting up my daily tasks and to-do's for the next three months.

"And nowhere in any of my goals, my objectives, my to-do's, is there anything that says, today I die. Dying is not on any of my lists. I can't die now. Like George Burns says, I'm booked. So I'm really not ready for this. Not yet. Maybe in another forty years or so."

But then I realized how tiny and unimportant all my plans were. And to my own surprise, I felt myself wanting to go with that Light. I became aware of how much I ached to stay up there, where I would be fully understood, where I would never face criticism or hostility or misunderstanding. No more aloneness, no dealing with those who could not understand. A place where the limits of mere human logic would never again be imposed on me. Where my creativity could bloom and blossom in an atmosphere of peace and acceptance and love.

The Light shone in serene patience, waiting for me to catch up with all the information I was trying to absorb.

Without any words, the Light asked me if there was anything or anyone that was keeping me connected to the earth. And before me, a star cluster of Light unfolded into a long, golden cord that had people and life events clustered all along its length. On that cord were all of my life experiences, through all of my lifetimes.

One thought system that floated on the surface of this core thought was my mother's grief. There was the grief she felt at parting, at leaving me behind when she passed on. There was the grief she was now feeling as she knew that I could not stay up there.

There was also a deep concern that flowed to me from the Light. How well was I holding up in my Earth life, under difficult circumstances? Was I keeping to the path that Divine Light had laid out for me? What did I need? What kind of help would be necessary for me to get through the problems and challenges of earthly living? Layer after layer of my consciousness was scanned by that all-knowing Divine Light. All parts of me were looked over, even the deepest realms of my subconscious and unconscious minds.

There was also healing in that scan, including an easing of what had been crippling migraines. There was the loosening of old fears and anxieties, and the beginnings of hope. And there was the lifting of deep grief and black despair.

As the scanning went on, I saw that the everyday "I," that part of me that took care of daily living, was only a tiny part of a far greater Intelligence that was wiser and vaster than the little everyday me. I became aware of facets of myself that I had never known existed.

Even as these thought-concepts unfolded within my awareness, I was also seeing a three-dimensional vision of my older son coming into my bedroom. He stopped and looked down at me, and he saw that his mother was dead.

I knew that I had to go back down to Earth, back down to my son. Grief cut through me. I wanted to stay, yet I could not. So I shook my head, and I spoke in a loud, mental voice, saying, "No!"

Words came tumbling out of me. "I have work to do. My writing. My singing. If I leave before I finish what I went down there to do, I will feel incomplete. I have my two sons. A beautiful daughter-in-law. A wonderful grandson. I want to see my grandson graduate from high school and college. And someday I want to see him married, with children of his own."

I stopped because I had run out of thoughts and out of words. I tried to catch my nonexistent breath to say more. But the Light sent me a gentle blessing, a soft approval of my choice. And suddenly that wonderful Light zoomed off, faster than any jet aircraft, until it was only a tiny speck of light in the infinite distance.

It all happened so quickly that I only had time for a sliver of startled awareness, and then a knife-edge disappointment. "Wait! Come back! How come we didn't get to talk more?" I called after the vanishing Light. "I've got such a lot of questions..."

But I was falling back down into that tiny earth that held the people I loved, falling back down to where I was so alone.

I struggled against it, fighting to go back up into those Light realms, to reach out and touch that Light just one more time. But I found myself whirling around and falling down and down. My life memories were spinning around me, flashing like thousands of brilliant pictures with bright cascading colors like a thousand tiny kaleidoscopes. And I remembered everything.

CHAPTER 2

Early on a cloudless morning in June of 1944, I looked out of the backseat window of our black, four-door Dodge sedan. I was looking really hard at our small brick home at 246 Holly Street in Denver, Colorado, with its green lawn and its mailbox. I could see a sign that my daddy had told me said "For Sale." And there was another smaller sign hanging down from it that said, "Sold."

I watched as my tall blue-eyed Swedish father climbed into the driver's side of a dented, rusty, mud-colored flatbed truck that he'd bought for very little money. The door of the truck squawked as Daddy slammed it shut. The truck's starter cranked over for almost a full minute before the engine sputtered into life.

The back of the flatbed truck was piled high with all our furniture and belongings. Our beds and our chairs and our sofa and even our dining room table. There were lots of cardboard boxes full of clothes and books. The round tub of our General Electric washing machine was stuffed with sheets and towels. And my mother's Gulbransen spinet piano was wrapped up in old blankets. Daddy had tied all our belongings down good and tight, and he'd lashed a great big canvas tarp over everything we owned.

As that rusty overloaded old truck pulled out from the curb, Mama put our black Dodge car in low gear, and we followed Daddy as he drove down the street. I looked back over my shoulder at the only home I could remember. I wondered what it would be like not to live in our home on Holly Street. Not ever again.

Our two-vehicle caravan slowly rattled past blocks of red brick homes where all the University of Denver college professors lived. Multicolored flowers grew in careful rows, and rosebushes bloomed with brilliant colors. Mama always said those bright green lawns looked as though they had been trimmed with nail scissors.

We drove until we finally got to the edge of the city of Denver. Daddy's mud-colored truck and our black Dodge turned onto a two lane highway that was clogged with long convoys of olive green trucks all jam-packed with soldiers and military equipment. The soldiers were all being trained to go and fight overseas, a long way from home.

I sat in the back seat of our Dodge, not saying a word. I leaned over and I wrapped my arms around our nervous half collie dog, Sparky, who panted and slobbered all over me as he climbed up on the back seat and licked my face.

I slid forward and rested my chin on the top of the front seat. I could see a small collection of tear-wet tissues on the seat next to Mama. And the farther south we drove, the bigger that mound of soggy Kleenex got.

Periodically, Mother choked out short sentences. "Our big, beautiful church." "Wonderful organ." "Associate choir director." "All my solo work..." Sounds of nose blowing. "Professor's Wives Book Club." "Cultural events." Sniffles. "Our beautiful home." Mother took a deep breath. "And what in the world are we going to do about getting Whitney piano lessons in some godforsaken place out in the middle of nowhere?"

For the next three days I sat silent in that back seat as, following Daddy, we left the major highway with its endless traffic jam of military transports. We chugged over near-deserted Colorado mountain roads, driving on through Leadville, Colorado, as we headed on down into northern New Mexico. I sat in the back seat of the Dodge, listening to Mama weeping and blowing her nose. I looked out the window and watched the scenery go by. I frowned at the Rocky Mountains and the intense blue of the New Mexico sky. I didn't know what our new home would be like. I didn't know what my life would be like. I had nothing but my dog Sparky to hang on to. Everything else had suddenly been turned into a big, scary mystery.

CHAPTER 3

It had all started late at night, just after New Year's Day of 1944. I woke up from a sound sleep, and I got out of my bed to go to the bathroom. When I came out of the bathroom, I was so sleepy I forgot to flush the toilet.

I heard my mama and my daddy in the living room, talking in low voices. "Liz-Beth," Daddy was saying, "We had a faculty meeting today." He looked over at Mother. "Dean Roberts told the professors that once this war is over, the number of students attending the university probably won't be enough to support a full size teaching staff."

Mother carefully placed both hands on the arms of her wing-back chair. She took a moment for a deep breath, and she said, "Why ever not?"

"According to the economists, we're going to have a worse depression after the war than we had back in the 1930s. That means almost no one will be able to afford a university education." Daddy said. "And since I've only been teaching at the university since June of 1940, that means I could lose my job."

Mother sat very still. And then she said, "What can we do?"

Daddy's blue eyes looked straight at Mother as he took both her hands in his. "Honey, I want to go down to New Mexico during spring break and have a look around. I want to see if I can find an electric power company that's up for sale."

Mother shook her head. "Daddy, we've discussed this a hundred times or more. Even if you do find an electric power company for sale, we don't have the money to buy it. I know it's your dream to run your own company, but that's all it can ever be. Just a dream. We could never actually afford to do such a thing."

"Well, I know one thing for sure," Daddy said. "If Dean Roberts was right, I may not have a job when this war ends."

He got up and paced the small living room. "Liz-Beth, I am so damned tired of living, year after year, with the threat of losing my job always hanging over my head. I'm tired of us having nothing of our own to fall back on. All these years of teaching, and what've we got to show for it? I'm in my forties now, so finding myself a teaching job in another depression would be just about impossible."

I sat down on the hall floor, and Sparky began licking my ear. I put my arms around Sparky, and I felt a tingle of fear. What if my daddy couldn't find work? What would happen to us then?

"Now Daddy," said Mother, "We have to look at things realistically. If there is a post war depression, it won't help if we're in over our heads in debt. That's if we could even get a bank to lend us the money to buy a power company, which I seriously doubt. Those layoffs Dean Roberts was talking about may not happen. And we're lucky you've got such a good job."

My father looked at my mother with eyes that held memories of the Great Depression. "How long do you think it will be before our luck runs out?"

Mother gave a slow shrug of her shoulders. "I don't know." And there was a long silence.

Finally, my dad gave a deep sigh. "Honey, I'm going to take Easter vacation time to go down south to New Mexico and have a look around. I've got nothing to lose doing that, and there may never be another chance for us to run our own company and start building ourselves some security."

Daddy's long face broke into a grin. "Besides I've always wanted to own something of my own. Being my own boss. Having my own company. That's the best thing for a guy like me."

Sitting up against the wall, I gave a big, silent yawn. And then Sparky and I tiptoed back into my bedroom where I climbed into my bed and fell sound asleep.

☆ ☆ ☆

The next day, despite all of Mother's carefully reasoned arguments, Daddy started digging out all the gas rationing stamps that he and Mother had so carefully saved up during the past two years of wartime rationing and doing without. And in early April of 1944, my father drove our 1936 black Dodge four-door sedan down south to New Mexico.

Our faithful old Dodge took my daddy all the way down south to Española and then on to Chama, even going as far east as the tiny town of Watrous. There the manager of the Watrous Power & Light Company told my dad, "If you're looking to buy a power company, you'd better talk to Refugio Martinez. He's the head of the New Mexico REA, and he lives in Las Vegas. Refugio's a major political power in this state, so you better talk to him before you even think about buying."

Way back early in the 1930s, President Roosevelt had authorized the building of electric power plants and power lines to serve consumers throughout rural and small town America. And since New Mexico was mostly small towns and farms and ranches, Roosevelt's Rural Electrification Administration, or REA, sold electric power to most of the state. So my daddy drove on to Las Vegas, New Mexico, to see Mr. Refugio Martinez.

It was a Sunday afternoon. The weather was overcast and chilly. Refugio Martinez was out in his back yard, chopping wood for the family stove, thumping large chunks of wood down on a big chopping block, swinging his axe up over his head, then bringing the axe down and splitting each fat piece of piñon wood lengthwise with a loud crack.

"So you're looking to buy yourself a power company," said Mr. Refugio Martinez.

Thump! "Okay, let me tell you something. You better not look around Watrous or any of that area."

Crack!

"The REA's interested in purchasing the Watrous power company for ourselves." Mr. Martinez picked up the next chunk of firewood. "You go on up to Pecos, and you talk to old man Wyner. He's the owner of the Pecos Light and Power Company, and right now he's got his company up for sale. He's got eighty-six, maybe eighty-seven customers for that power company of his. Total."

Thump!

Crack!

Mr. Martinez straightened up and stretched his back as he looked up at my tall, lean dad, to make sure he got the message. "Pecos is up in the high mountain country," Mr. Martinez said. "It's too small and too remote and too unimportant for the REA to bother with. You better go take a look at Pecos."

So Daddy used some more of his precious gas rationing stamps to fill up his gas tank, and then he drove the forty miles from Las Vegas on up to Pecos, New Mexico, where he made an appointment to talk to Mr. Wyner.

The next day, Mr. Wyner drove my dad all around Pecos, while Daddy kept rolling down the window on the passenger side, sticking his head out the window, and looking up. What he saw was galvanized iron electric wires sagging from undersized power poles that were gray with age and rotting at the base.

Finally, Mr. Wyner drove north for a mile or so. There the ramshackle power line came to a dead end, and there he stopped the car. "This here's the north end of Pecos. And up thataway is the Pecos Canyon." Mr. Wyner pointed to his left. "That dirt road over there, that's Republican Road. That's where all the Republicans in this town live, and there's not too many of 'em."

He ground the car into low gear and drove on past the two-track dirt road. "I never built no power lines down Republican Road. I'll be damned and in hell before some god-damned Republican ever gets a drop of electricity from me."

After lunch, Mr. Wyner and my dad went and looked over Pecos Light and Power Company's adobe walled power plant, with its weedy plant yard. And, like all men, they talked interminably.

Finally Mr. Wyner said, "Look here, Benson, if you're interested in buying, I'm sure as hell interested in selling. This goddamn power company's more trouble than it's worth. Buying this thing was the biggest mistake I ever made."

"Well," said my dad, "I sure am interested in purchasing. That's provided we can get the financing."

"Oh, you'll get your loan," said Mr. Wyner. "I'll see to that. I'll contact George Bloom. He's president of the First National Bank of Santa Fe. If anybody can swing you a business loan to buy this company and get you started up running it, it'll be George Bloom. He knows me. I've done a whole lot of business with that bank over the years. They'll treat you right."

Daddy said, "I've got until June when my contract with the University of Denver runs out. If you haven't found another buyer by that time, my wife and I will be moving down here. And then we can see about swinging that loan."

The two men shook hands, and the deal was made. There was nothing in writing. Back in 1944, in what was still the semi-Wild West, a man's word was his bond.

CHAPTER 4

It was after midnight when my parents drove our two aged vehicles into the big dirt parking lot next to the old Harrison House that was owned by Mr. Wyner. I was sound asleep in the back seat of the car, worn out by three long days of traveling. Daddy lifted me out of the Dodge and carried me into the small apartment. That night Sparky and I slept together on a mattress on the floor.

When I woke up at sunrise I could smell bacon frying and coffee perking. I sat up and looked around my new bedroom. It was small and shabby, with a carpet that needed scrubbing, walls that were painted a dingy beige, and windows that were dimmed with uncounted years of accumulated grime.

I got up and went into the bathroom and washed my face and brushed my teeth, listening to the clanking of the old plumbing.

I went into the kitchen where Daddy was standing over the stove. "Morning, kid," said my dad. "About time you got up. How about some scrambled eggs for breakfast?"

I yawned and said, "Where's Sparky?"

"Sparky's had his breakfast, and he's outdoors. As soon as you and your mother eat and get yourselves showered up and dressed, we'll go for a tour of the power plant."

Daddy smiled down at me as he cracked eggs into the frying pan and stirred them with a fork. He wasn't wearing the brown double-breasted suit with the vest and the gold watch and watch fob that he always wore when he was teaching at the University of

Denver. Instead, he had on a plaid work shirt and khaki pants, with high top workboots that were laced up with thin strips of rawhide leather.

I started eating my eggs while Daddy took Mother her breakfast, just like he did every morning. Mother came into the kitchen, dressed in a pale green blouse and brown skirt. “We’ll have to get this place cleaned up before we can even unpack,” she told Daddy. “It’s a filthy mess.”

“We’ll get someone in to help,” Daddy said. “And we need to get your office set up in the back room.”

Mother nodded. Her lips were tight and her eyes were red from so much crying. Daddy looked at her anxiously, but Mama didn’t speak to him. But I saw a small spark of interest in her eyes as she looked out the kitchen window at the power plant across the big dirt driveway.

After breakfast Daddy and Mama and I went outside into the early morning sunlight, and we began walking across the parking area to the power plant. Halfway across the dirt parking lot, Daddy stopped and pointed to the east. “Isn’t that the prettiest sight you ever saw?”

I turned and looked, and I saw mountains covered with pine and piñon trees. At the base of the mountains were houses that bordered green fields of hay and alfalfa. A line of tall cottonwood trees marked the flow of the Pecos River.

Off in the distance we heard a lone bird singing messages of love to his lady friend. But something was not right. I stood there and listened for a moment. Except for that bird, things were awfully quiet.

I turned around and I looked toward the road west of the power plant. “Where are all the cars?” I said. For there was not a car or truck or vehicle of any kind that I could see on that road.

“Most of the people in Pecos don’t own a car,” my father said. “They don’t have any money for buying cars, and with the war, all the gasoline is rationed. There are only a few old cars in Pecos, and they’re all stored away in the back of barns.”

My mouth fell open. “But how can people go anywhere without their cars?”

"They walk," said my dad. "Or they ride horseback. Lots of families have wagons. A few of them even have buggies."

"Pecos people ride in wagons and buggies?" I said. I looked up, wide-eyed, at the corrugated iron roof of the power plant with its two smokestacks. One smokestack was emitting small puffs of white smoke. "What's making that smoke? And what's that funny muff-muff sound?"

"That's the main power engine. It generates the electricity for the people of Pecos."

Daddy took some keys out of his pocket. He unlocked the padlock on the power plant door, and he opened it.

Inside the dimly lit power plant, the air was thick with the acrid smell of diesel oil. The floor was covered with a thick layer of oily brown dirt. And the muff-muff sound was really loud. It came from a squat cast iron engine with a flywheel about fifteen feet in diameter that kept on spinning around and around.

"Look over here." Daddy took my hand and led me around the side of the diesel engine. Mother followed in her office shoes, stepping daintily over a thick coating of oily dirt that covered the floor. Raising her voice to be heard, Mother said, "I take it this is the engine that's keeping the lights in Pecos on."

"Yep, it sure is. See that? The smaller housing off to one side, that's the generator." Daddy looked down at me. "That generator is putting out electricity for all the lights in Pecos."

Then he led Mother and me across to a switchboard that was twelve feet high and about ten feet wide. That big black board had all kinds of meters and dials on it, along with several great big, breaker switches.

"The electricity travels from the generator to the cables in back of this switchboard. And then it goes on out to the power lines. It travels through the power lines, and it goes all over Pecos. And that electricity lights up people's homes and businesses."

I gazed around, wide-eyed, trying to understand all I was seeing. "What's that over there?" I pointed to another smaller diesel engine.

"That's the backup engine. We'll start that engine up and run it during peak load hours. That'll be between sunset and about ten o'clock at night." Daddy smiled down at me. "This evening you can help me get that engine started."

"Wow!" I said softly to myself, so that Mother wouldn't hear me and tell me I couldn't.

Daddy looked over at Mother. "Isn't this something?" he said over the engine noise. "Aren't these engines beautiful?"

Mother turned her head and looked around her, dazed from the smell of the diesel oil and the sheer busyness of the chugging engine. "This all seems like a lot of work to me."

"Aw-w, heck no," said Daddy. "These old engines aren't gonna be any trouble at all. Why, every evening we'll come out here, just you and me, and we'll bring a couple of rocking chairs with us, and the two of us'll just sit out here and watch those big old flywheels going around and around."

Speechless at this declaration of marital togetherness, Mother stared at Daddy and then down at me. I stared up at Mother, and then I looked up over my dad. He had a smile on his face, and his eyes were the eyes of a man who has found his own personal spot in paradise.

✲ ✲ ✲

That afternoon, Mother and I walked over to Harrison's Country Store, a large stone building with a big front porch and a great big dirt parking lot.

No cars were parked in the parking lot. Instead there was a buggy or two and some wagons that looked like shallow wooden boxes on four wheels with a seat up front. The tired horses that pulled these equipages stood there with their heads low, dozing in the sun.

Mother and I walked into the store, and I stood there and looked around. One half of Harrison's Country Store looked like our neighborhood grocery store in Denver. There were canned vegetables on shelves, along with boxes of laundry soap, and lots of candy of one sort and another on shelves and counters, and a cooler where all the glass bottles of milk and cream and soda pop were kept well chilled.

I walked over to the other side of the store where there was all kinds of amazing hardware. There were great big wooden barrels held together by metal straps, and they were filled to the top with all kinds and sizes of nails.

There were even bigger barrels that had all kinds of horseshoes in them. And there was a collection of horseshoes of all sizes nailed up on the wall right above those barrels. Leaning against that wall was an assortment of shovels and rakes and hoes.

I felt eyes looking at me, and I looked over and saw a little boy staring at me with wide, dark eyes, not saying a word.

Finally I spoke. "Hi," I said.

There was no answer. The boy just looked at me for another minute and turned his head away.

"Why doesn't he say something?" I whispered to Mother.

"He probably can't speak English," she replied.

"But I thought everybody in America talked English."

Mother smiled. "Most do, but not all."

"Why not?"

"Lots of reasons," my mother murmured absently as she looked over dry goods shelves that were piled with shoes, cowboy boots and work boots, and clothes of all kinds and sizes, including blue jeans, bib overalls and work shirts.

Mother said, "We'd better go talk to the postmaster about renting a mailbox."

"Don't we already have a mailbox?"

"We will when we rent one."

"Where's the post office?"

"Right over there, at the front of the dry goods section."

I looked, and sure enough there was a big corner of the store that had been partitioned off. "I thought post offices were supposed to be in their own buildings," I said.

"In the bigger cities they are. In small villages like Pecos, the post office is wherever it gets put."

An hour or so later, Mother and I walked out of the store-cum-post-office, our arms loaded with groceries. More buggies and wagons had gathered out in the parking lot. Small groups of people spoke to each other in rapid fire Spanish.

I felt really strange because I couldn't understand anything they were saying. I stopped and looked over at all those people, at the men and boys, some in blue jeans and cowboy style straw hats, some in khaki pants, some in bib overalls that must have come straight from Harrison's dry goods shelves. The younger women were wearing cotton floral print dresses, while many of the gray haired women were dressed all in black.

What seemed like rows of dark haired, dark eyed children all stood stock still and stared at me, while the older people looked over at us. Several of them nodded courteously, and Mother smiled and nodded back.

"Why are all those old women wearing black?" I asked Mother.

"They are widows. Women whose husbands have died. Come on. We have to get home now."

"It's not very far to walk," I pointed out to Mother. "We live right next door to the store."

As we walked on, I heard soft words from the people who were looking at me. "*Rubia,*" was one word. Others said Spanish words that sounded like, "*La muchachita del hombre de la luz.*"

"What are they saying?" I asked Mother. "Why are they all looking at me?"

Mother smiled down at me. "They're saying you're very blonde," she told me. "And you know, you're a real cotton top with your pretty white-blonde hair. And they're saying you are the little girl of the man of the light. That's your Dad. They've named him *el hombre de la luz,* the man of the light."

"What have they named you?"

Mother looked a little self-conscious. "*La muñequita.* That means little doll. I think that's because I'm thin and I'm petite."

"What's petite? Does that mean short? Daddy says you're short." I turned around and looked back. "Do any of them talk in English?"

"Some of them do. But not all."

"What am I going to do when I go to school? How will I say anything to the kids if they can't talk to me in English?"

Mama smiled down at me. "Just give it time. You'll find ways of making friends."

"Maybe," I muttered to myself. School was going to be a really strange place if all the kids were like that silent little boy in the store.

I tagged along behind Mother with my head down, feeling homesick for Denver.

✲ ✲ ✲

That evening while Mother was cooking dinner, Daddy said to me, "Would you like to help me start the backup engine?"

I jumped up from the kitchen chair. "Okay," I said.

My dad and I walked over to the power plant and went inside, and Daddy took me over to the big flywheel that jutted out from the silent backup engine. He picked up a heavy six foot long stainless steel rod that was about three and a half inches in diameter. The rod gleamed brightly under the white metal shaded lights that shone down from the galvanized iron roof above us.

"Now," my daddy said, "I want you to help me get this engine primed."

I watched carefully while Daddy put one end of the stainless steel rod into one of the holes that were evenly spaced around the outer diameter of the huge, unmoving flywheel. About five and a half feet of the steel rod jutted out from the flywheel and angled up toward the galvanized iron ceiling.

Daddy moved out toward the high end of the rod and jumped up so far that both his feet left the ground as he grabbed the rod with both hands. The engine flywheel slowly revolved as Daddy's weight pulled the rod down almost to the dirt-covered floor.

"Now you can help me," Daddy said over the everlasting engine noise that filled the plant. He took the rod out of the hole it was in and thrust it into another hole higher up on the broad steel rim of the engine's flywheel.

I stood next to my daddy as the rod came slowly down. As soon as I could reach the rod, I jumped. I felt the resistance of the flywheel as the rod slowly descended toward the floor, turning the flywheel on its axis.

"Now let's do it again!" And Daddy and I repeated our jumps and pull-downs eight or nine times.

Finally my dad took the stainless steel rod and carefully laid it on the floor beside the engine. Then he led me around to the front of the engine and pointed down toward its base. Attached to the engine block was an automobile emergency brake that looked like it had been taken out of an old Model T Ford. "You take hold of that," Daddy said.

I put my hand around the emergency brake handle, and Daddy closed his large hand around mine. And then we squeezed the brake handles together and slowly pushed the emergency brake forward. The small diesel engine responded with an achingly slow turn of the flywheel as it coughed out a loud *"Whoo-oo-oomph!"*

I looked up at my dad in complete surprise. "Keep it up," he yelled as he grinned down at me.

The two of us kept slowly pushing forward on the brake handle. And then the engine coughed again, and it said "*Whoompf!… Whumpf!… Whumpf!… pop-pop-pop-pop-pop-pop!*" And the engine's flywheel spun around, faster and faster.

I looked up at my dad, and I hollered, "Wow!"

Daddy smiled down at me. "Now you can help me throw this backup engine online."

He took my hand and led me over to the big, black switchboard and pointed at two black-box voltmeters, their needles quivering with electric life.

"We have to wait for the voltage to reach this point," my daddy said over the noise of the two engines as he pointed at one of the glass cases that shielded the voltmeters.

Then Daddy placed his big callused, hand over mine, curling my fingers around the handle of the larger breaker switch. We stood there and waited for a moment as all the needles and dials on the switchboard moved and pulsed to the rhythm of the two busy engines.

"Now," said my dad. And together we moved that breaker switch up to the on position.

All of a sudden, the lights in the power plant shone brighter, then dimmer, then brighter, then dimmer, as the two diesel engines with their attached generators sped up and then slowed down, filling the power plant with their rumbling, popping, mechanical drumbeats, until they finally settled down, each muttering to its own stable rhythm as the spokes of the two flywheels whirled and pulsed in time to the syncopated rhythms of those two half-ton cast-iron diesel engines.

Daddy and I went outside. He locked the plant door while I looked up at him with wide eyes. Daddy smiled down at me. "I'll bet you're the only kid in America that's ever helped start a diesel engine and thrown a generator online."

Dizzy with exhilaration, I said, "I really helped you, didn't I. And I did all right too. Didn't I?"

"You sure did. Did you notice how those overhead lights all started oscillating when the engines came online?"

"Yeah," I said. "That was fun."

"That oscillation happens because there's no governor that keeps the power levels from fluctuating. So nobody in this town can own an electric clock, because when the voltage fluctuates like that, an electric clock will run faster and then slower, and then faster and then slower. And that means no electric clock in Pecos will ever keep accurate time."

My daddy and I laughed together, and he took my hand as we walked back to the apartment to get ready for dinner.

CHAPTER 5

After my dad had gone to every home and business that had electricity and read all of Pecos Light and Power Company's eighty-seven electric meters, my mother sat down in the office and inserted a penny postcard into her fourteen year old Olivetti typewriter.

Carefully she typed in the amount owed on the bill, then turned each postcard over and typed the name and address of the customer. Then Mother and I took all eighty-seven postcards over to the post office, where they were all mailed out to Pecos Light and Power Company's electric customers. In 1944, electricity cost our domestic customers $1.27. Our two dozen or so local business users, mainly gas stations, small grocery stores, and local mom-and-pop restaurants, had a rate of $3.57 a month.

Over the next three weeks, people walked into the tiny office at the back of the Harrison House, the women with folded dollar bills in their purses, the men pulling worn leather billfolds out of their back pockets. Mother took the dollar bills and made change, and then she stamped both the customer's copy and the office copy with a stamp that said Paid.

I watched carefully as Mother gave the customers their change. I wanted to learn how to do that. I knew I could stamp those bills paid, and I was pretty sure I could give the customers the right change.

✲ ✲ ✲

One afternoon Slim Watson, a sixty-five year old silver haired cowboy, walked in the office door, weaving slightly. The acrid aroma of cheap whiskey wafted from him.

As Mother stamped his bill paid, Slim took out a small bag of Bull Durham tobacco and some cigarette papers, and he proceeded to make a roll-your-own "cigareet". As he tapped the aromatic tobacco onto a small square of paper, Slim smiled down at Mother, leaned forward, and said with a slight slur to his speech, "Ha-ow'd the old-time cowboy take a bath?"

Mother sat straight up in her office chair. Before she could say a word, Slim said again, "Ha-ow'd the old time cowboy take a bath?"

Mother shook her head as she looked up at Slim. "You're pulling my leg," she said.

"Na-ah, na-ah, na-ah!" said Slim, waving his arms and scattering flakes of Bull Durham tobacco all over the floor, the desk, and Mother's Olivetti typewriter. "Na-ow, ha-ow'd the old time cowboy take a bath?" Slim swayed forward and beamed down at Mother.

"All right, I'll bite," said Mother. "How did the old time cowboy take a bath?"

"Wa-ll," said Slim, "He built hisself a campfire, and he heated up a can full of water. He dug hisself a hole in the ground, and he lined it with his slicker." A cowboy's slicker was a rain cape made out of bright yellow oilcloth. "Then that old cowboy, he poured that heated-up water into his slicker, and he jest climbed in, and he took hisself a bath."

Slim pulled himself up to his full six foot four and beamed down at my stunned Mother. "Na-ow ain't thet simple?"

Then Slim smiled a sorrowful smile as he said, "Life shore was better back in them old days. Things wuz a whole lot different back then. If'n I could find a trail that would take me back to them days, I'd git on my old cowpony and I'd go there."

With a hint of moisture in his whiskey reddened eyes, Slim picked up his change, put on his Stetson hat, and moseyed right on out of Mother's office.

☆ ☆ ☆

All during 1944 and much of 1945, the distant thunder of far off guns of war formed an unspoken background to our peaceful life. To me, the war was the occasional picture in the *Santa Fe New Mexican* and remarks made by a radio newscaster heard on our small wood veneered Motorola radio.

Memories of uniformed soldiers and sailors crowding into the downtown stores in Denver were fading, developing a dreamlike quality. And the snarling, whining roar of single engine fighter planes flying over our Denver home in thrilling and scary formations was a sound I would never hear again.

On certain days, especially Saturdays, the Harrison General Store parking lot, which was located right in front of the Harrison House, would be filled with flatbed wagons, buggies, buckboards, and surreys with the fringe on top. Pulled by tired and patient horses, these equipages would surround the occasional car or truck.

Seated in the surreys and buggies would be mothers, grandparents, and children, all waiting for the man of the family to come out of the general store with the few necessities that had to be bought.

Mothers and *abuelitas* would ask the man softly, “Is there mail?” And if they were lucky, there would be a penciled letter on tissue-thin paper inside an envelope that had a red, white, and blue border all around the edges.

The whole family would spend time looking over the envelope. Then they would tuck it carefully inside purse or pocket to read at home. Relief would hang in the still air. The family knew that one or two or three weeks ago their son or grandson had still been alive. Yet their relief would be laced with anxiety, with wondering about what had happened since the letter had been written. Wondering silently about what might yet happen to their own.

☆ ☆ ☆

Late in October, Mother went back to visit her family in Perry, Oklahoma. She was gone for almost ten days. Then one evening Mama called Daddy long distance and she said, "I'll be home on Saturday."

And the next Saturday morning, Daddy and I were standing out in front of the railroad depot in Rowe, New Mexico. It was a miniature depot and it had a second story where the stationmaster and his family lived.

Out in front of the Rowe Depot were two sets of bright, shining railroad tracks. As Daddy and I waited in the shade of the depot, he pointed and said, "Look way off over there. See that little streamer of smoke? That's Mama's train coming down the track."

I looked really hard, and way far away, I saw a tiny gray and black spot.

"Now listen hard, and pretty soon you'll hear the train coming."

I listened as hard as I could until finally I heard the tracks humming. And then I heard the distant sound of a locomotive as the black spot grew and began to take shape. "It sounds like our big power engine, Muff-Muff," I said to Daddy.

Daddy smiled and said, "It does, sort of."

Far off the mournful whistle blew. Daddy looked at me very seriously and he said, "I'm going to pick you up and hold you tight when that train comes in."

"Okay." I was excited at the thought of seeing the big railroad train from the same height as my tall father.

Moments later, the train came into the Rowe Depot, chuffing slowly. Steam came out of its brakes as it began slowing to a stop with a loud hissing and squealing of brakes and engine wheels slowly turning and rocker bars moving up and around and down, all creating a world of tremendous sights and sounds that were filled with the power that moved the black coal fired, smoke wreathed locomotive along the shining railroad tracks.

I hugged my arms tight around my daddy's neck as I watched, and I wondered how anybody had ever made anything as big as that black engine with its smokestack and its enormous wheels. How did they put it all together so it worked? But I couldn't ask because the noise from the engine and the steam hissing out from the brakes was way too loud.

At last the train slowed to a stop. Each of the train cars bumped into the car ahead. When all the jerking and bumping had finally stopped, the engine sat there like an enormous black horse, huffing and resting.

A black man wearing a train conductor's uniform got out and put down a step for my mother to step down from the train. He handed Mother her suitcase, and Mama came over to us and kissed Daddy. My father hugged my mother with one arm.

I wrapped both arms tight around my daddy's neck as I looked up at the passenger cars. I saw lots of young men in uniform, their faces all pressed up against windows, all of them watching my parents and me. Mother hugged me and kissed me. Then she said, "Let's give all those nice young men on the train a big wave."

So we smiled and waved as the locomotive blasted its loud whistle and started to puff out smoke. The cars all bumped and jerked as the long train began to move. The train wheels clacked as the long chain of cars moved past, going faster and faster. And my parents and I kept on waving at all those smiling young faces, and all those soldiers and sailors and marines waved back at us.

Years later, I would wonder how many of those young uniformed men had come back from the Second World War, and how many had been laid to rest in faraway graves.

CHAPTER 6

On a warm and sunny August day, I was playing out under the cottonwood trees in back of the Harrison House when I heard our office screen door slam against the wall. I looked up and my mouth fell open.

Not one time in my whole life had I ever seen my ladylike mother run. But now Mama ran up to me, laughing and crying all at the same time. She picked me up in her arms, and she hugged me. Between sobs, she kept saying, "The war is over! The war is over!"

How could the war be over, I wondered. I could not remember a time when World War II was not being fought.

CHAPTER 7

South of the village of Pecos lies the Pecos National Historical Park and the Pecos Pueblo National Historic Landmark. But back in the postwar years, the Old Pecos Ruins, as everybody called them, were just decaying adobe walls in the middle of a cow pasture.

Ever since 1838 when the few remaining Pecos Indians moved to the Jemez pueblo, the silent ruins had baked under the New Mexico sun. In the summertime, the occasional red Hereford or black Charolais cow could be seen grazing on gray green grama grass or wandering over ancient kivas and storerooms and living quarters that were all worn down dirt-filled bumps on the ground.

The mostly Spanish speaking people who lived in postwar Pecos were too busy rebuilding lives that had been disrupted, first by the Great Depression and then by the Second World War, to pay any attention to those deserted ruins. And the few tourists who came to Pecos all headed straight up the Pecos Canyon to go fishing. But in 1946 my parents and I got to see some real Indian dancing at the Old Pecos Pueblo.

Soon after the end of the war, everybody in Pecos and Santa Fe had started buying cars. My parents had bought themselves a second hand Plymouth, and every Sunday we drove into Santa Fe to attend services at a small Congregational church. The minister's name was Dr. Diefendorf, but everybody called him Doc.

Doc was a young man in his thirties, and he was short, bald, and athletically fit. And Doc's wide circle of friends included one New Mexico Pueblo Indian man.

The Indian man's name, as I recollect my mother telling me, was Tony White Cloud. He was a famous Indian dancer, and he came from the Jemez Pueblo. Mother told me that Tony White Cloud had even danced in Washington, DC. And she said that Tony White Cloud had taught Doc how to do Indian dancing.

And that was the reason the entire membership of the Santa Fe Congregational Church drove out to the Old Pecos Ruins one Sunday afternoon to set up for a summer's evening picnic and Indian dance. About twenty-five cars drove down the bumpy dirt tracks that led to the Pecos Pueblo, a procession of cars such as had never been seen by the people of Pecos.

Dad and Mother and I were all three of us crowded into the front sofa-seat of our Plymouth. The back seat was loaded with silverware, plates, and glasses, along with a great big platter of fried chicken, a couple of baked dishes, a serving bowl of green beans, a pumpkin pie made with Libby's canned pumpkin and rich cream and lots of sugar, and a big glass jar of hand squeezed lemonade sweetened with lots of C&H pure cane sugar from Hawaii.

We parked our car on the bare dirt, along with all the rest of the church people who were driving in. We got out of our car, and Daddy pulled out our card table while Mama started getting out the baked dishes.

Mama turned to me and handed me plates and silverware. "Here, Whitney. You take these and you carry them over to where your father will be setting up the card table."

So, walking very carefully, I helped my mother by carrying three plates and three sets of silverware and three napkins over to the north side of the old ruined church where a lot of wobbly card tables were being set up. Nearby, a few women began laying out casseroles on long trestle tables that were covered with red and white checked gingham tablecloths.

Looking over at the kids already playing in the surrounding thickets of juniper and piñon trees, I said, "Can I go play?"

"Don't go too far. Stay in sight," Mother said in an absent tone of voice.

I walked slowly past those trestle tables, looking at the rows of baked dishes and gallons of all kinds of ice cream, along with apple pies, cherry pies, cakes of all kinds and descriptions, and plates that were mounded with cookies. People who'd had so little during the dark years of the Great Depression and World War II now cooked up overflowing feasts for every church social.

I laughed and shrieked as all us kids played tag among the juniper trees, which were more like six foot evergreen bushes. After what seemed an endless time, we heard our parents calling, "Time to eat!"

But before we got to eat, one of the older men stood up and began saying a long and hard to understand prayer about blessings for this, that and the other. That old man prayed and prayed, and I squirmed and squirmed while my parents firmly held both my hands.

At last the prayers were over, and we went through the line, with the older people and church dignitaries going first, and kids and their parents going toward the end.

And then we all ate until we could hold no more. By the time we had all finished eating chicken and baked dishes and ice cream and pie and cake and cookies, the sun was going down.

While the women cleared the tables, the men lit a big bonfire, made from dry fallen branches that had been collected from the surrounding piñon and juniper thickets. And someone else brought out a big tree stump that was put to one side of the gathering group. And then everybody began settling down, some sitting cross-legged on blankets on the ground, others in creaky folding lawn chairs.

A gray haired Indian man, his hair cut in a pageboy with a red handkerchief tied around his head, came out from behind the great adobe walls of the old church ruins. He carried a really big Indian drum over to the large tree stump where he sat down, putting the drum between his knees. And he started drumming and singing an Indian chant.

The old drummer's call carried out over the long deserted kivas, out over the piñon and juniper and scrub cedar trees, out over the land where the Pecos Indians had lived for thousands of years. His voice echoed through the mountain air as sunset shaded into the pale lavender of a New Mexico dusk.

As darkness began to fall, the drumbeat became faster and the chanting sounded more urgent. From behind the thick adobe wall of the church came two dancers, one a Pueblo Indian man, the other a bald man whose skin was stained dark with some kind of natural juice.

My mother touched my arm as she pointed and whispered, "Look. That's Doc Diefendorf. And that Indian man with him is Tony White Cloud."

Doc Diefendorf and the Pueblo Indian dancer were both carrying big hoops on either arm, and as the great drum boomed and the drummer chanted, the two men began to do an Indian hoop dance. Their moccasined feet thudded into the hard packed earth, forming a counterpoint to the chanting and the playing of the gray haired drummer.

The big bonfire flickered and flared as the two dancers passed their hoops over their heads and arms, moving them down to their legs and their feet, then lifting the hoops over their heads once more and passing them down again while the chanting of the old man and the steady beat of the drum echoed back from the adobe walls of the old church. As the dance went on the sky darkened to a deep velvety black, and the old church ruins were silhouetted in black relief against a brilliant star filled sky.

I watched in fascination while dance after dance was performed, some with hoops, some with jingle bells circling the ankles of the two dancers, and some with both men just dancing, their feet thudding on the adobe clay.

And I, seven-and-a-half years old, became tireder and sleepier as the dances went on, until I finally fell asleep in my father's arms.

I seem to remember halfway waking up, opening my sleepy eyes and staring out into the circle of firelight. I cannot remember whether it was reality or dream, yet I saw the slender Indian man dancing, while trembling eagle feathers, black with white tips, fanned and feathered down his outstretched arms. The unending beat of the drum, the soft sound of the dancer's moccasined feet, and the timeless chanting of the gray haired singer called to the spirits of the ancient pueblo dwellers as the fading firelight rose and fell, setting the dancer into flight.

And I was held safe in my father's arms as my dreams went flying up, higher than the mesa, higher than an eagle's wings, flying all the way up to the blazing diamond stars of the Milky Way that banded the sky above the Glorieta Mesa.

CHAPTER 8

A few months after World War II had ended, Daddy started hiring young local men, some of them Spanish speaking veterans, to work on Pecos Light and Power Company's new power lines.

Most of those young men were in their early twenties. They were physically fit, and they had all the discipline that came from having been in the United States military and fighting in the most terrible war in history. It would take that kind of discipline for those young men to learn how to climb Pecos Light and Power Company's power poles and work with the hot wires, the electric wires that carried 2200 volts of electricity to people's homes and businesses.

Once my father had his men hired, he began building power lines all over Pecos. Every morning my father and his men would use strong thick wires to tie 30 foot power poles on either side of their pickup trucks and onto my dad's old Dodge car. My skinny father would slide in through the window on the driver's side, and he'd start up the old Dodge. Dad and the men in their pickup trucks formed a strange caravan as they drove out from that dirt parking lot and onto the washboard dirt roads of Pecos to begin their working day.

Most of the day, half of the workers would be down in holes that they were digging for those new power poles. All anybody could see of those young men were the shovelfuls of dirt that flew up and over the sides of the holes.

Once the holes were dug, Pecos Light and Power Company's antique winch truck, which some previous owner had painted a revolting baby-diaper green, would lift a power pole up off the ground. The men would guide the power pole into a freshly dug hole, and then they'd shovel dirt down into the hole and tamp the clay earth down around the pole so it was set into the ground real good and solid.

Finally the men would unroll bales of copper wire, and the wire would get lifted up onto insulators that stuck out from the tops of the power poles. The green winch truck would tighten up those copper wires, shining golden in the sunlight, until they had just the right amount of slack in them.

One time there was a length of wire that somehow got snagged, and as the winch truck pulled on it, the long copper wire broke in two with a loud *Spang!*

My dad just had time to yell, "Hit the dirt!" before that copper wire whipped through the air. Daddy and all his men lay flat on their bellies, hugging the hard ground as the broken end of the copper wire snapped back and forth over their heads.

Finally the wire hit a fence post, and as it whirringly wrapped itself around the post Daddy and his men slowly picked themselves up off the ground. My shaken father looked all around at his men and he said, "Are you guys all right?"

One of the young veterans sat up and grinned over at my dad as he said, "We're okay. It's just like being in the army."

All through the late 1940s and on up through the early '50s my dad would go on building power lines. "I've got to get those lines built now," he told Mama and me. "If I don't do that, the REA could build their lines straight over the mountains from Las Vegas. And then they could come right on down the Pecos Canyon, and charge extra low rates for their electricity, and cherry-pick all our customers. If that happens, we won't have any business left."

So Daddy and his men kept working every day, replacing all the old power poles in North Pecos. Then he built some brand new power lines in South Pecos and East Pecos. And not too long after that, he started building twenty miles of line up the Pecos

Canyon, all the way past Terrero and on up to Mountain View Dude Ranch.

☆ ☆ ☆

After the war, many of the smaller ranches up the Pecos Canyon were turned into dude ranches. And all kinds of dudes from all over the country would come west on vacation. All up and down the canyon, old corrals and barns were razed to make way for small log cabins built around a single great hall that served for dining and for evening entertainment, all for the burgeoning influx of the dudes.

In the mountains east of Pecos, in the Cow Creek area, "Honeyboy" Baltzley began renting out cabins by the day and by the week. The four Martin girls, Peggy, Dodie, Toodie, Babe, and their mother, ran their own super-efficient operation, raising cattle and horses, renting out cabins and guiding dudes on trail rides through the Pecos Wilderness Area.

☆ ☆ ☆

Early one summer morning in 1946, a newly arrived eastern lady came into the dining hall of the Pecos Valley Dude Ranch. "How did you sleep on your first night?" she was asked.

The eastern lady placed one hand on her palpitating bosom. "I didn't sleep a wink," she said. "I lay awake all night long, listening to the wild Indians beating on their tom-toms."

All the guests in the dining hall got very quiet, and the local waiters and cooks looked at each other in astonishment. There hadn't been any Indians living around Pecos since 1838.

"Listen!" said the tourist lady. "You can hear those wild Indians beating on their tom-toms, right now!"

Things got even quieter in the dining room. Everyone listened hard, and then they heard, far off in the distance, Arnold

Benson's power plant engines going "*muff, muff, muff*" and "*pop-pop-pop-pop-pop.*"

In addition to preserving native culture, Pecos Light and Power Company's diesel engines sometimes put on fireworks displays for the locals. When too much soot collected in the engines' smoke stacks, they would occasionally catch on fire, and showers of sparks would flare up a hundred feet or more. At night, this was a spectacular sight, with orange and gold and red sparks lighting up Pecos Light and Power Company's power plant and its surrounding work yard.

Daddy and his men would all be out there with garden hoses, spraying the plant roof and the smokestacks, cooling them until the fire died down. Then they'd clean out the smokestacks real good with extra large scrubbing brooms. And finally Daddy would restart the engines.

In 1947 progress came to Pecos Light and Power Company. My dad built a power line west from Pecos, and Public Service Company of New Mexico ran a line east from Santa Fe. The two power lines met at the tiny hamlet of Cañoncito, where Dad and his men worked with the hardhats from Public Service Company getting those two power lines hooked together. And from that time on, my parents bought electricity wholesale from the Public Service Company of New Mexico.

That first evening after we went online with PSC, Mother and Daddy drank a cup of tea to celebrate. But I went to bed early, and I cried myself to sleep, for I knew I would never again help Daddy throw a generator online, and help send Pecos Light and Power Company's homegrown electricity out to all the homes and businesses of Pecos.

And that was the beginning of the age of the power grid.

✲ ✲ ✲

The outside world began intruding more and more on the remote village of Pecos. Some of the local cowboys went to work for the freshly built dude ranches, turning their hands and their skills on horseback from wrangling cows and horses to wrangling dudes. The people of Pecos became accustomed to seeing long lines of tired horses with drooping ears, all listlessly following their leaders, all of them plodding down the main dirt road of Pecos.

Perched on the backs of those broken down nags were middle aged overweight lady dudes in stunning Western attire. Their red dyed and bleached blonde hairdos were topped by white, tan and black ten-gallon Stetson hats. Generous bosoms filled satin cowboy shirts that came in brilliant shades of maroon, lavender, peach and apple green, such as had never been seen in the Old West. Plump hips and thighs were squeezed into expensive cowgirl pants that ranged from tan or dove gray twill to ravingly new Levis in shades of inky blue. And expensive Tony Lama cowboy boots lolled in the saddle stirrups. Riding next to those visions of western splendor were small pony mounted buckaroos and buckarettes, all decked out in cowboy and cowgirl outfits, complete with holstered six guns that were loaded with caps. Local cowboys trotted back and forth on their spirited steeds, keeping the slow cavalcade moving along more or less in a straight line.

One June day Mother and I looked out the front window of the office and saw a tourist in his car come to a dead stop in the middle of the newly incorporated Village of Pecos's main dirt road. The driver sat there in his bright red convertible as several hundred red Hereford cows came bawling and bellowing along, taking up the entire road, separating into two streams of unhappy cows that flowed around the tourist's expensive convertible. The cow herd kicked up clouds of dust that settled all over the convertible's neon red paint and expensive leather upholstery—and all over the red-faced tourist who sat there shaking his fist and swearing at the top of his lungs.

Five or six cowboys rode on by the convertible, paying no attention to the raging dude in the driver's seat. They were too busy yipping and whistling at the herd, keeping the cows headed toward the cattle pens at Rowe, where they would be loaded onto railroad cattle cars and shipped out to the slaughterhouses and meatpacking plants located somewhere in the Midwest.

The bawling herd slowly moved on by the newly opened gas station next to the Harrison Country Store. Fishermen and their families were parked at the pumps, filling up the gas tanks of dusty station wagons and shambling pickup trucks that had silver bullet vacation trailers hitched on behind them. Sweating fathers went into the gas station to buy Coca-Cola's for themselves and their wives, and strawberry and orange sodas for the restless kids that came tumbling out of cars and trucks, some crying, others asking, "When're we gonna be there?"

Periodically one of the boys would start teasing his siblings and pushing his younger sisters around. Kid clamor would ensue as mothers shrieked, "Billy-Joe, you leave your little sister alone, you hear me? You better listen to me or I'll whop you a good one!"

But Billy-Joe never heard anything until Pop paid for the gas and came out of the station to rumble something at his wife, and then roar, "A'right, you kids, ever'body back in the truck! Where's EmmaRea?"

And a boy-voice would pipe up, "EmmaRea's in the bathroom, and she's got the door locked, and she says she ain't comin' out. And I need to go! Bad!"

CHAPTER 9

At the same time the Pecos power lines were being built, my parents had to move out of their apartment. So they built a house out of concrete block with a flat roof. Inside, there was only one room, because my parents ran out of money before they could get it finished. The windows were covered with plastic coated window screening that rattled loudly every time there was a breeze. The only privacy we had was in the bathroom.

One day my father went and bought some pine lumber and hired some local men to build one wall between the office and the living room and another between the living room and the kitchen. My parents slept in two bunk beds in a nook next to the kitchen, and I slept on our fold-out couch in the living room.

Our house was basic because it was designed by my engineer father. Like all engineers, Daddy believed in an informal interpretation of the Bauhaus rule that form follows function. What that aphorism really meant was, if it works, it's beautiful.

✲ ✲ ✲

When it came to animals, my parents had a soft spot for orphans and castoffs. After Sparky met his sad demise from being hit by a car driven by a drunk tourist, our new dog, Skipsy, came from the animal shelter in Santa Fe. And soon after that, a fat and yappy black and white stray pup was found hiding behind my parked bicycle. We named her Wimpy.

All our cats were local wild cats that we would feed and then wind up adopting. Most of our cats preferred to live out in the building that housed Pecos Light and Power Company's silent engines, where castoff clothes folded inside half open storage boxes provided warm beds to sleep on and where the cats had plenty of food to eat every day. My dad said the cats helped to keep the field mice away, although why any field mouse would ever want to go inside that old diesel smelling power plant remained a mystery.

One day my dad brought home a tiny abandoned colt. She was a beautiful little girl colt, with a reddish brown coat, a white blaze down her face, and a black mane and tail. She had three white stockings and one black stocking. I named her Pronto.

Since our new colt had no mother and she was still at the age where she had to nurse, Mama and I would heat up five or six baby bottles of milk and molasses twice a day and take them to our pasture. There was an ancient log cabin style barn with a small stable for two horses in the back. There we would hold the baby bottles, one after the next, as that tiny hungry colt nursed.

After a few months, my father said that our colt was ready to be weaned from the bottle. So we took a bucket of heated milk and molasses down to the pasture, and Daddy guided the colt's nose down into the bucket of milk. Pronto almost reared up, jerking her head back and splashing milk all over the dirt floor of the stable.

But my raised-on-a-farm father persisted, and twenty minutes later, Pronto was drinking the warm milk out of that bucket as though she'd been doing it all of her life. "In a few more months, we'll start weaning her onto drinking water and get her to eating hay and oats," my dad said. "But until then you're going to have to bring a bucket of warm milk down on your bike every day. You can sling the bucket handle over the bike's handlebars. And you'll get to feed her."

Over the next several months, Pronto grew from a gangly colt into a beautiful small horse. She was always more pony size than real horse. And while I loved playing with my miniature horse, I wanted a full sized horse that I could ride.

"Please, Daddy, can I have a horse of my own to ride?" I begged. And finally my dad said he'd see what he could do.

One day I came home from school, and Mother and Daddy said, "Let's go for a drive."

We drove down to our pasture, and Daddy stopped the car and we all got out, and my dad said, "We've got a surprise for you."

My parents took me back to the stable, and there, standing beside Pronto in the small corral, was a beautiful black and white paint mare, tall and slender and rangy.

"Here's your new horse," said my dad.

"You mean I can ride her?" I gasped.

Daddy grinned down at me. "You sure can. We don't have a saddle yet, but we've got a bridle for her. I'll put you up on her bareback, and you can walk her around a little."

Mother smiled at me. "Why don't we name her Mairsy Doats," she said. "Just like that Johnny Mercer song we sing sometimes."

Daddy put the bridle on my new horse, and then he lifted me up on her back. "Hang on to her mane," he told me. I grabbed the horse's mane and hung on for dear life as my father led Mairsy Doats around in small circles. After awhile Daddy said to me, "Why don't you take the reins now?"

I started reining the horse around in small circles that got bigger and bigger. Then, as my parents watched, I rode Mairsy Doats out across our twelve acre pasture.

I wanted to go faster, so I bumped my heels against the horse's side and clicked my tongue. And Mairsy Doats responded by going into a trot and then a slow canter.

I was thrilled with the feeling of having my very own horse under me, so I clicked my tongue once more, and the horse started to gallop.

Off in the distance, I heard my father calling to me, but all of a sudden I was too busy hanging on to my galloping horse's mane to pay any attention. We came to a small gully that ran through our pasture. And before I could stop her, Mairsy Doats lifted off and she jumped right over that gully.

Her front hooves hit the ground on the other side of the gully, and I fell off and hit the ground. I lay there on my back, with the wind knocked clean out of me. Mairsy Doats stopped and turned around. That horse gave me the most puzzled look, just like she was saying, "What are you doing down there?"

Mairsy Doats came up to me and put her muzzle down to touch my left cheek. For the very first time, I felt the whiskery softness of my horse's muzzle and the whuffling of her warm breath blowing against my face. My dad came running up to me and he said, "Are you hurt?"

"I don't think so," I said.

Daddy carefully felt my arms and legs. "I don't think you've broken anything." I stood up on my shaky legs, and he asked me, "Are you hurting anywhere?"

Too shaken to speak, I just shook my head.

And right away my dad lifted me up and put me back up on Mairsy Doats. "Remember," he said to me with a serious look, "Whenever you fall off this horse, if you're not hurt, then you get right back on her again. That way you'll never be scared to ride her."

I nodded, absorbing another one of my dad's life lessons. Whenever you fall off, you get right back up again and you ride your horse.

That lesson came in handy as, over the next several weeks, I began saddling and riding my horse almost every day. At first I only rode her in our pasture, but then my mother said, "As long as you have your two dogs with you, and you don't go too far, you can take your horse out of the pasture to ride. But you always have to put the saddle on her. The only place you can ride her bareback is when you're riding in the pasture."

So me and Mairsy Doats and my two dogs, Skipsy and Wimpy, all explored South Pecos from end to end. And after awhile I began riding over the juniper and piñon covered hills west of Pecos.

CHAPTER 10

Back when my father was teaching at the University of Denver, he would put on a brown double breasted suit every morning, complete with white shirt and maroon tie. If the weather was cold, he would put on a brown overcoat. And last of all, he would always put on his light tan fedora hat, just like the hat that Humphrey Bogart wore in the movie *The Maltese Falcon.*

Even after we moved to Pecos, my father wore that same fedora every day. He wore his hat when he went out to work out on the power lines. He wore his hat when he out went to see a customer who was having trouble with his electric service. My dad even wore his hat when he was working out in the plant yard.

But after three years of exposure to New Mexico sun, wind, rain, and snow, Daddy's hat looked to be showing signs of wear. The rim of the antique fedora kept flopping around Daddy's ears in comical style. Dark patches of sweat circled the crown. And I could stick my thumbs through the holes in that hat.

Mother kept saying, "Daddy, that old hat of yours looks just awful. You've got to get yourself a new hat."

But my dad would just shake his head and say to Mother in his Swedish accent, "Nope. Nope. This old hat does me just fine."

My father always had a fondness for old things. In fact, my father was never a consumer. He always figured that if you used what you had, you'd never want for more. Old cars, for example. Daddy liked old cars because he could work on them and keep them running like clocks. Old power plants too. Even after they had been shut down, Daddy loved our two power engines and their antique generators because, "By golly, they don't build 'em as good nowadays."

And Daddy's old hat just kept on getting more and more dilapidated.

One day Mother said, "Daddy, that old hat looks terrible. You go over to Harrison's Country Store and you get yourself a new hat." Mother's brown eyes twinkled up at Daddy. "Pecos Light and Power Company will even pay for it."

Daddy looked right back at Mother as he said in that mild tone of voice that spelled pure Swedish cussedness, "Now, Liz-Beth, there's not a durned thing wrong with this hat."

Mother used her final warning tone. "Daddy, that hat is absolutely filthy." She took a deep breath and she said, "It stinks!"

"Aw-w, what do I need a new hat for?" Daddy said. "This old hat's still got plenty of wear in it. Nowadays they don't make 'em like this."

And Daddy plunked his sweat stained fedora firmly down on his head. The rim of the old hat flopped around his ears as he marched out the front door, wearing his stinky hat, his plaid shirt, his khaki work pants, and his hightop work boots.

But with that hat, my mother figured both thrift and nostalgia had gone far enough. So one day when, for some obscure reason, my father was not wearing his hat, Mother took that tattered fedora, with its sweat stains and its wear and its holey crown, and she tossed it into the coal stove that we used to heat the living room.

"There," said Mother, brushing her hands together. "That gets rid of that old hat." Her brown eyes sparkled as she gave a short nod. This was one battle she'd managed to win.

I looked over at her. "Mama, that's pretty sneaky. Daddy's not going to be happy."

"Your father is just going to have to live with the fact that he's going to have to get himself a new hat."

About ten minutes later, mother's office helper, Annabelle Quintana, came out of the kitchen where she had been preparing lunch. Annabelle looked around and sniffed the air and said, "What is it that smells so bad?"

Mama sniffed, and Annabelle sniffed, and I sniffed as we all walked around the living room, looking for whatever was causing that unique odor.

"It smells like burning rubber," I said.

"Ohmigoodness," said Mother, "I wonder if it's Daddy's old hat in the stove."

Annabelle looked baffled. "You've got a hat in the stove?"

Mother and I looked at each other, but before we could say anything, Daddy came roaring through the front door. "Liz-Beth!" he called out.

Daddy came into the living room and he stopped cold. "Lord God Almighty, what smells so bad in here?"

There was an awkward silence, but Daddy didn't notice. He kept sniffing and walking around the room until he finally stopped in front of our coal stove. "Did somebody put something in this stove?" Daddy asked as he lifted the latch on the stove door and swung it open.

Out puffed a cloud of dirty gray smoke. Bending over and peering, my dad said, "What the heck is that thing?"

He picked up the poker and he stuck it in the stove, and he brought out a shapeless smoking mass of charcoaled felt. A cloud of foul smelling smoke puffed up from the felt, which had not caught fire, but had simply smoldered and wilted. Sparks rimmed and edged all the holes in the melted crown.

Annabelle put a hand over her mouth and nose. "I'd better go open the kitchen door," she said.

As Annabelle scooted off to get some fresh air, Daddy looked at Mother. "This is my hat," he said in dismay. "Who put my hat in the stove?"

My dad looked over at me. I looked back at him, not saying a word, widening my eyes to look innocent, keeping my mouth tightly shut, trying not to laugh.

"Did you know anything about this?"

"Nuh-ahuhhmmm," I mumbled. But Daddy didn't even notice. He kept looking down at his hat. Almost all the sparks were dying, and there was a steady stream of stinky smoke rising up to the ceiling of our living room.

Mother, caught between laughter and remorse at the distress on my dad's face, said, "Daddy, I put your hat in the stove."

Daddy stood there with his smoking hat hanging off the tip of the poker. His shoulders were bent, his face the picture of woe. "You put my hat in the coal stove?"

Then my father did something he never did. He took the name of the Lord in vain. "Well, I'll be god damned," my father said. "I'll just be god damned."

Mother didn't even rebuke Daddy for using bad language. "Honey, I'll get you a new hat. I promise."

My dad looked ready to weep. "It won't be the same." He paused for a moment of grief. "They don't make 'em like this old hat. Not anymore they don't."

CHAPTER 11

On a clear day in the summer of 1949, I was in my bedroom, getting dressed to go down and ride my horse. I buttoned my shirt, zipped up my jeans, pulled on my black cowboy boots, and grabbed my cowboy hat off the shelf of my closet. I walked into the living room, heading for the front office to tell Mother that I was going to go for a ride on Mairsy Doats.

Suddenly, a stark and screeching scream began piercing through the office door, going on and on. I went to the door and opened it. Then I stood there with my eyes wide open.

Standing in front of the gray metal filing cabinet was my father. His back was flat up against the front of the filing cabinet, and he had both his hands upraised, palms out. And he kept saying, "No, no, no. We can't do that."

Standing in front of my father was Bob Winslow's new wife, Irene Winslow. She had a wadded up bunch of money clenched in her fisted right hand. She kept shaking that fist and the money right in my father's face. And she kept on screaming words to my father that no lady ever used. "You take this money, you goddamn fucking son of a bitch! You take this money right now!"

My dad was shaking his head and saying, "No, no, no. We cannot accept anything less than full payment of your electric bill. That bill is over five months in arrears. We must have complete payment of the total amount owed before we can reconnect your electricity."

The shrieking voice coming out of that purple lipsticked mouth went up even higher. "You fucking bastard! You've got to take this money right now! You better take this money now, you fucking son of a bitch! If you don't take this money, I'll make you wish to god you had!"

I looked over at my mother, sitting there silently at her desk, her arms folded, her lips tight, her brown eyes flashing fire. Standing next to Mother was the office assistant, Annabelle Quintana. Her eyes were wide with shock. And right next to the front door stood Cipriano Lujan, a young man whose parents owned a small grocery store in East Pecos. He was leaning back against the wall, his gaze steady, his eyes alert and observing.

Mother sent me a look, then gave me a quick nod as her eyes glanced over toward the front door of the office. I knew my mother was telling me to get out of there, so I tiptoed around that woman with her wine red hair, her strange looking hat, her citified purple suit, her stilted shoes, and her foul screaming mouth.

Without a sound, I opened the front door, and I slipped out, closing the door behind me. I walked to the front corner of the building, and I softly called to our two dogs. "Here, Skipsy. C'mon Wimpy."

Skipsy, our half collie dog, came around the corner of the house with her head down, moving toward me with a cringing sideways trot, edging away from those screams that came knifing right through the office windows.

Behind her, Wimpy's fat short legged sausage body scampered over the ground as she headed toward me at a frightened run. Both dogs looked up at me as if to say, "What's going on?" But I couldn't tell them, because I couldn't understand it myself.

"C'mon," I told the dogs. "We'd better get away from here." We headed off toward the horse pasture, with the dogs running ahead of me, then circling back, asking for quick reassuring pats on their heads.

When I got to the pasture, I didn't saddle Mairsy Doats. I just slipped her bridle on, and I rode her bareback. My horse and my two dogs and I spent the next several hours wandering among the juniper trees at the base of the small hill at the back of the horse pasture.

My head was swimming and dizzy, and I kept having the funniest whirling sensation in my stomach. I couldn't stop thinking about that screaming woman and all those bad words coming out of her misshapen mouth. After a long and quiet time, I leaned forward and put both arms around my calm and beautiful Mairsy Doats's neck and gave her a long hug, just so I wouldn't feel so scared.

When we got back to the barn, I slipped off the bridle, and fed Mairsy Doats and Pronto generous portions of hay and alfalfa, with a helping of oats for dessert. And then I made sure their water tank was filled up.

Every time I thought about going about back to the house, my feet started dragging and my knees felt weak, so I stayed with my horses as long as I could, petting them and talking to them. Finally I started walking home along the back way, through thickets of juniper and piñon and brush cedar. My two panting, slobbering dogs stayed in front of me, crossing back and forth with a quick, nervous trot.

When I got home and opened the front office door, everything was silent. I tiptoed into the living room, but there was no one there. I opened the door to the hallway, and I could hear my parents through their bedroom door, talking in low murmurs.

The office door banged open, and a man's voice hollered, "Hello! Anyone here? Where the hell is ever'body?"

Quick heels came tapping on the hall floor, and Mother opened the door to the living room. Her face had a set look as she walked across the living room and into the office.

"What the hell's goin' on here? I come in here to pay my electric bill, and there ain't one single soul in this here office."

"I'm sorry," said my mother in a tight voice. "We're having a difficult day."

The man gave Mother a shrewd look. "I'll bet it was that goddamned Winslow woman," he said in a calmer tone of voice. "I saw her and her fancy blue Cadillac when I come out of Harrison's store."

"I'm afraid I can't—"

"That woman's a poisonous bitch. She's sued her first husband, that Santa Fe architect, for big money, more times than anybody can count. And she almost took Chuck Charles of Charles Santa Fe Cadillac to court. God knows what she had on him. Chuck ain't never said a word to nobody, but he hates that woman like poison. How the hell d'you think she got herself that fancy Cadillac of hers? That so-called husband of hers sure as hell can't afford to pay for no car like that one. Old Bob Winslow ain't got shit in his bank account."

My white-faced Mother murmured something inaudible. She took the man's money, made change, and marked his electric bill paid. After he left, Mother sat behind her desk, looking off into the distance, her eyes filled with worry.

☆ ☆ ☆

A few weeks later, Mother sat down with me on our divan. She was holding a sheaf of long papers in her hand, of a kind I had never seen before. They all had a funny-looking stamp down at the bottom, with signatures at the bottom of the page.

Mother said, "Whitney, I have some bad news."

I looked at Mother soberly. I already knew this had something to do with that awful Winslow woman.

"Your father and I are being sued."

My mouth fell open, and I said, "What for?"

"You remember the day that Irene Winslow came in and tore into your Dad?"

"I remember." As if I could've forgotten.

"She's claiming that your father took her money out of her hands. And she claims that he stuffed that money down the front of her dress, inside her brassiere."

"What?" I said, sitting up straight. "That's dumb! Daddy would never, ever do anything stupid like that. Besides, you were sitting right there. And Annabelle was standing right next to you. And that young guy from across the Pecos River was there too. So how can that crazy woman even say anything like that?"

"Well," said Mother, "That's what she's claiming." Mother looked at me with a serious expression on her face that frightened me. "And that makes you a very important witness in this case."

I felt a weight of overwhelming responsibility settle down all around me. "I wish I'd stayed in the office with you. Then I could've been a witness about everything."

Mother shook her head. "No, you did just the right thing. When you went outside, you looked all around the front of the office and the house, and you saw Irene Winslow's Cadillac. And you saw no one in that car, and you also saw that there was no one outside our house trying to look in through our office windows."

"That's right," I said. "Just me and the dogs were there. That's all there was."

"So that means Irene Winslow can't claim she had a passenger in her car who saw what was going on. Or that there was someone looking in our windows who could verify her story. So you did exactly the right thing."

I sat back and relaxed, just a little. "So what are we gonna do?"

"Your dad and I have made an appointment to see our lawyer, Fletcher Catron."

A lawyer, I thought. And I was a witness. Maybe I would have to be in front of a judge and a jury in a courtroom. The whirling sensation settled inside my stomach and then inside my head where it kept on spinning around. "So what's going to happen?"

"I'm afraid I just don't know."

And that was the beginning of our seven-year ordeal.

☆ ☆ ☆

From that time on, Mother would get a tight look on her face whenever she went to the post office to pick up the mail. And at least once a week she would come back with her face white and strained. She would open very official looking envelopes, and take out documents that were long and involved, and she would look them over.

Whatever was in those papers, it was never good. In the evenings both my parents would go into their bedroom and shut their door. I could hear the sounds of their voices talking until I closed my bedroom door at night.

☼ ☼ ☼

As a child, I was always a good sleeper. But my parents started to suffer from insomnia. Mother would get up every morning with red eyes. All day she would be snappish and edgy, and then she would almost break into tears as she apologized to me and to my dad.

And my father kept on working harder and harder every day, building more power lines, hooking up more customers for electricity. In addition, we had recently bought the Pecos Telephone Company from Mr. Wyner. So now both my parents were working twice as hard as they had before.

Mother told me, "I'm having to do the billing for the telephone customers, which takes almost as much time as getting the bills out to all our power customers. And all that extra work doesn't bring us in any more money. That darned phone company just keeps on breaking even."

One afternoon I found my mother in the bathroom, taking a vial of tiny pills out of her purse. "I went to a doctor in Santa Fe to get something to help me relax," Mama said. She looked down at the pills. "These are called codeine. The doctor in Santa Fe said that they will help calm me down during the day and help me to get some sleep at night."

Mama looked over at me. "I want your dad to take these. We just can't go on without getting any sleep at all." She looked away, and then she took a deep breath and gave a sharp sigh. "I just don't know what else we can do," she said.

What the Santa Fe doctors failed to tell my parents, and what few laypersons knew back in 1948, was that codeine was made from the juice of the opium poppy. My mother and father did not know that this drug was closely related to morphine and heroin. The doctors did not tell them that codeine was habit forming, nor that taking codeine could seriously impair their thinking processes. Both my parents would have been shocked and disbelieving if anyone had told them that they were in real danger of becoming a pair of pharmaceutical drug addicts.

The first fatality that resulted from my parents' use of mind-altering drugs was our family life. That warm closeness and the laughter that we had shared died. From that time on until the end of their lives, I would never be able to communicate with my parents again. Every time I tried to talk to them I found myself unknowingly talking to a wall of drugs.

CHAPTER 12

Daddy always started his day before dawn. He would get up around four o'clock, and he would spend the first hour or so of his day eating his breakfast in the kitchen while he read the morning paper. Then he would go out and look at the sun coming up over the mountains to the east of Pecos.

One morning he began reading a series of articles in the *Saturday Evening Post* that were groundbreaking journalism for the late 1940's. Those articles were about rape. Back in 1949, no one ever talked about rape. In fact, no one ever discussed anything about sex in public. So at ten years old, I wasn't quite sure what rape was, but I knew it was something bad.

One morning I snuck that issue of the *Saturday Evening Post* out of the house, and I took it down to the horse barn. I sat on bales of hay, and I read. That article said that there were women who were being made to have sex with men against their will.

Which confirmed what I already knew—that horses had a lot more sense than humans. No one had ever heard of a horse doing any such thing. Horses, I thought, were infinitely better than people. I took that copy of the *Saturday Evening Post* back home, and put it back in our magazine rack, and I forgot about it.

But not my father. As one article after another was printed in magazines and newspapers, he became more and more frantic at the thought of rape. The Pecos-Santa Fe area, which probably had one of the lowest crime rates in America at a time when crime statistics were low to begin with, now looked to my father like a nest of vipers. Not the people we knew, of course, but some unknown person could always be out there, lurking.

One warm summer day, my father told me, while he was making himself some toast and coffee, "Come September, we're going to be sending you down to Las Vegas. You'll be going to school and boarding there during the week, and you'll come home Friday evenings on the bus. And you'll be home for weekends."

I stood there without saying a word while a thousand thoughts spun around inside my head. My father had always known what was good and safe for me, so he must be right about this. But there was a dark and whirling space inside me that kept getting bigger and bigger.

I tried to speak, but for a moment I couldn't make a sound. Finally I said, "Why can't I go to school during the day in Santa Fe, like Jane and Rose Gardner do? They get to come home from school every day. They get to live at home with their parents."

My father shook his head, his voice rising sharply. "Crime rates in Santa Fe are too high. We can't have you going to school in Santa Fe."

"But we go to church there."

Daddy's eyes sparked as he looked at me. "It's too dangerous for you to go to school in Santa Fe." My daddy turned away from me and started eating his toast and drinking his coffee. He opened up the *Santa Fe New Mexican*, and he started reading.

After a silent moment, one of our workmen came to the kitchen door and asked if he could pick up his weekly paycheck. Immediately, Dad got up. "Sure. Right away." And he called to Mother, "Liz-Beth."

The two men walked through the door toward the front office, while I stood there in the kitchen, thinking hard. Daddy wasn't mad at the men that worked for him. He wasn't mad at the rest of the people around him. And he wasn't mad at Mother. Why was he so angry with me? But the more I thought about it, the deeper the mystery became. And the black hole inside me kept growing and twisting.

CHAPTER 13

I remember sitting between my parents on a prim and proper couch in a small front room with waxed and glossy hardwood floors and vacuumed area rugs. Three weeks ago, my father had told me, "We've found a place for you to board in Las Vegas."

My eyes must have shown my misery. But nothing more was said.

And now I sat there, looking at a fat middle-aged woman with short iron gray hair, sitting across from us in a wing backed chair. She wore a flowered housedress and a vast pinafore apron. Her lips were curved in a chilly smile, and her cold gray eyes appraised me and found me wanting.

I looked away from her, looking at the white walls where there were shelves with well dusted porcelain figurines. A few pieces of carnival glass glowed inside dark and forbidding and absolutely useless glass front cabinets.

Mama looked down at me with the anxious look she always had when she wanted some adult to like me. To think I was good enough, I thought resentfully. "I do hope you will get along well down here," Mother said to me.

The fat woman looked over at me and said with false heartiness, "Of course she will. We will get along very well, won't we, Whitney. You may call me Auntie Em."

Another smile flitted across her thin mouth, showing teeth that were small and precise and white.

A cold knot of dread settled into my stomach as my parents went out and brought in my suitcase filled with brand new school clothes and school supplies. And then my parents walked out the door without even saying good-bye. I saw them through the front window, getting into their new Plymouth station wagon and driving off.

I was left standing alone in a cold, barren living room. "Well now, Whitney," said Auntie Em, all pretense of affability gone, "It's time you went upstairs and unpacked. You're living in my home now, and you will have to obey all the rules. Dinner is served promptly at five-thirty."

I left the living room and climbed dark and narrow stairs that went up to a small dormer bedroom. The walls were painted a pale gold. Yellow curtains with figured patterns swayed in the sunlit window that was open to a hot September breeze.

My suitcase lay on the white counterpane of the creaking double bed. I unpacked my new school clothes. I picked up my duffle bag, and I took out my school supplies and placed them on the small desk in the corner nearest to the door. Then I put the suitcase and the duffle bag on the floor of the closet.

I sat down on the creaking bed and looked around. Strange pictures hung on the walls. Children dressed in styles from the 1920s watched as elves played under spreading oak trees and fairies perched on flowers. I sat there, staring at those pictures until the nauseating smell of frozen fishsticks in a frying pan drifted up the staircase.

I heard a call from downstairs. I opened the bedroom door and went down and stood just inside the kitchen door, looking at the white painted table that stood in the exact center of the kitchen. On that table, I saw places set for two.

"Aren't you going to wash your hands before you eat?" Auntie Em looked at me as though I were an orphan child off the streets. I looked back at her, knowing I was here only because forty dollars a month was going into Auntie Em's purse. I said nothing, just walked silently into the bathroom and washed my hands.

As we sat down at the table, Auntie Em looked across at me and said, "Do you say grace before you eat?" A small pain began growing in my left temple as I shook my head without making a sound. I had no reason to thank God for being in this place.

Auntie Em gave a "Hmph," that was half sniff. "You're Presbyterian, aren't you? In this house we have always been Methodists."

As though Methodists were better than Presbyterians, I thought resentfully.

"We will say grace before every meal. Fold your hands, please."

I clasped one hand with the other and bowed my throbbing head while the grace was given by Auntie Em. "We thank thee, Lord, for this food for the nourishment of our bodies. Amen."

I opened my eyes and saw Auntie Em's pale blue eyes looking straight at me. "You may pick up your fork now."

I took the fork in my left hand and looked down at the limp rectangles of breaded frozen fishsticks that had been incinerated in Crisco. A modest helping of canned green beans sogged beside the fish sticks.

Dinner was silent. I ate looking only at my plate, carefully cutting each fishstick before I put it in my mouth, making sure that not one bit of food fell off my fork. I was eating, not because I was hungry but because I knew I had to. Already I knew that I could make absolutely no mistakes in this house.

After dinner, Auntie Em said, "I listen to the radio for two hours in the evenings. Do you have any favorite programs?"

"No, ma'am," I replied softly, like a small animal that seeks to move silently to escape a sensed danger.

"Then what would you like to do?"

"I would like to go up to my bedroom and read." I had brought some Cherry Ames and Nancy Drew books with me.

Auntie Em nodded with a sharp dip of her head. "Then you do that. Your father says you are supposed to be in bed by nine o'clock. Be sure to set your alarm for seven fifteen every morning. You will need to make your bed in the mornings, and you must keep your room neat. I don't like climbing those stairs, so you will be doing all the housework up there."

I climbed the steep and narrow stairway to the airy bedroom, grief making my eyes gritty with unshed tears, the sense of desertion a tight trap clenching my heart. I shut the door at the top of the stairs. I walked over to the bed, and I put my face down on the pillow. And I started to cry without making a sound, so that I wouldn't be heard over the sounds of tinny laughter that came from the floor model radio in the downstairs living room.

At eight thirty I began getting ready for bed. I went downstairs, into the dark bathroom, and I brushed my teeth and washed my face. I went upstairs and I put on my new pajamas, and then I got into bed and I put out the light. I lay there in that strange bed, absolutely still and silent as a black depression settled over me. My father and mother no longer wanted me. I had been abandoned to a hostile stranger, and I didn't know why.

Finally, being young and healthy, I fell into a deep sleep with no dreams that I could remember.

✲ ✲ ✲

The next morning I woke up when the alarm went off at seven fifteen. I dressed in my new school clothes, and I brushed my hair. When I went downstairs to use the bathroom and-brush my teeth and wash my face, I saw a plate of breakfast rolls on the table.

Auntie Em was nowhere in sight, so I took one of the rolls and went back upstairs to get my books. I knew that I had better keep that roll hidden, so I put it in a kleenex and stuffed it in my book carrier. I walked back downstairs and out the back door, silently closing the door behind me.

I bit into the cold roll as I walked the two blocks to school, to register myself and start my first day in a new school in a strange and terrible town.

CHAPTER 14

In the 1950's Las Vegas, New Mexico, was a small remote town with a colorful history. Founded in the eighteenth century, the town soon became a trading center. Ranchers, businessmen, and farmers came to Las Vegas to stock up on needed supplies. Billy the Kid was a regular visitor, and on one occasion he got himself arrested in Las Vegas.

After the Santa Fe Railroad came through in the 1880's, the town turned into a farming and ranching center, a health spa, and a tourist town. A number of well-off people built two and three story Victorian homes with all the latest in fine furnishings, complete with gas lighting. A few years later, they had newfangled electric lights installed. Those who could not afford mansions built themselves smaller brick homes that were snug and comfortable.

In 1894, Highlands University was founded. And in 1931, the beautiful art deco style Ilfeld Auditorium was built on the university campus. Everyone basked in the glow of the money that would come flowing in forever.

But during the Great Depression, the town's economy collapsed. And right up into the early 1950s, while the rest of the country prospered, Las Vegas was still locked into its own longstanding recession that was bitter even by New Mexico standards.

Every morning as I walked to school, I went by grand old homes that had been subdivided into dingy apartments. Their outside walls and roofs were weather stained, and most of the houses had little paint left on them. Inside the houses, wainscoting and walls were painted chalky shades of green or buff or pinkish-orange. The ornate tin ceilings had been painted over, and the floors were covered with cheap linoleum.

There were few jobs in 1950s Las Vegas. Some husbands went out of town and found jobs doing roadwork for the State Highway Department. Others found work in construction wherever they could, even going out of state for weeks or months at a time.

Young couples who had bought homes at the end of the Second World War were now locked into owning homes that were unsalable. So the wives stayed at home to raise their children alone, living on whatever money their menfolk could send home to them. In those days, of course, women with husbands and children almost never had jobs of their own.

In the Old Town area, around the plaza, there were some of the poorest people in the whole of the America. Homeless men and women, all of them dressed in filthy ragged clothing. They looked like they were literally starving to death, as some of them may have done.

It was true then, as it is now, that after wars and during recessions, people become locked into their fears. So the people of Las Vegas were fearful and angry in the face of endless hardship. Back in 1950, Las Vegas was a tightly knit and bitter town of about twenty thousand people.

It was not a friendly place for a twelve year old seventh grade girl to be cut adrift. Especially since her parents were known to own and operate a power company, which meant that they must be very well off, which was actually not the case. But every kid in Las Vegas knew that I got to leave that hopeless town to go home on weekends and in the summers, while the people around me were stuck in that dead end community. No wonder hardly anyone, whether child or adult, would speak to me. But all that was something my twelve year old child's mind could not comprehend.

CHAPTER 15

One day when I was in eighth grade, I walked into the band room, and I said to the band director, "I want to learn how to play the flute."

The band director was an older man, in his sixties, and he was nearing retirement. He looked at me with tired eyes, and he said, "We have a flute you can use. Woodwind classes are after school, Mondays, Wednesdays, and Thursdays from three o'clock to four thirty. I'll put you on the signup sheet."

That weekend I brought my school flute home to Pecos, and I showed Mother how I could blow air across the hole in the mouthpiece to make a sound.

For one moment, Mother looked at me and her eyes really connected with mine. "We'll have to get you a flute of your own," she said. "It'll need to be secondhand because that's all we can afford, but I think we can get you a flute to play."

So I went to woodwind class three times a week, and I began learning how to play my very own nickel plated secondhand flute.

Most evenings I would go upstairs to my room after dinner, and I would practice. Not too much. And not too loud. I didn't want to attract any unwanted attention from Auntie Em.

✲ ✲ ✲

In all that wilderness of loneliness, there was one twelve year old girl that lived next door. She played clarinet in junior high school band, and I played the flute. We began walking home after school, busily talking to each other about the things that junior high school girls talk about. I had had best friends in grade school, and it had been fun to have them over to play. And somehow I was still in that childhood frame of mind. So one day I said to Janeen, "I'd really like for the two of us to be best friends."

I can't remember Janeen's response, but I do remember overhearing her mother coming over that evening and saying to Auntie Em, "I don't want that Whitney playing with my daughter. I don't want her talking to Janeen or having anything to do with her. There's something wrong with that girl."

Then the two women looked over their shoulders and they saw me. Both women turned their backs and began talking to each other in low, ominous murmurs. I walked in the back door of Auntie Em's house, wondering what was wrong with me.

From that day on, Janeen's attitude completely changed. She and the other girls began talking about me. Whenever I came near them, they would all stop speaking, and they would stare at me with eyes that looked as glazed as playground marbles.

One day I overheard them talking about me as I came into a classroom. I sat down and I broke into tears. "I know what you're doing," I cried, "And I don't like it. You don't have any right to talk about me behind my back."

One of the girls looked at me and said, "Oh, who cares what you think. You're just a stupid—" And she stopped and smirked at me, then looked around at the rest of the class.

I looked around as well, and not one of those girls was meeting my eyes. I sat there at my isolated desk, and I started sobbing. "Stop being mean to me," I cried. Looking at Janeen, I said, "Why do you hate me? What have I done?"

Janeen's head came forward, and she clenched her hands. "I'm not being mean to you."

"Yes, you are," I cried. "You're talking about me behind my back. Telling lies about me. You and all the rest of them. You're all mean and you're all hateful."

Another girl snapped back at me. "Why should we care what you think? You're such a liar. Nobody believes anything you say."

"I am not a liar," I said, my Sagittarius soul wounded to the core. "You've all been saying bad stuff about me and doing mean things to me, and you know it." I put my head down on the desk and tried to control my tears.

"What a baby you are," said Janeen. And the other girls shrugged their shoulders and turned their backs on me.

From that day on, I began walking to school with my head bent, looking down at the ground to hide my anger and my pain. And the rumors, whatever they were, spread like grassfires in a high wind.

✡ ✡ ✡

Christmas had always been my favorite holiday. The chemistry sets my dad got for me, the occasional doll from my mother, the blue spruce Christmas trees with their lights and decorations, the warmth, the laughter, the music, all brought security into my life.

Now, every day throughout that holiday season, my mother went over to the post office to get the mail, and every day she brought home more long envelopes that were stuffed with all kinds of legal documents.

In the evenings, after the Pecos Light and Power Company office was closed, my parents took those legal papers into their bedroom and closed the door. Walking alone to my bedroom at night, I could hear the now familiar sounds of my mother weeping, while she and Daddy talked in low voices. Until at last there was silence.

CHAPTER 16

The next three school years crawled slowly onward. One weekend I tried telling Mother how much I hated being boarded out in Las Vegas. "Mother, I don't like it down at Vegas," I said. "None of the kids like me. They make fun of me, and they look at me like they hate me. Nobody will even talk to me."

Mother had just taken her evening pills. Her eyes were filmy with the drugs, and she looked at me dreamily. "Oh, I wouldn't worry about that. Kids in junior high school are like that. It was the same way when I went to school."

My already withered hopes began to die in my heart. I knew better than to try and persuade my dad to change his mind. Might as well try to grow a tree on a boulder as plant a new idea in my dad's stubborn Swedish head.

Monday morning came way too soon. Dad got me up before dawn. He fed Mother and me breakfast, and then he put my suitcase of freshly washed clothes in our car. As Mother and I got into the car, my stomach began to roil.

Driving down to Las Vegas, I didn't say one word. Finally Mother looked over at me and she snapped, "I don't know why you won't talk to me. I drive you down to school so that we can have some talk time together, to have some closeness, and you won't say one word to me."

I couldn't say anything to that, so I just put my head down and started reading my latest Nancy Drew book. I only looked up when we drove by Starvation Peak, a round butte with a small, flat top. Legend had it that centuries ago, the Spanish conquistadors had attacked a group of Indians. Finally, the Indians climbed to the top of Starvation Peak, and the Spanish camped all around the bottom, and there they stayed until the Indians had all starved to death.

I stared up at Starvation Peak. I knew that Mother was taking me back to that starvation town I'd been dumped into. And I didn't know why.

Finally, I spoke. "Mama," I said, "Isn't there anywhere else I can go to school?"

Frowning, Mother glanced over at me and gave a sharp sigh. I could tell she was still mad because I hadn't talked to her. "Well," she said, "The only other thing I can think of is to send you back to Oklahoma, where your uncles live."

Fear congealed like iced Jell-O in my stomach. My parents were actually thinking about sending me away forever. I might never see my dogs or my horses again.

I froze, sitting absolutely still and silent on the sofa-like car seat. An inner knowing rose up in me, a clear understanding. From now on, I would have to be the perfect child. Absolutely good in every way. Never complaining. Never crying. Never letting anyone know anything at all about what was going on inside me.

But what had I done that was so bad my parents didn't want me anymore? What was so awful about me that I had become an abandoned child? Why had I been sent away from home?

I could not bear the thought of my father doing anything bad to me, so I considered the situation and came to the conclusion that it must have been my mother who had been the behind the scenes manipulator that sent me away from home because she was jealous of my close relationship with my father.

But in reality, it was the codeine. That opium-based narcotic was what did the real damage. All during the 1940s and the '50s and the '60s, no one knew the real story of the side effects of mind altering drugs, particularly the long term effects. And looking back, that does seem strange. How could they not have known?

But in those days, the collective paradigm held firmly to the belief that modern medicine, which had already done away with smallpox, diphtheria, typhoid fever, pneumonia, and so many other killer diseases, was infallible. Soon, the medical profession told us, there will be a cure, not only for cancer, but for all the world's ailments. It will only take a lot of money and a little time, and the whole world will be filled with happy, healthy people.

My father subscribed wholeheartedly to those views, right up to the end of his life. One time he told me, "You've never had to see anyone die of pneumonia, the way I saw my father die when I was sixteen. It took four men to hold my father down. Nowadays if you get pneumonia, you just go to the doctor's office and get yourself a shot. That's a miracle. Modern medicine has done that for us."

Today America's bright dream of achieving universal good health through medical research has dimmed. According to the United Nations, the American medical system is now the poorest of any developed country in the world. And the antibiotics that my father had such faith in are increasingly helpless against today's rapidly mutating bacteria. Medical progress is now measured in steps rather than leaps.

But back in the 1950s, I was a child who witnessed, all unknowing, the pharmaceutical companies chemical numbing of my parents' capabilities to love, to empathize, to truly be there for their daughter. I was a helpless and unknowing witness to a chemically induced freeze drying, a suspension of all the higher level emotional faculties in the minds and hearts of two good people.

Within weeks after starting on codeine, my two strong, intelligent, and loving parents had been reduced to a dependency that meant their emotions vacillated between sudden angry outbursts, shaking night terrors, and an eerie, dreamy detachment from all the closeness of family life. They could still run their business, but we would never again have a warm family life or a real home.

☆ ☆ ☆

By ninth grade, I was spending more and more time alone in the upstairs bedroom of Auntie Em's home. And when puberty hit, I started experiencing severe cramps. Two or three days a month, I would stay home from school. All day long, I would just lie in bed, with black thoughts swirling all around me. But by then Auntie Em took very little notice of anything I did. I wasn't sure if she even knew I was in the house.

Finally, my parents got a letter in the mail from the school principal. I had an unexcused absentee rate that was unacceptable. And I was flunking almost every course I was taking. That afternoon, my father came storming up the stairs to the bedroom in Auntie Em's home, where he saw me lying in bed on a school day. He pulled the curtains open, and he yanked the blankets off the bed and onto the floor and he said to me, "You get up out of that bed right now!"

I sat up and looked at my dad, my eyes blinking in the light. "I can't," I said. "I'm sick, and I hurt all over. I don't feel good."

My dad never raised his voice when he was angry, but it carried anyway, and his words could be heard throughout the entire house. "I don't want to hear one word out of you. You get up out of that bed right now, and you get dressed, and you get yourself down to that kitchen," he said. "And you bring all your schoolbooks and all your papers with you."

I got up, and I dressed with shaking hands. When I came downstairs, my arms loaded with schoolbooks and spiral notebooks, my father was seated at the kitchen table.

Auntie Em was sitting straight up in her kitchen chair, right across from us. Her eyes were wide as she looked over at my angry father with his electric blue eyes. I would've enjoyed the look on Auntie Em's face, except that I was a lot more scared than she was.

My father said to me, "You haven't been handing in your algebra assignments. And, according to the principal, you're making D's and F's in every one of your classes. So from now on through the end of this school year, I'm going to be driving down here every evening. On weekends you'll be at home all day Saturday and Sunday, working until you get caught up in your math, along with every other assignment you'll need to hand in."

For the next several hours, my dad and I worked on algebra. I didn't dare cry. When he got up to leave for home, he said to me, "I'll be here tomorrow afternoon right after school."

Finally, Auntie Em spoke up. “Mr. Benson, I think you’d better find another place for your daughter to stay. I’m not one to allow any unpleasantness in this house. My health won’t stand for it.”

My father gave Auntie Em one glance. “Whitney will be coming home in a few weeks for summer vacation. We’ll find her another place to stay for the coming school year.”

No one ever argued with my father when he spoke in that tone of voice. It was a deadly calm command. Even Auntie Em was left without words.

For the next nine weeks, a great silence fell over that house, and over Auntie Em. Every afternoon after school, my dad and I would work at the kitchen table for three or four or even five hours. By the time school let out for summer vacation, my math, my English papers and my social science assignments were all up to date. My grades on my final report card jumped from D’s and F’s, all the way up to B’s in all my subjects. I even made a B-minus in algebra.

On the last day of school, my parents came down to Las Vegas and packed up all my stuff. My father spoke to me only once on that drive home. “We’ve found you another place to stay. You’re grown up enough now that you don’t need to have adults around to take care of you. From now on you’ll have a studio apartment of your own. And you’ll have an allowance of five dollars a week for food and spending money.”

I breathed a deep sigh of relief. For the first time since I could remember, I would have some real privacy. No more Auntie Em. And five dollars a week in the 1950s was a lot of money. But the shabby town of Las Vegas didn’t look all that much better to me.

✲ ✲ ✲

After we got home I lugged my suitcase into my bedroom and opened it up. Then I unpacked everything I’d brought home, and I hung all my clothes in my closet. I closed the suitcase and put it away, and then I sat down on my own bed in my own bedroom, which was a strangely vacant room. Whenever I slept in that bedroom, I felt like a visitor.

I remembered the time when I was little and my father had me sitting in his lap. He was telling me about the day I had been born. "Your mother went through a real hard time having you," my dad said to me. "The doctor even thought they might have to do a Cesarean section."

"What's that?"

"That's when the doctor goes into the womb and lifts the baby out through an incision he makes with a surgeon's knife. But at the last minute, Mama went into real hard labor, and you finally came into the world."

"Where were you?" I asked.

"I was out in the waiting room for the fathers, and I thought it never was going to end. When I went into Mama's hospital room after you were born, and I held you in my arms for the first time, I was really thankful." Daddy shook his head. "Boy, was I relieved that you'd finally made it."

Now, sitting on my bed in our silent house, I felt a sharp longing for the time when I could talk to my dad, really talk, just like we used to.

CHAPTER 17

In a life where everything seemed to be in upheaval and there was no order that I could see, the Pecos mountains became my refuge. On the warm summer mornings, I would saddle up Mairsy Doats. And me and my two dogs and Mairsy Doats would all head up into the mountains.

Along the way we would pass by a dried up tailings pond that was left over from the days when there had been gold and silver and copper mining up the Pecos Canyon. The ore from the mine was loaded onto small tram cars that clacked over narrow railroad tracks, going up and down pine covered mountainsides, traveling all the way to the mill. That was where the gold and silver and copper and lead were all refined and then shipped out.

The mine had closed down after the Second World War, and the mill had long since been torn down. But the tailings pond was still there with its smell of chemicals. No plants grew on that dry cracked clay. No lizard, however small, darted over its surface.

Once we got past the smelly tailings pond, the Glorieta Baldy fire road turned into a two track dirt trail that wound through piñon covered hills and climbed on up into the mountains. I would ride along those tracks until the brushy piñon and juniper trees gave way to pine trees and green meadow grass that was sprinkled with wildflowers of assorted shapes and sizes and colors. To the north I could see Pecos Baldy, with its icecap that never completely melted. And toward the east were green mountains with a road that led to Cow Creek and the hamlet of Upper Colonias. I could turn my head and look over my shoulder to the south where the majestic Glorieta Mesa loomed, giving me a sense of safe enclosure, of order in a world where my daily life was chaos and confusion.

I would ride up that beautiful mountainside until I was so high up that I could look way down at Pecos and see the houses, each one no bigger than a tiny matchbox. There were always a few cars driving along the roads, and they looked as small as the heads on the pins my grandmother used when she sewed.

The only sound was the wind in its endless mystery, turning the pine and fir trees into living, moving creatures as it whispered and sighed endlessly through their branches. I always wanted to ride my horse to the top of Glorieta Baldy. But that great and beautiful mountain always receded ever farther away from me. So when the sun began to head west, I would reluctantly turn Mairsy Doats toward home.

The gentle New Mexico mountains taught me to use my intuitive mind, to silently absorb the shapes and colors and sounds and beauties of the world around me. And they taught me that riding horseback was not like riding in a car. When you were on a horse, it took real time and patience to get somewhere.

The wordless peace that I felt in the mountains taught me about God. I can still hear the voice of God, whispering to me in the soughing of the wind and gently speaking to me from the deep green branches of the pine trees that grew on the steep mountain slopes.

☆ ☆ ☆

The next September was the start of my sophomore year in high school. My parents had rented a one room studio apartment on the second floor. It had a tiny kitchenette in one corner, and the bathroom was across the short hall. This was located only a few houses away from Auntie Em's place, but it was far enough removed that it seemed to me like another world.

Mother and Dad spent half a day moving me in, and then they left to go back to Pecos.

My new landlady was well up in her seventies. She lived downstairs, and she was deaf as a post. Across the hall from her lived another little old lady who always wore black dresses with lace collars and who sat in her chair and did almost nothing from day to day. She too was deaf. Both women were very quiet and rather sweet, so I dubbed them the Deaf Old Dearies.

Living in the apartment may have been part of the reason why I began to enjoy schoolwork. I didn't have the everlasting noise and bustle of living in a house that was really an extension of a busy company office. And I was free from the nightmare of Auntie Em and her cronies.

One of my first assignments in my sophomore year was to write an essay on Abraham Lincoln. I went to the school library and the public library to do research on Lincoln and the Civil War. That was when I found out how much I enjoyed doing research. Spending time reading in a library and making notes was quiet and informative.

When I got my paper back from the teacher, there was an A+ at the top. The teacher said that this was one of the top essays from all her English classes. In geometry I worked diligently, determined not to have to live through another fiasco like my freshman algebra course. I kept my math grade up to a C, and I got B's in most of my other courses, an A in English, and a more or less automatic A in band, where all you had to do was show up and play to get the grade. I even put in time practicing my flute.

✲ ✲ ✲

Architecturally, Las Vegas, New Mexico, was a beautiful town that had been frozen in time and left to slowly decay. On warm evenings I would walk by whole blocks of homes that were Norman Rockwell perfect. Each house had a porch and a lawn with trees and flowers.

As the sun went down there would be a few moments when the lights inside the houses would go on, but the drapes were not yet closed. Lace curtains gave a softness to picture window views of overstuffed chairs and sofas. Dark Victorian end tables held family

Bibles that were inscribed with the names and the birth dates of long grown sons and daughters. On the walls hung pre-World War II prints of idealized landscapes and framed photographs that all blended into dreams of a time lost and gone.

Every fourth or fifth house had a big gold star glowing dimly from one of the windows. Those were the homes of gold star mothers, women whose sons had been killed either in World War II or in Korea.

I would walk past all those homes, carrying a book in my hand, reading in snatches about the history of philosophy or excerpts from the writings of Albert Schweitzer. I even had dreams of becoming a medical doctor in Africa, just like Schweitzer.

One evening as I was walking down a tree lined block, a car pulled up beside me and stopped. The back window rolled down, and I saw Betty Rolandson, a girl I knew in school.

"Hey," she called to me.

I waved and kept on walking.

"Hey!" The call was insistent.

I turned and looked as Betty rolled down the back window of the car and stuck her head out. "You wanta go for a ride? C'mon, ride with us. We'll drive you home."

I shook my head and Betty said, "Oh, c'mon. It'll be fun."

I shook my head again, then shrugged my shoulders, hesitated, and finally said, "Well, okay. I guess."

Betty opened the car door. "Hurry up. We haven't got all night."

Hesitantly, I walked to the car and got in. Betty reached across me and she slammed the door as the young man in the driver's seat gave the car the gas. Tires squealed as we sped down the street, going well over the speed limit.

I looked at the three boys in the front seat. The driver was an older boy who had graduated from high school two or three years before. His name was Carl. He was tall and blond, and he was dressed in a Western shirt and cowboy boots. Carl turned and gave me a flash of a practiced smile. The other two boys kept their backs turned.

Betty moved forward and leaned over the front seat. She put her right arm around Carl's neck and kissed his left ear. Shocked, I slid back in my seat, wondering where we were going. I felt strange and frightened. This was not the Betty I had seen in school, friendly and laughing with all the other kids.

Carl looked back at me and gave me another smile. Quickly I looked away, but not before I had seen his smile widen.

Betty moved even closer to Carl, playing with the top button of his shirt. "How 'bout we go out to the strip along the highway?" she said.

"Yeah, we can do that."

One of the other boys spoke up. He was short, dark-haired and sullen. "Let's go by the red light district. It's about three blocks over."

"You don't have to tell me. I know where it is," Carl said. He spun the wheel, and the car squalled around a corner. Betty squealed and gave a high, shrieking giggle.

"I'd like to go home now," I started to say, but there was a burst of speed as we careened around another corner, and I grabbed the window crank to hold on.

A moment later the car slowed to a crawl as Carl drove down the street. Here and there a red light gleamed dimly in a darkened window. There were no streetlights illuminating the tiny stucco houses that abutted the cracked and battered cement sidewalk. The street was deserted.

"Guess they're not open for business tonight," said the boy in the right-hand seat.

"Don't know why," Carl said. "Old Judge Gutierrez runs this red light district, so there's no way they're gonna get raided."

Betty squirmed and shrugged her shoulders. "This is so boring," she said. "Let's go someplace fun."

"You got it, baby," said Carl as the aging Ford shuddered into a U-turn. "We'll go out on the highway to one of the clubs, and we'll look for a little action."

Betty put her head forward, her rabbit teeth nibbling on Carl's neck. He kept one eye on the road as he turned his head and kissed Betty on the lips.

"Maybe we'd better let Whitney go home," said Betty, giving me a too friendly smile.

I said nothing. I was afraid to speak or move. I just hunched over, clutching my book, as the car raced down another street.

Carl glanced back at me and he saw my unsmiling face. "We'll put her down here," he said.

The Ford went weaving over to the side of the street. Carl stomped on the brakes, and the old Ford squealed to a stop. Betty reached across and opened the door. "See you tomorrow. At school."

"Okay. Yeah. I guess," I mumbled as I slid out and stood up on shaking legs.

Betty gave me a satisfied cat smile. "Bye." She waved one languid hand as she and the boys started laughing at me. Then she slammed the door as Carl gave the old Ford the gas. The Smittys rumbled as the car fishtailed down the street and screeched around the next corner. And the sound of the car slowly faded.

I stood there, all alone under the dim and silent light of a street lamp. I looked around, wondering just where I was and how I could get home safely. I started shivering from the chill in the air. The sun had gone down, and in the darkening evening, all the homes had their curtains closed. Light gleamed around the edges of those tight, protective curtains.

I began walking as fast as I could, from one street lamp to the next, heading in what I hoped was the right direction to get home. At the end of the fourth or fifth block, I looked down the street to my right. I saw the public library at the center of the park, and I knew I was just a few blocks from my apartment. I started running as fast as I could, hoping that Carl and Betty and those strange boys would not come back to try and pick me up again.

When I reached the front door of the house where my apartment was, I stood a moment as I gasped for breath. Then I took the house key out of my pocket and unlocked the door. I ran up the stairs, knowing the two deaf old ladies who lived there would never hear me.

I went into my studio apartment, and I closed and locked the door. I was shaking, and my knees were so weak I didn't know if I could keep from falling down. I knew I could never go out for a walk in Las Vegas again. All those nice houses with their neatly trimmed lawns suddenly seemed like a gloss, an iridescent surface glowing on the top of stagnant sewage that had a spider at its center named Judge Gutierrez. The judge that ran all the whorehouses and strip joints in Las Vegas. The judge who kept sending my parents all those legal papers that made my mother cry for hours on end.

Everything and everyone in Las Vegas was warped. All the kids at school. All their parents. All the people of Las Vegas, every one of them, were living under some kind of dark and evil spell, cast by Judge Gutierrez. Las Vegas was a horrible, evil town, and I was incarcerated there for what seemed like forever, serving a six year prison sentence for crimes I had never committed.

CHAPTER 18

One warm spring day, my Aunt Sybil called Mother long-distance from Perry, Oklahoma. "Day before yesterday, Mother Wilson started seeing double. This morning she called and told me the doctor had put her in the hospital. So I went to the hospital during visiting hours to see her, and we talked. Mother Wilson looked just fine. She told me her vision was clearing up, and that she felt good, and the doctor had told her that she should be ready to go home by the next day.

"Then all of a sudden, Mother Wilson sat straight up in her bed, and she looked up toward the ceiling with the most surprised look on her face. And when she fell back on her pillow, she was gone."

"Gone," said my mother to my father that evening after work. "Just like that."

✲ ✲ ✲

I don't remember anything about my grandmother's funeral, which was held at the Perry Memorial Chapel. I do remember one of the neighbors saying afterward, "Eighty years is a good long life. When it's your time, and you've got to go, that's the way to do it."

All the family and the neighbors agreed. They all said that Grandma Wilson had lived a rich full life. But my mother said to me, "An awful lot of people die in their seventies, so anyone who lives a full eighty years has to have lived a rich full life, just by virtue of having survived for so long."

The day after Grandma Wilson's funeral, my dad took me to the station and put me on the train. I had to get back to school in Las Vegas. So I got on the train, and I sat there all alone as the train whistled its way across Oklahoma and New Mexico.

I got off the train at the Las Vegas Railroad Station and took a taxi to my apartment. I lugged my heavy suitcase upstairs. It bumped against my knees with every step. I went into my studio apartment, and I closed the door behind me. And I carefully unpacked my clothes.

At last I gave a sigh, and I sat down on the floor and put my head down on the seat cushion of my one and only chair. And I remembered my grandmother.

Grandmother Wilson was a plump and tiny woman. Her eyes were blue, and she wore wire-frame glasses. Her long gray hair was pinned up in a knot at the back of her head, and her dresses were flowered, like all grandmothers wore back then. Her black lace-up shoes had sturdy heels and black shoestrings that were always tied in a nice tight bow.

I was eight years old when I Grandma caught me filching some unbaked cookies that were on a plate right next to a buttered cookie sheet. I thought she wouldn't notice if I just took one or two cookies, but she did.

Grandma laughed at me and shook her head and said, "Naughty girls who steal raw cookies don't get to eat any cookies when they're baked." But of course I snitched some of the freshly baked cookies too.

When I was born, Grandma Wilson made a hand sewn quilt for me. It had beautifully embroidered yellow roses appliquéd on large squares of white fabric. I used that quilt on my bed until it finally wore out, when I was married and in my twenties. Then I told my mother, "I feel guilty about not keeping Grandma's quilt in the cedar chest. If I had taken better care of that quilt, I'd still have it."

Mother looked at me in surprise. "Oh no, honey," she said. "That quilt was meant to be used. It was nothing fancy. It was just an everyday quilt."

Grandma's quilt had been an everyday work of art, like the crocheted back and arm covers that covered her living room chairs; like the fine handmade lace that Grandma sewed on her own dresses; like Grandma's painting of a woods with a stream running through it; like the beaded purse that Grandma made way back around the year 1895 for Little Mary, Grandma's youngest sister who died of diabetes at the tender age of ten.

When my Grandfather Wilson passed away, Mother had used some of her small inheritance to buy twelve acres of pasture land where our two horses, Mairsy Doats and Pronto, grazed on the grama grass that grew on the acreage. There was also a gray house that had a steep pitched red roof. My parents had divided the house into two rental apartments. But the back apartment was too small for most people, so it was usually empty. That was where Grandma Wilson stayed when she came to see us.

I was ten years old when my grandmother first came to visit us in Pecos. Grandma liked to travel, and she had never been to New Mexico. So she came and stayed with us for the summer. Looking back, I'm sure my mother must have told her about the lawsuit. And Grandma Wilson must have wanted to be near her only daughter.

I was happy to see my grandmother, and when Mother told me I would be staying down in the small apartment to keep Grandma company, I was even happier. That first night, after we had climbed into the double bed and turned out the light, Grandma Wilson began telling me about her girlhood growing up on a Kansas farm, way back in the 1880s. The saddest part was when she told me about her mother's death.

"When Little Mary was born, my mother became terribly ill. Grandma Bean, who lived on a farm about a mile down the road, had delivered Little Mary, but there was nothing she could do for my mother. She just kept on getting sicker and sicker, until she could hardly move. I was only thirteen, but I stayed home from school. I nursed Mother, and I took care of Little Mary.

"One evening I went down to the spring house to get some cold water. As I was walking back to the house, carrying the water, I heard the sound of angel wings rustling in the trees. I knew my mother was gone. The angels had taken her. And when I got back into the house, why so 'twas." Grandma always used funny words like 'twas, and 'twill be.

"How old was Great-Grandmother Hosie when she died?" I said.

"She was thirty-seven years old." My grandmother sighed. "From that time on, I stayed home and kept house for my father and my two brothers and Little Mary. Sometimes I would be so tired at night I couldn't sleep and I couldn't move. I would lie in my bed and listen to the clock ticking. I could even hear our cat walking across the floor."

All that summer I took lessons from my grandmother in how to paint with oils. Grandma and I would each stand in front of our own easel, and she would show me how she painted her landscapes. Then I would try to paint the way she did, except that I would put horses in my pictures.

Grandma Wilson taught me how to sew a fine hemstitch, and she taught me how to embroider. She wanted me to learn how to knit and, goodness knows, I tried. But all I got was a snarl of yarn that Grandma laughingly unraveled and wound up into a ball. I knew that my Grandma Wilson, who painted and made quilts and baked rich and buttery sugar cookies, was just the right sort of grandmother to have.

Sitting on the floor, with my head down on the chair in my Las Vegas studio apartment, I finally began to cry. I stood off at a distance in my own mind, and I watched myself as I cried. I kept wondering if I was crying for real, or if I was just doing what I thought should be done. Were any of my feelings real? Or was I just pretending to be able to feel?

CHAPTER 19

By my junior year, I had settled into my own grade-point level of a B-plus average. But whenever I was alone in my apartment, away from hostile and prying eyes, I began letting my imaginative wings take flight. I read book after book on philosophy and religion, haunting the library and the one small bookstore in Las Vegas. And I wrote, and I thought.

In my senior year, my English teacher looked at me in astonishment when I started making A's on written assignments. I ducked my head, and I toned down my writing to make B's. That way I felt safer. It was far better in that town for me not to be noticed.

✡ ✡ ✡

In my baby book, there was a story Mother wrote about me, back when I was three years old and we were living in Denver.

I was sitting on the floor, playing with my toys, when Mother came into the living room and sat down at the piano and began warming up her voice. Going up and down the scale, she sang softly, "Ha-ha-ha-ha-ha." Then taking the chord up a half step, she sang again, "Ha-ha-ha-ha-ha." And on up the scale by half steps.

I got up and went over and climbed up on the piano bench. And there I sat, right next to Mother, singing her vocal exercises, right on pitch, matching her note for note.

Smiling down at me, Mother kept playing and singing her vocalizations as I sang along. Finally I looked up at Mother, and I said, "Ha-ha all gone now." And I wriggled down off the piano bench and went back to playing with my toys.

There never was a time when there was not the sound of singing in our little family. My mother had a beautiful, light soprano voice, which extended up to an effortless E above high C. By the time I was eight, Mother and I were singing duets for Kiwanis and Rotary Club meetings, including Eddy Arnold songs like "I Gave My Love a Cherry without a Stone."

When I was a sophomore in high school, I asked Mother, "Could I sing in the adult choir with you?"

Mother looked at me thoughtfully. "I don't see why not," she said. "I'll talk to the choir director about it, and if she says it's all right, then I'll bring the music home and we'll rehearse when you're home on Saturdays."

And that's what we did. Friday and Saturday evenings, Mother and I would go over the anthem for the Sunday church services. And every Sunday morning, Mother and I would climb the stairs to the small choir rehearsal room with its battered upright piano.

After a quick run through of that Sunday's anthems, the choir members would put on their choir robes with satin surplices, which were something like enormous collars. Then we would all file into the choir loft and sing.

✡ ✡ ✡

In my junior year, I joined Rainbow Girls, an organization for the daughters of Freemasons that met every two weeks at the Masonic Lodge in downtown Las Vegas. The lodge was on the second floor of the Ilfeld department store, an old stone building that had been built in the late nineteenth century. The lodge rooms looked like they had been there forever, with their worn carpeting and their walls with dark wood paneling.

Inside the lodge meeting room were four dark and imposing wooden chairs. Each chair looked vaguely thronelike on its dais. And there were metal folding chairs that seated the gathered Masons, the Eastern Stars, and the Rainbow Girls.

In the center of the floor was an altar and seven chairs arranged in a semicircle. Seven high school age girls sat there in their finest formal dresses that had floor length skirts and layers of scratchy netting. Each of those young women stood for a virtue. Love, patience, charity, and so on. I was in the first chair, which was "Love."

At one of the first meetings I attended as "Love," there was an initiation of new Rainbow Girls. I had to give a long memorized speech on the virtues of Love. I stood up and I opened my mouth—and I promptly forgot my entire speech.

In front of my father, assorted Masons, Eastern Stars, and half my classmates, I stood there, red-faced. Stammering and sweating, I felt the bottom of my world drop right through the second story Masonic Lodge floor.

Soon after that disaster, I was summarily relieved of my office as "Love," and I was relegated to the very bottom rung of Rainbow Girl officialdom. I was appointed choral director.

Once every two weeks, the Rainbow Girl chorus would meet after school for rehearsal, and the accompanist and chorus and I would go over the music for the upcoming meeting. I had never before conducted a choral group, but I sang in our church choir, and my mother was assistant choir director. So I did what Mother did. I cleaned up ragged endings and shaky starts. I talked about musical expression and about the meaning of the words.

At first, most of the Rainbow Girl chorus looked at me as though I had suddenly sprouted another head, but one visiting Rainbow Girl alumnus told me, "This group sounds better than it ever has. You're doing a good job."

I wound up directing the Rainbow Girl chorus for the better part of two years.

CHAPTER 20

Early one Monday morning, I boarded the Greyhound bus that drove through Pecos every day and stopped briefly at the Casanova to pick up passengers. I got on the almost-empty bus, and I sat down and gazed out the window. I was not happy about going to Las Vegas for another endless school week, but I would soon be out for the summer. Next year I would be a senior, and that meant I only had one more year until I could leave Las Vegas.

A sailor sitting in the seat right behind me leaned forward and said, "Hi."

I turned and looked at him. I hadn't even noticed him when I boarded the bus. He was smiling at me, and he said, "Are you going to Las Vegas? I'm going there to visit my parents. My name is Stan."

I looked at him with interest. "Did you go to school in Las Vegas?"

He grinned as he shook his head. "We lived in Colorado," he said. "My parents just moved to Las Vegas last year. My dad's a teacher, and my mother's taking education courses at the university. As soon as my leave is up, I'll be going to Pensacola, Florida, for flight training."

As we talked, I felt at ease with him. When we got off the bus in Las Vegas, he said, "Would you like to write to me?"

I was astonished. Hardly any boy had ever looked at me with interest. And here was this young navy man, and he wanted to write to me. "All right," I said as my cheeks reddened with feelings I could not control.

The next week I told Mother about the young man who wanted to write to me. She said thoughtfully, "Well, I don't suppose it can hurt anything for you to write. You might want to meet his parents. He said they were teachers?"

CHAPTER 21

I remember sitting in Ilfeld Auditorium, a gray stone building, in my cap and gown. It was June of 1956, graduation day, and I was relieved to be finally getting out of Las Vegas, New Mexico, my personal Alcatraz.

When we got home to Pecos, along with my suitcases and my few personal belongings, I said to Mother, "I'm so relieved. Now I'll never have to go down to Las Vegas again."

Mother's eyes looked over at the corner of the office, and she said, "Don't be too sure about that. With all our legal expenses, the only school we can afford to send you to is Highlands University in Las Vegas."

"Oh, Mother, you can't mean that!"

"Well, I just don't know where else you can go. The University of New Mexico is way too expensive, and the community college in Santa Fe, well, I'm just not sure. I don't know if they have good teachers there or not. It's just gotten started."

"Maybe I can apply for scholarships."

Mother gave a short laugh. "Oh, nobody will ever give you a scholarship. They'll think since we own a power company we're filthy rich." She shook her head. "You'll just have to go to Highlands in Las Vegas."

Doom clamped its gray tendrils around me as I stared at my mother. "I hate Las Vegas," I said. But Mother wasn't listening.

✲ ✲ ✲

There were twenty of us high school kids from the First Presbyterian Church of Santa Fe that traveled to a small town in southern New Mexico to attend Presbyterian Youth Synod.

We were right in the middle of the Eisenhower years, a time of frozen dreams, of Cold War nightmares held rigidly in check. The Korean War was etched in history. And just two years before Senator Joseph McCarthy had been censured by the Senate and had fallen from power. The unending reality of the A-bomb and the H-bomb hung over our world like darkened thunderclouds.

But that morning I was with a group of high school kids from all over the state, sitting in a hot and steamy Sunday school room listening to adult volunteers lecturing us on Presbyterian tenets.

I can't even remember what those tenets were. What I do remember is that a whole lot of boys talked to me. And during one lunch break, I became, of all things, a volleyball star. I was amazed when I managed to serve a volleyball across the net twenty times in succession. It was a one time only feat, and it won me new friends.

One of the volleyball players had his hair styled in a ducktail, and he had brought a windup 45 rpm record player. He had only one record to go with it. It was Bill Haley's brand new release of "Rock Around the Clock." I suffered through listening to Bill Haley singing "We're gonna rock, rock, rock till the broad daylight" over and over again, each time louder than the time before, until by the three hundredth replay of "Rock Around the Clock" I had learned to hate that song.

On the final day of Youth Synod, we gathered at the church for an evening worship service. All us girls wore dresses with full skirts and crinoline petticoats and tightly cinched waists. The boys wore suits and ties, with their hair slicked down and combed back.

I talked to one redheaded boy, handsome and tall in his suit and tie. There was that agonizing shy attraction between us that we only feel when we are teenagers. As I walked into the sanctuary with the group from the First Presbyterian Church of Santa Fe, I was fantasizing myself sitting next to the red haired boy.

This Presbyterian church had just built themselves a brand new sanctuary. The church pews had been bolted to the floor on the evening before Youth Synod began. The windows, which would soon be glazed with stained glass, now had clear glass in them that let in narrow bands of burning hot summer sunlight. At the back of the sanctuary the upstairs balcony was a jumble of lumber and carpentry tools.

There was the smell of unfinished construction, an odor compounded of fresh paint, raw cement floors and newly varnished wood. Every cough, every rustle or rattle of paper programs, every scrape of shoe soles across the uncarpeted concrete floors echoed throughout the sanctuary's great vaulted ceiling with its cross-braced beams and rafters. It was like attending a worship service inside a big bass drum.

To add to the noise, there was construction work being done on a four-lane thoroughfare a block or two away from the sanctuary, so traffic had been re-routed. What seemed like hundreds of cars and noisy trucks kept passing by just outside the sanctuary, creating an unending mechanical clamor.

I sat in the pew with my head bowed, fuming to myself. I could not worship. I could not quiet my mind to pray, not with that background of endless noise disturbing my peace.

The preacher led us through the invocation and the Bible readings. I went through the motions of reading the responsive readings and singing the hymns with my mouth turned down in an inverted bow. Finally we reached the moment in the worship service when the preacher intoned, "Let us pause for a moment of silent prayer."

The church's organ hadn't been installed yet. A small baby grand piano began playing softly over the sounds of coughs and rustlings and the sounds of cars, motorcycles, and great, long trailer trucks, all downshifting as they drove past the front door of the sanctuary. Sitting in that pew, I bowed my rebellious head, fully prepared to be angry and disappointed at missing my time of peaceful inner stillness.

All of a sudden an absolute silence fell over that sanctuary. There was not one small sound, from within or without. It was as though that entire group of three hundred teenagers, all in one simultaneous moment had decided to hold their breaths, while all those noisy cars and trucks had been directed by some agency to take other routes, far away from this holy place. It felt like we were being held inside a suspension of stillness.

Startled by the intensity of the silence, I opened my eyes and looked up at the minister standing in the pulpit with his white haired head bowed. Then my eyes, of their own volition, looked up at the huge overhead rafters of the sanctuary ceiling.

My mouth slackened into amazement and my eyes widened, for I was looking up at a great Eye that gazed down at me from the rafters. At once transparent and solid, this Eye was an enormous orb of golden white light, surrounded by streamers of brilliance.

My heart skipped beats as my breath stopped flowing in and out of my lungs. Transfixed, I gazed up at the immense Eye that was pouring an all-fulfilling Light down upon me.

That Eye looked deep within me. I could tell that it knew everything there was to know about me. All my dreams, all my doubts and questionings, all my secret sixteen-year-old wonderings about boys and sex, all my resentments and my faults and my tears, all my prayers and dreams for the future, all my hopes and all my fears. I could hold nothing back. Within that suspended time, I saw myself and I knew myself completely. Everything that I was, I knew. Even the smallest details of my life came flooding into my mind. And for the first time since my childhood, I knew that I was loved.

That great Eye poured love into me with an intensity I could never have imagined. Its ineffable sweetness enfolded me with a love that was far greater than any human love. The Great Eye was tender, it was caring, and it cherished me. It knew me, and it valued me for being exactly who I was. I sat there, looking up at that beauty, feeling so much love that I felt my heart was bursting wide open.

Just when I felt I could not take one moment more, the Great Eye faded and the silence receded. A rattletrap of a car drove by with banging rods and a clattering of various engine parts. The sounds of leather soled shoes scraping across the raw cement floor of the sanctuary echoed aloft, as the shaken minister raised his head and said in a trembling voice, "Let us pray."

When service was over we all walked through the great sanctuary doors and out onto the front porch. And all three hundred of us kids stopped and stood there without moving, standing on the broad flagstone porch of that church sanctuary. We were a sober, silent bunch of teenagers as we stood there with our heads bent, all of us studying the toes of our shoes.

Then we started sneaking looks at each other out of the corners of our eyes. And the whisperings began. "Did you feel that? Kind of like, I don't know, really peaceful?"

"Yeah, I did. Did you?"

"Yeah, I did."

"You did? You felt it too? I thought I was the only one."

The whispers and murmurs went on all around, while the handsome red-haired boy and I looked at each other in mutual astonishment. We had experienced something together, he and I. We didn't know what it was, yet we knew, regretfully, that we would never see each other again.

On that day, we had experienced something that maybe nobody else in the whole world had ever known as we had. We had all felt that peace. We had all been in that timeless bubble. We had all been the receivers of Divine Love.

I didn't know if any of the other kids on that great big flagstone church entrance had seen that Divine Eye, and I wasn't about to open my mouth and ask them. They might think I was crazy or something.

But I knew what I had seen. I knew what I had felt. And I knew it would never leave me. I knew that Divine Eye would keep watching over me for as long as I lived.

CHAPTER 22

The very next Sunday, our astonished Sunday school teacher at the First Presbyterian Church of Santa Fe listened to our excited group as we told of having felt something, experienced something. But we didn't know what it was.

Taken aback, our teacher said, "I'm going to ask Dr. Joseph Haroutunian to come in next Sunday and talk with you. Maybe he will know something about this."

Dr. Joseph Haroutunian was an eminent Presbyterian theologian. That summer he was on sabbatical, taking time off from his teaching duties to write a book, and he and his family were living in Santa Fe for a year.

So one week later, all of us were sitting in our Sunday school classroom, talking nervously while we waited for Dr. Haroutunian. When he finally came in the door, everyone fell silent.

Dr. Joseph Haroutunian was a short, slight Armenian man in his fifties, with gray hair and intelligent dark eyes. He wore a conservative suit, and he carried himself with the dignified reserve of an eminent divinity school professor. He stood at the front of the Sunday school class, listening to us kids as we tried to describe the indescribable.

"It was like nothing I ever felt before."

"It was like God knew everything about me, and it was all okay."

"It was something I couldn't understand, but I knew it was there."

After the class had stopped talking, we all sat there in frustration because we couldn't really find the words to tell about what had happened to us.

For a moment, Dr. Haroutunian stood there in deep thought. "It seems to me," he finally said, "That you have had an experience of the Holy Ghost."

I sat there amazed. That Great Eye I had seen, was it really the Holy Ghost?

Dr. Haroutunian went on to say, "Whenever we talk about spiritual things, we must be careful to define our terms. I define the Holy Ghost as the hands of God working through man."

And then I thought, "That brilliant Eye was real. This man has his doctorate in Presbyterian theology. He's a world famous scholar, and he is saying that what I saw and felt was real."

Today, Dr. Haroutunian's words would be called a validation of spiritual experience. Of course, in those days we had no such term. Yet we all knew that something extraordinary had happened to us. And Dr. Haroutunian told us it was all real, and it was all true.

After that summer ended, Dr. Haroutunian went back to his teaching job. A few years later, he was appointed to the chair of Systematic Theology at the Divinity School of the University of Chicago. In 1968, Dr. Haroutunian unexpectedly passed away.

Looking back, I understand how fortunate we were to have Dr. Haroutunian talk to our high school Sunday school class. How many people who have gone through visionary experiences or near death experiences, come back to this earth after being in the presence of Divine love, only to have well-meaning therapists and doctors debunk their experiences, using harsh unyielding materialist reductionist platitudes.

"Your daughter needs to be examined and possibly put in a psychiatric ward." Or, "Your family member has serious brain damage." "Your daughter is hallucinating." Or even, "Your child needs to be put into a mental institution."

There are numerous stories of needless tragedies that happen as the result of an unyielding materialism that does not hesitate to sacrifice young lives even as it attempts to preserve its own preeminence in the domain of human thought.

How much better it was for me to know that I was a child of the Holy Ghost, the Holy Spirit, the hands of God working through men and women. Even working through young people like me. On that bright Sunday morning, Dr. Haroutunian's words and his wise informal spiritual counseling were God's direct gift to me and to all of us who heard him speak that day.

CHAPTER 23

Two weeks later, I began taking summer courses at Highlands University, in Las Vegas, New Mexico. My major was chemistry, which was what my dad wanted me to take. I would also be taking a math course and basic chemistry, along with some required coursework.

I was miserable. I had been shipped back to the prison I thought I had broken out of when I graduated from Las Vegas High School. And I had no particular love for chemistry. I was only taking math and science to keep my father happy. I didn't know what I really wanted to be doing with my life.

I felt like banging my head on the dorm walls. But I didn't want to upset my parents, because after seven years of legal harassment, the case of Winslow v Benson was finally coming to trial. And Judge Gutierrez had made sure that the venue was in Las Vegas and that he was the trial judge.

✲ ✲ ✲

On the third day of the trial, Mother came by the dormitory and picked me up. On the way to the courthouse, we stopped by the bank to withdraw some money.

In the way of gossipy small towns, the middle-aged bank clerk had heard all about our court case. "That Irene Winslow is one nasty woman," said the clerk. "She's as tough as an old boot."

"Do you know her?" asked my astonished mother.

"Oh, good lord, honey," said the bank clerk, "Everybody in the Las Vegas business community knows her. Irene Winslow is Judge Gutierrez's mistress. She runs the judge's whorehouses in the red light district over on Fifth Street. Irene Winslow and Judge Gutierrez are as thick as any two thieves can be."

Standing beside Mother, I shivered, remembering the hair raising ride Betty and her boyfriends had taken me on the year before. I remembered seeing the tiny houses with their red-shaded lamps glowing from deserted windows. I recalled hearing the sound of squalling tires as Carl's old Ford with its snarling Smittys had sped down those silent darkened streets where not a soul could be seen.

"That explains it," said Mother as we left the bank.

"Explains what, Mama?"

"It explains why one of the Winslow woman's lawyers is Judge Gutierrez's cousin by marriage. And her other lawyer is the judge's son-in-law. I've known for a long time that there was more to this lawsuit than we ever knew." Mother looked at me, her mouth set in a straight thin line. "I don't think we're going to have much luck with this case."

✡ ✡ ✡

Inside the Las Vegas courthouse, a uniformed woman led me to a bleak room, paneled in dark varnished wood. This was the room where witnesses waited to be called into the courtroom to testify.

Annabelle Quintana and Cipriano Lujan were already there, sitting in dark leather covered chairs with sagging seats and ragged edges. As she shut the door on us, the uniformed woman said, "Don't talk about anything concerning the trial."

All three of us, Annabelle and Cipriano and I, sat for the next hour and then the next, waiting in almost total silence. A sort of legal limbo. At last the uniformed woman reappeared. She looked down at the paper in her hand and said, "Cipriano Lujan?"

Cipriano stood up, and the woman said, "Come with me."

Once more, the door closed. And Annabelle and I waited.

After another long silent time, the woman reappeared and said, "Annabelle Quintana?"

I sat in that dark, silent room all alone, listening to a cheap dusty clock ticking from a shelf. Sharp blades of sunlight pierced through venetian blinds. I watched the dust motes floating in the bands of sunlight. I felt like I was in a far off place where, if I was still enough, I would never be found.

After the clock had slowly ticked its way through a full half hour, the uniformed woman opened the door. She opened her mouth in what seemed like slow motion. The sound of her words sank into the varnished wood floor with a leaden sound. "Whitney Benson? You've been called."

I stood up and took a second to lock my knees in place, so that I could stay on my feet. Then I took a deep breath and followed the uniformed woman, who had already turned away from me. I put one foot in front of the other as I walked down a long, dimly lit hall with dark wood paneling.

The uniformed woman turned left, and I saw a heavy dark wood door being held open. Another uniformed woman stood in the open door, impatience on her face, her head jerking as she beckoned to me. I walked through the door and entered the courtroom.

The walls of the stuffy courtroom were paneled in heavy, dark wood. Overhead two fans circled, trying in vain to move the overheated air. The wood floor creaked under my feet as I walked toward the witness box. I saw the jurors, all of them Spanish except for one Anglo man. I turned and faced the courtroom.

Directly in front of me sat Irene Winslow, dressed in a tight purple suit. Her hair was purplish-red, and her lipstick was a darker shade of purple. Drops of sweat trickled down her heavily rouged cheeks, leaving pale runnels behind them. Seated next to her were her lawyers, both of them writing on legal pads.

Seated at another table were my father and mother and their lawyer, Fletcher Catron, all watching me with anxious eyes.

The clerk administered the oath and I sat down, right on the edge of the witness chair. Fletcher Catron stood up and came toward the box. He said to me, "Now, Miss Benson, will you please tell the court exactly what you saw in the office of Pecos Light and Power Company on the morning of June thirteenth, 1949."

I opened my mouth to speak, but before I could begin, a Spanish man standing next to the jury box began translating Fletcher's words into Spanish. The strangest thing about testifying in that misbegotten trial was that I had to pause after almost every sentence, waiting for the translator to translate everything that was said from English into Spanish. The translator was there because some of the older Spanish men on the jury spoke not a word of English.

The translator fell silent, and I was able to speak. "Yes, sir," I said to Fletcher Catron. "I was in our living room, getting ready to go down to ride my horse, when I heard someone in the front office screaming horrible words, really loud."

The Winslow woman's older lawyer rose and spoke. "Objection."

"Sustained."

Fletcher glanced over at the judge. Then he turned back to me and he said, "What did you do after you heard that disturbance in the front office?"

"I walked over and opened the door between the living room and the office, and I stood in the doorway, looking into the office."

"Exactly what did you see?"

"I saw my father and Irene Winslow."

"Was there anyone else in the office?"

"Yes, my mother was sitting behind her desk. Annabelle Quintana, her office assistant, was standing in back of my mother. And a young man named Cipriano Lujan was standing next to the front door, waiting to pay his power bill."

"And then what happened?"

"Mrs. Winslow had a lot of money in her right hand, and she was shaking her fist at my father. She kept on telling him that he had to take that money."

"Where was your father?"

"He was standing in front of the filing cabinet, and he was backed as far away from her as he could get—"

"Objection," said the older lawyer.

"Sustained."

"Did your father at any time move toward Mrs. Winslow, or make some motion with his hands toward her?"

I shook my head. "No, he did not."

"Did your father at any time touch Mrs. Winslow in any way?"

"No," I said, hoping my voice was not quivering. "He did not."

"What did your father do?"

"Mrs. Winslow kept on shaking her fist in my father's face. She had twenty dollar bills in her fist, and she kept telling him he had to take that money. And my father kept telling her no. He said that she and Bob Winslow were more than six months in arrears on their bill, and my father kept on saying he would not accept less than the full amount of the power bill."

"And what did you do?"

"I looked over at my mother, and she nodded toward the front door. So I walked past Mrs. Winslow—"

"Did Mrs. Winslow look at you or speak to you, or take notice of you in any way?"

Again I shook my head. "No sir, she did not."

"What happened next?"

"I walked to the front door, and I opened the door and went outside, and I walked around the corner to call my dogs."

"Did you see anything or anyone at that time?"

"I looked around, and all I saw was Mrs. Winslow's blue Cadillac parked in our office drive."

"There was no one else there?"

"No sir," I said. "No one else was there."

"What did you do then?"

"I left to go down to the horse pasture and ride my horse."

Fletcher Catron looked up at the judge and said, "Your Honor, I have no further questions."

I looked over at the table where Irene Winslow and her two lawyers sat looking at me. The younger lawyer rose and came toward me.

"At the moment you walked into that office, was your father standing with his back to you?" the young lawyer asked.

"No." I replied. "He was backed up against the metal filing cabinet."

"Was he between you and the front door?"

"No, he was not. He was off to my right, and Mrs. Winslow was standing in front of him."

"Did he at any time move away from you toward Mrs. Winslow?"

"No, he did not."

"Did your father at any time raise his hand to Mrs. Winslow?"

I straightened my shoulders, and I sat up ramrod straight and shook my head. "No sir, he did not. That's not the way it was." I took a deep breath. "I can draw you a sketch map that will show you exactly where everyone was in that office."

The young lawyer walked back to his table and brought me a pencil and paper, and I drew a rough map of the office and the people in it. I marked the door to the living room where I had been standing. I marked where my father stood, where Mrs. Winslow stood, and where my mother and Annabelle Quintana and Cipriano Lujan had been. And I drew a dotted line to show where I had walked through the office to the front door.

"Your Honor, I would like to submit this in evidence," the young lawyer told the judge.

For the first time, I looked up at the judge's bench, and I got a good look at Judge Gutierrez. He had a head that was round and mostly bald, with strands of gray hair plastered across the top to try and hide the baldness. His eyes were a light colorless blue, and his heavy dark jowls were oily and sweaty. To my surprise, he did not wear a judge's robes. Not even a suit or a tie. His shirt collar was open, showing gray hairs clustered over the top of a sweaty T-shirt, and the thin cotton fabric of the shirt strained over the most enormous belly I had ever seen on any man.

I looked back at the young lawyer as he held out a pencil to me. "Please initial this sketch for the court," he said.

I wrote WAB on the paper. The young lawyer handed it in as evidence, and then he said, "I have no further questions."

Fletcher Catron rose. I got down from the witness stand as he came toward me. Quietly Fletcher said to me, "If you would like, you can take a seat in the courtroom." I nodded, and then I went over and sat right behind my mother and my father. I watched as my father was recalled to the witness stand. The Winslow woman's lawyers showed him my map along with several other papers, and they began asking my dad a lot of mind numbing questions.

I turned and looked over at the hot, tired jurors, all of them men. The one young Anglo juryman looked full of himself. The rest them just looked overheated and exhausted. At four o'clock the judge recessed, and Mother took me back to the university.

The trial went on as I studied for my final exams. Then on the fifth evening Mother called me on the phone in the dorm room.

"Well," her voice came over the phone, "The verdict is in. We lost the case."

I sat silent for a moment. Then Mother gave a deep sigh.

"What do we do now?" I asked.

"Fletcher Catron will argue for an appeal to the New Mexico State Supreme Court," Mother said. "But I don't put much hope in that."

The next afternoon I walked into chemistry class to take my exam. As I sat down at my desk, a high school classmate, Robby Hill, walked over to me. "Have you seen this?" he said to me, slapping a copy of the *Las Vegas Optic*, the town newspaper, down on my desk.

With a chill, I saw a headline about our case on the front page of the *Optic.*

"How do you like that? Man, I guess that shows it all."

I just sat there and looked at Robby. His words held no meaning for me. An outsider, an alien, was what I had always been. And I had no use for what any of those Las Vegas people thought of me or mine.

Just then Dr. Stacey, our chemistry professor, came in the classroom, carrying his briefcase. He came over to me, and he looked at me with concern in his eyes. He spoke in a quiet voice, "Do you want to take the exam now, or would you rather wait for a day or two?"

Pride kept my back straight. "I'll take the exam now," I said. And I did. I wound up with a "C" in chemistry for the summer quarter.

☆ ☆ ☆

"After the trial verdict was in," Mother told me that weekend, "Your father and I went to get a cup of coffee in a coffee shop just across the street from the courthouse. And one of the jurors in the case—an elderly Spanish gentleman—came over to our table and spoke to your father."

The old man said to my father, "Mr. Benson, I feel really bad about what happened in that courtroom."

Out of sheer surprise, my father sat down in his chair. "Thank you," he said. "I appreciate that."

The old Spanish man stood there and shook his head. "You don't know what it was like in that jury room," he said. "The foreman of the jury, he didn't listen to anything we tried to tell him. That foreman, he just passed around the papers saying that you were guilty, and he told us we'd better sign them right away. He said that any of us who didn't sign those papers, that Judge Gutierrez, he would take all our land and our homes away from us. The foreman told us that we would lose everything we had unless all of us did what we were told. He said we'd better sign those papers right away, and we'd better not even try to argue with him."

My father and mother stared up at the bent old man. "That's right," the old juror told my parents in a shaking voice. "That is what happened in that jury room."

The old Spanish juror took a moment to control the tears that were filling his eyes and to steady his voice. "Mr. Benson, I am a poor man, and my house and my farm, those things are all we have. Without that, my family wouldn't have nothing."

Tears began trickling down the furrows of the old juror's creased face. "I signed that paper, and it makes me feel real bad that they would make me do such a thing to you. Because I think you are an honest man. But I couldn't do nothing, because Judge Gutierrez, I knew he would take all my land and my home away from me and my family. That judge, he's a really mean man, and I knew he would do that. And so I signed the paper."

The old Spanish man looked straight at my father. "I am very sorry for what I did to you."

"That's all right," my father said to the old farmer. "Believe me, I understand."

But the old man was beyond comfort. Without another word, he turned and walked out of the coffee shop with his shoulders hunched and his head bowed down.

✡ ✡ ✡

The following week, Fletcher Catron went before Judge Gutierrez and presented preliminary arguments for the appeal.

Mother called me at the dorm that evening, and she said to me, "It was almost comical. The original judgment was for twelve thousand dollars, but every time Fletcher mentioned the words 'state supreme court,' the judge knocked off another thousand dollars. Finally, Fletcher got him down to one thousand dollars, total judgment, and the representatives of our insurance company, who were at the hearing with us, told us that we should settle."

I went into shock. "Why do they want us to settle? Won't the court of appeals throw the case out?"

"Fletcher and the insurance people told your father and me that under New Mexico state law, the only thing the higher courts can do is to send the case back down to the same lower court, with the exact same judge for retrial. Fletcher said that if we did that, and we had another courtroom defeat, people would start to think that where there was so much smoke, there must be fire."

There was a long silence, and then Mother's tired voice came over the telephone, "We've done all we can do."

"I know," I said.

A silent moment passed. Then Mother and I said a quiet goodbye, and I went back to my studies for the last of my exams.

✡ ✡ ✡

A week after the trial, Mother drove down to Las Vegas and went to the county clerk's office. By dint of sheer determination and a tenacious insistence that she would stay there in that office until they gave her what she wanted, she was able to obtain a copy of the complete transcript of Winslow v Benson. Mother brought that trial transcript home, and she guarded it like gold.

✡ ✡ ✡

About six weeks after the trial ended, our lawyer, Fletcher Catron, went by the county clerk's office in Las Vegas to pick up a transcript of the trial for his office records. He gave the paperwork to the clerk, and she went off, and after a long period, she came back and said, "Mr. Catron, we've looked everywhere and we don't have the paperwork on Winslow v Benson.

Fletcher blinked once or twice, then asked the clerk to go back and look again. She did, and she came back with an embarrassed office supervisor. "Your paperwork is not in our files," the supervisor told Fletcher. "It's not in the files or anywhere else we can think of to look. We're terribly sorry, but we don't know where your trial transcript is."

When Fletcher told my parents about this, my mother produced her copy of the trial transcript for Fletcher's office staff to make a copy of it.

"They'll find the transcript," Fletcher said, without much optimism in his voice.

"They won't find it," said my mother. "None of those records will ever be seen again."

And they never were.

CHAPTER 24

On the day I completed my final exams, I went down to the local jewelry store, and I bought myself a white gold engagement ring and a matching wedding ring. They were the least expensive rings in the store. The engagement ring had one tiny diamond in it with two even tinier diamond chips on either side.

And then I wrote Stan that we should set our wedding date. It was the only thing I could think of that would get me out of Las Vegas, that horrible town where I had been imprisoned for over six mind numbing years. Stan wrote to me and said it was okay with him. And somehow or other, the date for our wedding was set. We would be married on the day before Christmas of 1956.

I was all of seventeen and a half when I first began wearing the engagement ring with the tiny white diamond shining from its center. When I first put it on, I was alone in the dorm room. I felt like my whole right hand and arm were weighted down. But I could see no other way to escape my endless imprisonment in that terrible town of Las Vegas, New Mexico.

✡ ✡ ✡

During the months leading up to my wedding, I kept having black doubts fold their wings around my aching head. It was nothing I could put into words, just a paralyzing sense of self-doubt.

One morning I said to Mother, "I don't know whether I can do this."

But it was not one of Mother's good days. She looked up from her chair with a flash in her brown eyes, and she snapped at me, "Well, if you don't get married now, you'll probably never have another chance."

So I had doubts on the one hand, and a terrible fear on the other of never being able to marry, and I had no idea why that was so. A part of me knew what Mother had said could not be true, but I had no answer for her, no way of disproving it.

The next Sunday I listened, mortified, as Mother talked with a friend in the church choir about what I'd said to her. "Well," Mother finally said, "Every young bride gets pre-wedding jitters. I had them," she said to her friend. "Didn't you?"

"Yes," said the other woman as she nodded her head. "I certainly did."

I stood silent. Maybe what I was feeling was normal. Maybe this fear, this sense of dread, was just a part of being in love. But it felt more like desperation.

On the other hand, this was the 1950s. More than one of my classmates had gotten married right out of school. It just seemed to be what everybody was doing. So if I wanted to be normal, if I wanted to prove that I could belong, then getting married was the only way I could think of to do that.

Looking back, it seems strange to me that I never stopped to think that Stan and I had seen each other only three times. Once when we met, once when he came home from leave the previous Christmas, and once in Colorado, the previous summer when the Naval Cadet Choir sang in Boulder.

I had written Stan letters every week or so, but there were no confidences between us. No easy sharing of common interests. Certainly no passion, and no declarations of love. In fact, Stan and I barely knew each other.

The weirdest signpost, or lack of one, was that Stan never told me he loved me. And I never even brought up the subject of love. Not once. I just assumed that since we were getting married, it had to be love. And if I was in love and I would be a married woman, that was the way it would have to be for the rest of my life. Black depression would settle around me with that thought, so I kept on putting it out of my head.

As the wedding invitations went out and the gifts began coming in, I felt a suffocating panic. I wanted to run somewhere, anywhere. But I couldn't back out now, not without horribly embarrassing myself and my family.

I tried once more to talk to Mother. "Is this the right thing for me to do?"

Mother shook her head. "You're the only one who can know that," she said and turned her head away, looking at something I couldn't see.

And so, Christmas Eve of 1956, just four months after the court trial, Stan and I were married in the sanctuary of the First Presbyterian Church of Santa Fe. My two friends, Roberta and Heidi, were my bridesmaids, and Stan's older brother was his best man.

I wore a floor length wedding dress of white satin that had seed pearls embroidered on the bodice. It was the most beautiful gown I had ever owned, and for one moment as I walked down that aisle, I dreamed of cherishing my wedding dress for years to come. I thought that maybe someday I would see my daughter wearing this gown.

After the wedding and the reception, Stan and I were showered with the required four-point-three cups of rice. The two of us got into Stan's second hand automobile with "Just Married" spray-painted all over it. Half a dozen tin cans were tied to the back bumper of the car. As we drove away, those cans clittered and clattered over the pavement with an empty sound.

When we came back from our honeymoon at the Grand Canyon, I carried the tiny beginnings of a son in my womb.

CHAPTER 25

In the spring of 1957, Stan was stationed on Coronado Island. We lived in a sandy mobile home park, located just yards from the beach. Stan usually took the car, so most days I didn't go anywhere. I stayed alone all day in a thirty foot mobile home. By the middle of the afternoon, the cool ocean breezes turned into hot winds that blew gusts of rattling sand up against the side of the metal walls of the trailer.

We had no television, only a small, plastic portable radio that played endless renditions of popular music that I didn't care for. And there were no bookstores anywhere close by. So I spent the hot afternoons reading the few books I had on my meager bookshelf.

To keep from being overwhelmed by morning sickness, I began to sleep late. That lasted until Stan came home one day and found me in bed at ten thirty in the morning. He went into a rage. "What are you doing in that bed?" Stan said . "This place is a mess, and you've got nothing better to do than lie around all day. Why aren't you washing the dishes and keeping the place looking nice?"

Feeling like a child who has been told she is unworthy, I crept out of bed and bathed and dressed, saying nothing. Silence was best, I was finding out. Because, as I had long known, no matter what I said or did, it would never be good enough. The best thing was to be quiet and unnoticed.

From then on I got up and dressed, then sat and read and tried to eat. I washed my dishes while trying not to retch at the sight of congealed bacon grease and the smell of morning eggs. In the afternoons I walked on the flat beach and gazed out at the flat slate blue of the Pacific Ocean and then at the dry and barren land around me. There were no more dreams of what I could be. There was only the barren reality of a young married woman's life back in 1957. Washing dishes and vacuuming and being miserably pregnant. I was as flat as the sandy beaches and the gray ocean waters.

I knew if there was anything wrong with this marriage, it was my fault. In fact, *Ladies Home Journal* and the other women's magazines of the time said it was the woman's duty to adjust. That was her only option. For me that meant just getting used to it, making it through somehow, from one empty day to the next.

I thought back to what my high school English teacher, Mrs. Skylar, had said when I told her I was thinking about getting married. "Hmph," she'd sniffed. "Out of the frying pan and into the fire."

Now that fire was a white hot sun that beat down on a trailer whose still and humid air could not be cooled by the rattling swamp cooler in our front window. Other girls in my age group were going to college while I sat on the beach, watching gray naval vessels cut through leaden waters. I gazed after them as they headed out, away from this heat soaked place, going over the horizon, going where there was excitement and newness. Somewhere, anywhere that was not here.

☆ ☆ ☆

One day, while I was lying down, reading in bed, my baby moved. Such a tiny sensation. I put down my book, wondering what this was, this flutter like the wings of a tiny bird stirring in my lower abdomen. I looked down at my beginning-to-swell stomach, and I felt it again. A fluttering, wriggling thrill.

"I'm here," the little traveler floating inside my womb announced. "I'm here, and I'm not going anywhere. I'm here to stay."

Showers of happiness rose up in me. A love such as I had never felt burst and fountained in my heart, filling me with the same bliss I thought the angels must feel when seeing the full light of God.

Then terror split me open. Suppose I wasn't good enough to be a mother. Suppose I could not raise this child. Suppose something happened. This baby could die of some disease or other. It could be killed by a car that ran over it. It could die because I could not care for it well enough. Because I was never good enough. I lay there in that hot, airless bedroom, in a state of panic, staring at the wood veneered trailer walls, while the late afternoon sweat poured off me.

Then once more I felt that fluttering, the sweet movement of a new life inside me. Never mind, I silently told the tiny bird inside my body. We'll find ways of making it. We'll make it together, you and me. The two of us will make it, somehow.

✲ ✲ ✲

Arnold was six months old when Stan came home from six months of temporary duty in Alaska. He seemed more relaxed and happier. We moved to Hayward to be close to Alameda Naval Air Station, and we spent time on weekends going up in the hills and painting while our baby slept in his carrier. Stan played with him and seemed to enjoy being a father.

The next year went by quietly enough. Yet there was a sense of foreboding I could not shake.

Arnold grew into a toddler, and he was super active. White-blonde hair, blue eyes, active, curious, fussy. He was a handful. Whenever Arnold napped, I would try to meditate. This was something I thought was new to me, but in fact it was exactly what I had been doing since I was eleven, or even before. I can't remember when I didn't do it. I just got very quiet and began doing what I called listening to the silence.

But now strange things began happening. I would feel a humming vibration in the soles of my feet that moved on up my legs and into my abdomen and then up into my chest. I thought, What is going on? What is happening to me? I'm trying to have a quiet moment and here I am, feeling like a human vibrating pad. What is this?

After awhile, I began getting frightened. I didn't understand why my peace was being broken into by these unpleasant vibrations. I would get up and move around restlessly, wanting something, but not knowing what it was.

And once again there was friction building between Stan and me. But I kept on thinking, Once we're out of the navy and we move back to New Mexico, things will be better.

CHAPTER 26

Shortly after the trial Irene Winslow divorced Bob, and she moved to Santa Fe. And soon after that, our pastor, Dr. Robert Boshen, called my father into his office after church one Sunday.

"I have difficult news for you," Reverend Boshen said to my father. "A member of our church has heard rumors that you attempted to sexually molest a woman named Irene Winslow. This member is asking the board of elders why our church has a sexual molester teaching our high school Sunday school class."

My father shook his head in despair. "What can I do about this? That woman will never stop her lies about me. And rumors run through this area like wildfire."

Reverend Boshen said to my father, "Go home and put together all the legal documents you have on the case. And go by your lawyer's office. Get copies of whatever you need to put together a complete paper history of the court case."

My father looked over at Dr. Boshen for a moment, and understanding dawned. "I can go and see those people who have called the church, and I'll ask them to go over all the court documents." Dad paused and thought for a moment, and then he said, "It's a good thing Elizabeth made certain we got our copy of that trial transcript."

After the conference and a quiet prayer with the minister, Dad went home and got out his big, fat leather briefcase, the one that he'd used when he taught electrical engineering at the University of Denver. He and Mother put in a copy of the trial transcript along with all the other legal documents, notices, and letters that had accumulated over those difficult seven years. And then Dad called and made the appointment.

A week later my father drove down a tree-lined Santa Fe street and parked his car in front of a quiet adobe style home. Dad walked up to the front door and rang the doorbell. A short man with sparse brown hair and a round face came to the door, and my father said to him, "Mr. Blalock?"

"That's right," the man said, looking at my father with suspicion in his eyes. "And you're Arnold Benson?"

"Yes sir, I am."

"Well, you'd better come in." Mr. Blalock opened the door wider and stood to one side as my father entered. Without offering to shake my father's hand, Mr. Blalock led the way into the dining room, and said, "If you want to lay your papers out, I'll go through them."

As Dad laid out the papers, Mr. Blalock looked over at him with hostility in his eyes. "I have to tell you," he said, "These are serious charges, and I know you lost that case. So I don't want to hear any excuses from you about this matter."

"I won't give you excuses," my father replied in a firm voice. "I'll just lay all the papers out, and you can examine them for yourself. You and I will go through these papers, and you can ask me any questions you like, and I will answer them. And then you can draw your own conclusions."

Mr. Blalock gave my father a look of deep skepticism as the two men sat down at the dining room table. "All right. Let's start in."

For the next hour and a half, the two men sat hunched over the stacks of papers on Mr. Blalock's dining room table. They went through one legal document after the next. And gradually, a puzzled frown came over Mr. Blalock's face.

"This can't be right," he said, looking down at the trial transcript. "This testimony you've got here in the court transcript is nothing like what we were told, my wife and I."

He got up from his chair and went down the hallway calling, "Dierdre, would you come in here and take a look at this?"

A short, chubby woman with a valentine-shaped face and inquisitive eyes came out of the bedroom. "Take a look at this," her husband said to her. "This trial transcript is nothing like what we've been told."

The wife sat down and began to read. After going through some of the papers, she looked up at my father and then over at her husband with a frown on her face. "What on earth was going on here?"

"Well, it sure beats me," her husband said.

And the two of them sat there with my father for another two and half hours, poring over the trial transcript, the depositions, the court notices, and all the rest of the paperwork.

Finally Mr. Blalock sat back in his chair and shook his head. "This sure does beat anything I ever heard of. I never knew of anything like this happening to anybody."

Mrs. Blalock leaned forward and asked, "Why on earth did it take a full seven years for this case to come to trial?"

"Elizabeth and I suspect that Judge Gutierrez and the plaintiff's lawyers were waiting as long as they could before the statute of limitations ran out. Maybe they were hoping that one or more of our witnesses would move away or be unavailable to testify at the trial. But as you saw in the transcript, all three of our witnesses testified."

"And Irene Winslow had no witnesses to testify to her story?"

"No, she did not. Not a single witness."

A shocked silence filled the dining room. Finally Mr. Blalock said, "My God. This can't be happening in our country. This is America. Things like this aren't supposed to happen here."

Mr. Blalock looked down at all the papers spread out over the dining room table, and then he came to his feet. "Mr. Benson," he said, "I owe you an apology. When you came in that door, I took one look at you and I was thinking sure as the world that I was looking at a guilty man. Just as guilty as the devil himself.

"Now I know I was wrong about you, and I want you to know that I am sorry about the terrible injustice that was done to you and your family." And Mr. Blalock took my father's hand and shook it.

This, of course, was not the end of Irene Winslow's machinations. For the next several years, Reverend Boshen would make the same dreadful call to my father. And time after time, with patient persistence, my father would make phone calls to set up appointments.

And a few days later, he would go and talk with yet another alarmed family about the facts of the Winslow v Benson case. And each time his listeners would go through the same stages of hostility, skepticism, suspicion, doubt, and then on to puzzlement, and finally dawning enlightenment.

More than one of the wives wound up in tears as the entire story of seven years of unremitting persecution by the corrupt Judge Gutierrez and his mistress, Irene Winslow, that vindictive whorehouse madam, was told to them.

More than one person asked my father, "Why didn't you fight this on appeal?"

Dad replied, "Our lawyer told us that if we did take this case to the court of appeals, the only thing that could be done under New Mexico law would be to send the case straight back to the same court and the same judge for retrial. And we knew what the results of that would be. Our lawyer and the insurance representatives told us that if people heard we lost the same case twice, they might be convinced that where there was that much smoke, there had to be fire." Dad's mouth tightened. "That was one of the hardest decisions we ever had to make. I sure wanted to fight it. But we really had no choice."

Finally, however, even the Winslow woman had had enough. Santa Fe in those days was a small town of right around twenty-five thousand people, and more and more people began asking about that trial transcript, which so thoroughly discredited all of Irene Winslow's rumors. Over time the rumors abated, and my parents were able to get on with their lives without further slanders and harassment being leveled at them. As for Judge Gutierrez, within four years he was voted out of office, and he disappeared from sight.

I was proud of my father and mother for fighting the good fight. My father was a man who had faced the threat not only of losing his business but also of having his manhood smeared by a pair of criminal minds. It took many years and the bearing up under untold burdens of anxiety and downright terror. But year after grinding year, both of my parents stood up to Judge Gutierrez and Irene Winslow and all their evil rumors. And because of sheer Swedish tenacity, my dad, along with my determined Irish mother, ground those false charges into the dust. In the end, our little family won the battle in the court of public opinion.

Yet that victory came at a terrible price. Both my parents were now addicted to a powerful pharmaceutical called Miltown.

Hollywood had made Miltown famous. One star after another proudly proclaimed the wonders of living a life without anxiety. The comedian Milton Berle even wisecracked, "I'm thinking of changing my name from Milton Berle to Miltown Berle."

In the 1950s, the drug was easy to obtain. Doctors wrote out liberal prescriptions, and pharmacies would automatically refill those prescriptions. There were even rumors of some pharmacies selling Miltown over the counter, without a prescription.

Overnight, America had become a nation of respectable middle class men and women who had been turned into walking pharmaceutical addicts. Like my parents.

CHAPTER 27

In 1959 Stan became a civilian. We moved our mobile home back to Albuquerque, and Stan began going to the University of New Mexico full time to earn his degree in mathematics. He and Dad had worked out a deal so Stan would work for my father on weekends and during summer vacations. My parents would pay Stan's school tuition plus our living expenses. That meant Stan and I and my parents, would all be on short rations, but it would also mean that within two years, Stan could finish up his degree and find himself a good job.

That first summer, Stan got a phone call in the middle of the night. It was Dad, and he told Stan, "You'd better get down here fast. We've got a major power line down."

"Where is it?" a startled Stan said.

"It's right behind the Adelo general store. Some kid ran his car off the road, and it snapped the power pole off at the base. You'd better get yourself down here as fast as you can."

Without waking me, Stan got dressed, and he headed out the door.

The next morning, a very young Arnold and I walked the short distance to the power company office. Mother met me at the door. "Right now Pecos, Rowe and Glorieta are without electricity and telephone service."

"Good grief," I said. "What happened?"

"Some teenage kid was driving home from the local Bucket of Blood Bar. He'd just gotten his driver's license, and he'd managed to buy himself an old junker. The kid was drunk and speeding when he came around that curve. His car sailed off the road and went careening across the open field, and it slammed into the power pole and snapped it off at the base."

"Heavens," I said. "Is the kid okay?"

"Oh, he seems to be just fine," said Mother. "Which is more than I can say about Pecos Light and Power Company. Daddy and the men are working to clean up the mess and set a new power pole."

I sat down in shock as Mother said, "All the wires on the pole snapped. There were live electric wires that were snapping back and forth, all over the place, until the main breakers shut down. It's going to take Daddy and his men at least two days to get our main power line up and running." Mother's lips tightened. "Once the backup batteries in the dial switchboard room go dead, Pecos Light and Power Company and Pecos Telephone Company will both be out of business."

The next thirty-six hours crawled by. All the power and all the telephone service in Pecos, Rowe, and Glorieta went dead. The office was silent. Word of what had happened had gotten out, and nobody came by the office to complain.

Periodically one of Daddy's men would come into the office to get the keys to the supply room. The men said almost nothing. Their faces were grim, and their work clothes were grimy with dirt and sweat.

Stan did not come home that night. Nor did my dad. My father and his men worked all night, and all the next day, getting the new power pole set and putting up the crossbars for the electric wires. Then they patched the electric wires, pigtailing the breaks soundly, so those hot wires wouldn't pull apart when they were pulled up on the pole. And finally they hung a couple of new transformers.

Right around midnight of the third night, Dad and his men had most of the repairs completed. My father engaged the breakers on that main power line, and electricity was restored to most of Pecos, Rowe, and Glorieta.

"You can all go home now and get yourselves some rest," my dad told his men. "We'll finish the rest of this job over the next week or so. And then," my father said in a grim voice, "I'm going to go have a talk with that young man and his family."

It was a bone weary group of men that finally went home to their families at about two o'clock that third morning. Stan came in our apartment quietly and got undressed. I was already in bed and, sound sleeper that I was, I didn't hear Stan come in the door.

An hour later I came wide awake in the dark. I heard a strange buzzing noise that seemed to go on and on. I got out of bed, and I went into the hallway and listened. That buzzing sound seemed to be coming from the bathroom.

I opened the bathroom door and stood there, blinking in the light. I saw Stan, lying on his back in the bathtub. His long legs were spraddled out in the black cold bathwater, and his chin was resting on his chest. He was lying there in the filthy bathwater with his mouth hanging wide open, sound asleep and snoring away.

I walked over to Stan, and I shook his shoulder. "Stan," I said.

"Ummphh?"

"Stan, wake up. You need to take a shower and get into bed."

"Hnhrr," said Stan.

It took nearly half an hour to get Stan into bed. And when he had pulled up the covers, he turned over and slept like the dead until eleven o'clock the next day.

☆ ☆ ☆

A few days later, my father went to see the grandparents of young Georgie Varela. Both parents had died years before, and Georgie was being raised by his grandfather and grandmother. That little family of three sat huddled together on their couch. Their faces blanched when my father handed the grandfather a bill for $350 in 1960s money. "This is just for the materials," my dad told Georgie and his grandparents. "I'm not going to charge for the labor, because you could never pay all that off."

"Mr. Benson," said the grandfather, "We'll give you what money we can. But we don't have this kind of money. I don't know how we'll be ever able to pay you back."

My father's face was stern. "I don't want you paying me one penny of that money. I'm putting Georgie on Pecos Light and Power Company's payroll. This young man is going to work off what he owes the company. And that means every last penny of it."

Then my father turned to the white faced teenage boy sitting next to his grandfather, and Dad said to Georgie, "You be at our office at eight o'clock tomorrow morning, and you'd better be right on time."

For the next six months, Georgie worked for my angry father and Pecos Light and Power's angry workmen. And by the end of that time, Georgie had paid back every cent he owed Pecos Light and Power Company.

I happened to be in the office on the day when Georgie came in after work to talk to my father. "Mr. Benson, I know I was wrong doing what I did, and I'm sorry," Georgie said. "Now the money's all paid off, what I owed you, and I'd like to keep on working for you. My grandfather thinks you're a good man to work for, and I would like to go on working for you."

"Well, Georgie," said my dad, "I don't think you're a bad kid. I think you're just a young man who made a real serious mistake and got himself into a whole lot of trouble. But you came in and you worked every day after school and on weekends, and I think you've turned into a good worker. So we'll keep you on the payroll for now, and we'll see how it goes."

It turned out that it went pretty well. Georgie Varela worked for my parents until they finally sold the power company in 1967. He wound up becoming a lineman, working on what the linemen called the hot wires, the ones that carried 2200 volts of electricity in them.

While he was still in high school, Georgie played on the Pecos High School basketball team. In his senior year, there was a tournament down in Las Vegas. In one game Georgie jumped up to catch the basketball and he came down off balance. He stumbled backwards, crashing through the big double doors that opened out into the lobby of the gym where the game was being held.

As a red-faced Georgie came back through the doors and onto the basketball court, one Pecos leather-lungs up in the stands stood up and yelled, "Hey, Georgie, there goes Mr. Benson's power line again!" And all the Pecos basketball fans sitting in the stands roared with laughter.

CHAPTER 28

After graduating from UNM, Stan began working as a programmer at Lovelace Medical Center. By that time we had two sons, and we had bought our own three bedroom home. And for the time being, the storms in our marriage were being held at bay.

One warm summer day I was lying down on our couch in the living room. The kids were playing out in the back yard, and Stan was at work. Without any warning, I suddenly found myself floating up near the ceiling of the living room. I looked down, and I could see my body lying on the couch right below me.

I was a floating blob of clear crystal, and I was bobbing around, bumping up against the living room ceiling like a weightless balloon. Coming out of the center of me was a strand of what looked like clear jelly that connected me to my body.

I looked down at the room below, and it was like I was viewing everything through a fish eye lens. Some things were in sharp focus, like our LP record player. Other parts of the room were rounded or somehow distorted in shape.

I felt a kind of upside-down amazement, and I said to myself, I think I'm in a pickle. How do I get down from here?

The instant that thought came, I grew flippers! They looked like embryonic arms and legs coming out of the four corners of the spherical me.

I desperately wanted to move, so I paddled my arms and my legs like I was swimming, but instead of moving forward, I found myself spinning around. Maybe this is what it's like being on a spacecraft, I said to myself. I'm a weightless astronaut.

Once more I moved my flippers, trying to swim through the air the way a swimmer moves through water. Instead, I began spinning around and around. When I tried turning myself in the opposite direction, I began spinning the other way around. I stopped trying to swim as despair hit me. I asked myself, how am I ever going to get myself back into my body?

I looked over at the corner of the room, and right next to the front window I saw a friendly face with long blonde hair and intense blue eyes. "Archangel Michael," I said, not knowing where those words came from, "Please help me."

And suddenly, without any awareness of having moved, I found myself once more lying on my back on the couch, staring up at the ceiling. I got up to go check on my sons in the back yard. As I moved across the living room I felt like every part of me was a sandbag, weighted down with cement.

I dragged myself to the kitchen door and opened it and looked out the door. Arnold was up in a big elm tree, where he wasn't supposed to be. When he saw me, he started climbing down.

Four year old Philip was holding a broken branch from our willow tree. He was waving the branch up and down, dipping the tip of the branch in his plastic wading pool. He looked up and saw me standing in the doorway. "Look at me, Mommy," Philip said. "I'm fithing."

I smiled at him and said, "Have you caught any fish yet?"

Philip looked up at me in frustration and replied, "How tan I tatch any fith? Dis pool ain't dot no fith in it!"

Laughter silvered up in me, and suddenly my body felt lighter. Even in my strange world of visions and out-of-the-body experiences, there was some order and normality after all.

CHAPTER 29

That next fall I started back to school. I enrolled at the University of New Mexico's music department, and soon I was sweating assignments in basic music theory. Harmony, the study of the structure and progression of musical chords, was a closed mathematical system all its own. Music history was something I enjoyed. Singing with the UNM chorus was a leap of joy for me. But piano was difficult, and the voice lessons that I took with one short-lived voice teacher after another were dismal.

For my own pleasure, I took a course in Shakespearean tragedies, taught by a humanities professor named Katherine Simons. I still have a yellowed mimeographed examination paper with one of her exam questions. "Explore the grays, not merely the blacks and whites, in Shakespeare's two portraits of evil: *Hamlet*'s Claudius and *Othello*'s Iago. Note particularly the presence and the functioning in each portrait of the Elizabethan concepts of reason, will, appearance, and reality."

I spent a long time pondering those four concepts. Reason. Will. Appearance. Reality. What was the job of reason in my two worlds, outer and inner, logical and intuitive, everyday living on the one hand, and the psychic and spiritual world on the other?

Which of those two kinds of experience constituted reality? Which was mere appearance, my inner world or the outer everyday world?

✲ ✲ ✲

One Saturday morning, I was working in the kitchen when I heard a scream and then the sound of Arnold crying. I ran to the kitchen door, down the back steps, and across the backyard to where my son was lying on the ground.

"What happened?" I asked Arnold.

But he was crying so hard he couldn't answer. After a little bit, he stopped crying and he stood up. I held him as we walked into the house. I put Arnold in his bed, and I asked him again, "What happened?"

"I was up in the tree," Arnold sniffled. "And the branch started to break and I fell down."

I sighed. I had loved climbing trees when I was a kid, and I knew the sense of freedom it gave. But I had to say, "Maybe you shouldn't climb any more trees."

Another sniffle came from the pillow. I stood there for a minute while Arnold got quieted down and his eyes began to close. Then as I turned to go out the bedroom door, Arnold said to me, "Mommy, I can't move my arm."

I turned back, and I carefully felt my son's right arm. I could feel the break in the middle of his forearm. I spoke to my son very softly. "You wait right here and you lie still. I'm going to get something to put around that arm."

In a minute I was back with a copy of *Life Magazine* and scissors and string. I carefully wrapped the magazine around my son's broken forearm. Then I wrapped the string around the magazine, and I tied it tight.

I gently lifted my son down from his bunk bed while Philip watched, wide-eyed. "Come on," I told both my boys. "We're going to go see the doctors about this arm."

I shepherded my two frightened boys into the emergency room at Lovelace Clinic, and two hours later, Arnold's arm was in a cast.

"It's a clean break," the doctor told me. "He'll have to keep the cast on for the next seven or eight weeks. He'll be staying in the hospital overnight, just to make sure he's all right."

The next twenty-four hours were miserable. I was facing exams, so I had to go to class, but I was in so much pain and anxiety that in violin class I was bent double over the music stand in front of my chair. My throat was so full of pain that I could only hold it in by clenching my teeth tightly together.

The day after his misadventure with the tree, Arnold came home from the hospital. And almost overnight, my son changed from being an active running and climbing boy. He turned all that energy inward, and he became a quiet, introverted dreamer.

CHAPTER 30

By the time of my sophomore year at UNM, the atmosphere in our home had turned into a black-rimmed thundercloud. Years later, my mother told me that whenever she came down to see us, she always had to leave for home sooner than she'd planned on doing, simply because she couldn't stand the tension in our house.

That tension kept building day by day. Still, I ignored the darkening clouds as much as I could. I figured that maybe I could hold those clouds at bay, that maybe they would not get any darker than they were. I was still hoping against hope that somehow the marriage would work out.

I began to talk with Stan, to try and share some of the experiences I was having. I asked him to pray and meditate with me in the evenings, and for a few weeks we prayed together. But then Stan began working late almost every evening, and the shared prayers slowly died out.

I told Stan about the fact that I could sense other people's feelings, sometimes even hearing their thoughts in my mind. I was trying to work up to telling him about my experience with the Great Eye when I was seventeen. I thought perhaps this would help our understanding of each other, that we might be able to communicate better.

Then came the day when I walked out to the parking lot near the education building where Stan was waiting to take me home. I got into the car and I shut the door. And Stan turned to me and said in that low, cold voice that spelled trouble, "I want you to know, Whitney, that I've called your parents. I told them to come down here immediately. I said this is an emergency. I told them you should be put into the Las Vegas State Mental Hospital."

I sat there, my jaw slack with shock. Then a wave of anger came over me, and I opened my mouth to protest.

A quiet angelic voice spoke to me in tones that were clear and firm. The voice said to me, "Be absolutely quiet. Do not try to argue. This is a dangerous situation for you. Don't be afraid. Just do exactly as we guide you to say and do, and we will see you safely through this."

I sat in silence all the way home, staring out the side window of the car, until our car turned into the driveway and parked next to Mother and Daddy's station wagon.

I walked in the front door of the house. My parents were sitting side by side on our living room couch. I saw the fear in their eyes as they looked up at me. I smiled at them as I put my books down on the table and sat down.

No one said a word. Finally we began talking about things in general. About how their drive had been coming down from Pecos, about how the work at the power company was going. Finally Mother looked at me with a worried expression in her eyes, and she said, "How are you doing, honey?"

Taking a deep breath, I said, "I'm doing fine." My voice came out sounding confident and serene. A puzzled look crossed Stan's face as I added, "My courses are going well. I'm carrying a B-plus average in my classes."

Stan just sat there, and he stared at me. He looked like he was asking himself, "What's she going to say next?" I kept on talking with my parents until about an hour later when they left to go back to Pecos. Once the car had driven off, Stan turned to me and said, "Well, Whitney, I hope that's a lesson to you."

I said nothing at all, just went on into the back bedroom where Arnold and Philip were playing on our bed. The serenity that had flowed into me while I was talking with my parents drained out of me, and I felt shaky and exhausted.

I remembered one time when I was playing flute in the Las Vegas High School band. The school's young new band director had somehow gotten us a gig playing an afternoon concert at the Las Vegas State Mental Hospital.

It was the strangest experience to play John Philip Sousa marches in front of several hundred mental patients. Most of them just stared at us without blinking or applauding. Others moved in odd ways as they sat there listening. One sad young boy who was in our junior class in Las Vegas High School sat right up in the front row, looking defiant, daring us to look back at him, or to say anything to him. But the most shocking moment came when an older man began to cry and scream piteously. Right away, two husky men in khaki pants and white shirts lifted that patient up out of his chair and hustled him out a side door.

And now the man that I was married to had tried to get my parents to commit me to that very same insane asylum. And I knew for certain this was not the end. Stan was a bulldog. Once he fastened onto something he never let go.

Sitting there on our bed, I knew without a shadow of a doubt that I would never be safe as long as I was married to Stan. And I knew that if anything happened to my parents, I would be in real danger. So from that day forward, I kept all communications with Stan limited to necessities and inconsequentials. And the thunderclouds ripened.

CHAPTER 31

One day a psychology professor told the class, "No thinking person can believe in God. No thinking person can believe in life after death. No thinking person can believe there is such a thing as an independently existent mind. No thinking person can believe in the reality of the human soul. No thinking person can believe there is such a thing as any value to this accident we call life. There are only the laws of chance."

That meant Dr. Martin Luther King, a Christian minister, was not a thinking person. Nor was Gandhi. He was a practicing Hindu. Nor was the Dalai Lama. Nor Mother Teresa. And how about Isaac Newton. He was an Arian Christian, which meant that while he believed in one God, Newton did not believe in the Trinity. Newton wrote more books about theology than he did about science or math. Not only that, he was a practicing alchemist. Does this mean that Sir Isaac Newton was not a thinking person?

But back in the 1960s, even more than today, such questions fell on deaf ears. At most universities, pure reductionist intellectualism reigned supreme, even in the arts. In music classes we had lectures on aleatoric music, which consisted of composing music by throwing dice.

As for God, he had nothing to do with anything, for God was dead. The philosopher Bertrand Russell, in his essay, *A Free Man's Worship,* had written the materialist's epitaph for God and for all of humanity. "Such, in outline, but even more purposeless, more void of meaning," Russell wrote, "Is the world which Science presents for our belief..."

> That man is the product of causes which had no prevision of the end they were achieving; that his origin, his growth, his hopes and fears, his loves and his beliefs are but the outcome of accidental collocations of atoms; that no fire, no heroism, no intensity of thought and feeling, can preserve an individual life beyond the grave; that all the labors of the ages, all the devotion, all the inspirations, all the noonday brightness of human genius, are destined to extinction in the vast death of the solar system, and that the whole temple of Man's achievement must inevitably be buried beneath the debris of a universe in ruins—all these things, if not quite beyond dispute, are yet so nearly certain that no philosophy which rejects them can hope to stand. Only within the scaffolding of these truths, only on the firm foundation of unyielding despair, can the soul's habitation henceforth be safely built.

Bertrand Russell's view was extreme. But back in those days, any college student who dared to express a belief in God or any lasting value in human life, other than purely subjective, would find herself immediately put on the defensive.

And any woman in the 1960s who dared to talk about having out-of-body or other visionary experiences would have been considered a subject for psychological examination. While witches were no longer burned at the stake, any education major in the 1960s who said she had visions of God would have been in real danger of not graduating. And she certainly would not have been able to find a job after graduation.

So Stan's attempt to ship me off to the state mental institution had some powerful supporters. And if talking about my vision of the Great Eye could get me a one-way ticket to a mental hospital, then maybe I was crazy. Was I going insane? I didn't know.

The one thing I did know was that I could share my visions and my out-of-body experiences with no one. Those experiences were radioactive, and if I talked about them with any person around me, my career as a teacher would be over before it got started.

CHAPTER 32

One fall day, our young violin instructor came into the classroom all out of breath. "Sorry I'm late," he said to the violin class. "I've been rehearsing with the UNM student orchestra and our soloist for the upcoming concert."

Later, as he took a moment to work with me, the instructor said, "Your fingers are way too stiff. There's a whole lot of tension in your playing. Come to the concert tomorrow night. Sit down close to the front of the hall, and watch the soloist's hands. That guy's fingers are so relaxed on the bow and the fingerboard they look like wet noodles."

After classes that afternoon, I went to the music department office and volunteered to hand out programs for the concert. And the next evening I was sitting in the front row, right next to the aisle where I would have a clear view of the soloist's hands.

The lights went down, the audience murmurs quieted, and the conductor, Kurt Frederick, walked onstage carrying a violin. Then the soloist came onstage. There was an audible gasp throughout the hall as people realized that the soloist's legs were encased in heavy braces. Absolute silence fell in Popejoy Hall as the twenty-something violin virtuoso, using two canes, walked to the front of the orchestra. He sat down on a metal folding chair, and Kurt Frederick handed him the violin. Popejoy Hall was blanketed in a deep hush. No whispers, no creaks of chairs. Not even a cough or the rustle of a program.

The conductor lifted his baton and gave the downbeat, and the orchestra played the opening bars of Tchaikovsky's violin concerto. Then Itzhak Perlman lifted his Stradivarius, and he began to play.

I sat there, realizing that now I knew what it meant to be transfixed. Perlman's playing was so brilliant, so filled with emotion and youth and zest and the sheer love of music that I literally could not move.

The end of the first movement came. Not one person in that hall stirred. Not one sound as the second movement carried us deeper into the world of Tchaikovsky in all its heartbreaking beauty.

The third movement was so intense I could feel myself levitating. I had forgotten all about watching the violinist's fingers. I never even noticed them. All I could do was live inside the world of music that was being created just for me.

The final chords were played, and the conductor gave the cut-off. The audience sat in silence. We all knew that we were in the presence of a great artist.

After a long, quiet moment the applause began, almost timidly. And then it spread around that great concert hall until it grew into a solid roar of sound as we all stood and applauded and cheered while Itzhak Perlman bowed to the audience from his metal folding chair.

After the concert was over, I drove my car through deserted late night streets. I pulled up at one stoplight, and a cop car pulled up on the other side of the intersection. I was still so dazzled by Perlman's playing that I stepped on the gas and went right through the red light. I found myself driving right on by two of the most astounded cops I had ever seen in my life. Both those cops stared straight at me through the windshield of their cop car as I ran that red light right in front of their faces.

The moment I realized what I had done, my hair stood straight up on my head. I made a fast left turn, and before those two startled policemen could get their black-and-white in gear, I was gone.

I zipped my car around several curvy streets and managed to get myself thoroughly lost. And then I laughed all the way home. How could life give me anything more beautiful than the music I had experienced that evening.

CHAPTER 33

For three solid years, music theory and harmony had been my personal black beasts. I had struggled through two years of harmony, and I nearly flunked my first semester of musical form. I managed to pull a C out of the course by paying a friend to tutor me.

However, in my senior year all that hard, unremitting, brain-cracking labor began to pay off. That was the year I took advanced courses that included orchestral conducting as well as composition and orchestral arrangements.

For my final exam, I composed and arranged an orchestral piece that was about fifteen minutes long, and then I copied out the parts for full orchestra. The day of the final exam came. I stood on the podium to conduct the University of New Mexico Student Orchestra as they played my composition.

I lifted the baton and gave the downbeat. Waves of sound filled the orchestra rehearsal room as my baton arced and flowed through the air, giving the players the beat, the expressive movements, the meaning of the music. Everything was coming from the center of me. At that moment everything in my life was good.

As the last chord was played, I held the fermata, and then I gave the cutoff. The orchestra rehearsal room fell silent. There was a moment of silence, and then the entire student orchestra broke out in spontaneous applause. The very same young orchestra players that had played Tchaikovsky's violin concerto with

Itzhak Perlman were applauding my piece and my conducting. They were applauding me.

Afterward I stood in a daze out in the hall. When my conducting and composition professor came out of the rehearsal room door, he shook his head and said, "I've never heard of any undergraduate composition being applauded like that. That was good."

He gave me a brief smile and turned and walked away. And I stood there, feeling like I'd won a big blue ribbon.

CHAPTER 34

It was my final semester before graduation, and I was already starting to book job interviews. I had finally begun to realize that I had selected a career path that offered only limited job opportunities, and I was hoping against hope that I would find placement somewhere.

So my evaluations in classroom music practice teaching were all important. And one in particular, the evaluation of my elementary classroom music teaching by a professor from the department of elementary education, made me tremble. I had never met Dr. Gilbert, the evaluating professor, and I had no idea of what he would be looking for. I spent much of the night before my evaluation lying in bed staring up at the ceiling.

Next morning I woke up with my mind in a fog. I got the boys dressed and ready for school, and I took them to the babysitter's home. Then I drove to the elementary school where I was doing my practice teaching. The class and their teacher were out on the playground, so I had a quiet moment to lay out music instruments and song books.

The bell rang and the children and their teacher came into the classroom. Once the children were seated at their desks I took over the class and began teaching the music lesson.

Just as the children were singing their first song, the door to the classroom opened, and a gray haired Professor Gilbert came in and sat down at the back of the room. My heart gave a leap, and I found myself short of breath.

But I took a deep breath, and I went on with the lesson. I concentrated on three basic skills singing, playing, and music reading. First the children sang two songs they already knew while playing rhythm instruments. Then I had all the children stand up and clap and play some rhythms that I had written out on the chalkboard. Finally, I had two small groups of children come to the front of the classroom and move through the steps of a dance.

After the lesson was completed, Professor Gilbert got up and walked quietly out the rear door of the classroom. I gathered up instruments and textbooks. I smiled at the children and their teacher and said a quick goodbye.

As I walked down the hall, Professor Gilbert came out of the teacher's lounge. For a moment, he and I looked at each other in mutual surprise. Then he said, "I'm glad I caught you. I can give you your evaluation sheet right now."

He handed me the paper, and I looked down at it. At the top of the page was a blue penciled A-plus.

I gasped and looked up at Professor Gilbert, who was smiling at me. He said, "I want you to know this is one of the finest lessons I've ever seen from any student teacher. You held your class together, you stressed each concept, and you took them through each activity, and you timed it all just right. It was a treat to watch you work."

I could not speak. I just stood there, tears gathering in my eyes, feeling such happiness as I had never felt before in my whole life.

"Take this sheet home with you and look it over," Professor Gilbert said. "And then return one copy to my office with your signature. And good luck to you." And with a final kind look, Professor Gilbert left, walking briskly out the front door to his next evaluation.

I stared down at that paper, with its passport to a new life and a future in teaching, and I walked down the hallway toward the front door of the school. Under my feet were two small golden clouds. I will be a teacher, I thought. I will go out into that working world, and I will be good at what I do.

CHAPTER 35

By August of 1967, I had completed my undergraduate course work. I had been on the honor roll three times. My graduate record examination scores were in the ninetieth percentile for my general courses and eightieth percentile for music.

Did I feel ready to begin my teaching career as I drove out to Bernalillo to begin my first day as an elementary music teacher for the children of Sandoval County, the third poorest county in the nation? Not for one moment. I was a twenty-eight year old college graduate, a soon-to-be divorcée and single mom, a green-as-grass first day schoolmarm, and I was terrified.

Bernalillo Elementary School had a small music classroom located in a freestanding building used for the janitor's room and for storage. Inside the music room was a piano, an inexpensive record player, some classroom rhythm instruments, a set of chromatic bells, a lap harp and songbooks, and thirty metal folding chairs. I was happy to be in that room. I knew that the kids and I could play and sing and dance, and none of the regular classrooms would be disturbed.

The first class arrived at the door of the music room right after the morning bell. Twenty-three first grade children silently filed in and sat down. The classroom teacher smiled at me and went back to her room to catch up on some of her paperwork, and I was left alone with eighteen Spanish kids and six Pueblo Indian kids. Twenty-four pairs of dark eyes gazed at me without a blink.

I looked into those eyes and I was overwhelmed. Those children were now in my hands, and they would either learn music, or I would have failed them. And that I would never do.

I smiled down at a tiny Pueblo Indian girl with dark hair that curved around chubby cheeks. Her face never changed expression. But after a moment's thoughtful consideration, small lights came on in those two black eyes. I smiled at the rest of the class and saw their faces start to relax. And in classic teacher fashion, I began the class by saying, "Good morning, boys and girls."

There was not a murmur in reply. After a silent moment, I said, "My name is Ms. Bengtson, and I'm going to be your music teacher."

The silence was as thick as peanut butter. My voice got a little too bright. "We're going to sing a song I think you already know. It's called 'Are You Sleeping Brother John.'"

More silence. I handed out rhythm instruments. Several sets of sticks. Small drums with red circular sides. Jingling tambourines. And finally four metal triangles.

I gave the last triangle to a tiny boy named Benito, who was about half the size of the rest of the first graders. His round face had a tough expression that came from Benito's being the youngest in a family with eleven older sisters. His family lived in a two bedroom home, and his teacher had told me that Benito spent most of his time at home fighting for his life.

The teacher had warned me beforehand that the pint-sized Benito was a holy terror. "Every other kid on the playground is scared of him," she said. And she looked at me with a certain pity in her eyes. "Let me know if you have any problems."

Now I gently took Benito's left hand, and I curled his index finger around the silvery metal triangle. I placed the triangle beater in his right hand, and I helped him strike the triangle with the beater.

The triangle gave out a beautiful *Ting*, and Benito's angry eyes opened wide. He looked up at me with the wonder of a child who has seen his very first Christmas tree. I smiled down at him as we began to sing "Brother John." And I realized this was why I became a teacher. In that moment I knew I was supposed to be exactly where I was, doing exactly what I was doing.

✲ ✲ ✲

For the rest of that first week, I worked on settling in to my teaching schedule, which involved traveling between elementary schools.

Mondays, Wednesdays, and Fridays, I taught at Bernalillo. On Tuesday and Thursday mornings, I drove to a three classroom elementary school in Algodones. In the afternoons, I drove up into the mountains to the small school in the mountain town of Placitas. And then I drove back down the steep mountain road to Bernalillo where I taught more afternoon music classes.

I had a tight schedule. Before school began, I had taken the schedule I had originally laid out to the principal, a gray haired woman with a long, square face and a jutting jaw.

She looked it over and then she glared at me. "This is not the schedule you're going to have." She dropped my carefully laid out schedule in her wastebasket. "Here's the schedule I've already made up for you."

And she shoved a paper with times and schools scheduled in square blocks during the week. I looked it over, and I said, "This will mean that I have only thirty-five minutes to pack up instruments and music books and then drive from Placitas back to Bernalillo. I'll need time to set up for my final two music classes in the late afternoon. Could we rearrange this schedule so that my last stop of the day would be in Placitas?"

"Those teachers and their principal don't want you up there the last hour of their day. They have other activities scheduled. That's your schedule, right there." And before I could open my mouth, she added, "And it's your responsibility to be back in time to take your afternoon classes."

"There is one other thing," I said. "The road up to Placitas is slick and dangerous in snowy weather."

The principal leaned forward in her chair. Her eyes burned holes in the air. "I'm not interested in excuses. Every other teacher in this school teaches all day every day. As far as I'm concerned, the time you spend driving between one school and the next is free time for you, and you're not getting one minute of driving time you don't absolutely have to have."

I walked out of that office in a state of gloom. Jobs for elementary music teachers were not plentiful, and it looked like I would have to go back to school and start taking evening and summer classes to qualify for elementary classroom certification. Because sooner or later, I was going to have to find myself another job. And in the meantime, I'd better not put a foot wrong.

CHAPTER 36

On the twenty-first day of September 1967, I went to the Bank of New Mexico and deposited my very first paycheck, totaling $479.38 after taxes and deductions.

That evening I told Stan, "This marriage is over."

Stan sat there and looked at me. "I didn't know anything was wrong," he said.

"This marriage has come to an end," I said. "You can move out this weekend."

✲ ✲ ✲

The following Saturday, I stood out on the front porch of what was now my home. Stan was packing all his belongings into the back of his car. Arnold and Philip were both sitting in the front seat. I watched as Stan's Rambler moved off down the street, turned the corner, and was gone.

I went into the house, and I shut the front door. I stood there and looked around the living room, and I listened to the silence. I thought to myself, I am alone in this house.

I had never lived in a place that did not have someone else in it. Even the studio apartment in Las Vegas had the downstairs deaf old dearies. Someone else inside the four walls, someone else walking across the floor, someone else putting a dish away. But in this house there was only silence.

I walked down the hallway with gentle steps so the pain in me would not awaken, and I went into my bedroom. I opened the door of the half empty closet, and I took down the dress bag that hung in the back.

I laid the bag down on my bed and unzipped it. I lifted out my white satin wedding dress with its embroidery and its glowing seed pearls. It was the most beautiful gown I had ever owned. I sat down on the bed, and I stroked the lustrous satin skirts. I lifted up my crinkled bridal veil. One marriage, I thought. Eleven years of my life.

I carefully laid the tulle bridal veil on top of the wedding dress. Then I folded the satin dress into a bundle with the white veil crushed inside the seed-pearled folds of the gown. I picked up the gown, and I carried the slippery satin bundle down the hall, through the kitchen, and out the back door.

I walked around to the side of the house, and I lifted the lid on one of our three metal garbage cans. Then I stuffed and pushed and pummeled white satin and bridal veil all the way to the bottom of the odiferous garbage can. For a moment I stood there, looking down at black streaks on what had once been my white wedding dress.

I held up my left hand, and I gazed at the two white gold rings on my ring finger. One ring for engagement, the other for wifedom. The tiny diamonds of the engagement ring flickered in the sunlight. They were the only diamonds I had ever owned.

I slid the engagement ring and the wedding ring off my ring finger. I turned my right hand over, and I watched as the two rings landed on top of the shapeless satiny whiteness streaked with greasy, smelly stains. I put the garbage can lid down over the white corpse of a misbegotten marriage.

The garbage would be collected on Tuesday.

I went back into the kitchen, and I washed my hands, over and over again. I no longer had time nor place in my life for white satin, for tulle bridal veils, for white gold rings with diamonds. No time to waste on false hopes.

A dark rage burned inside me, held in check only by the ice of unshed tears. Years of tears, silenced by cold will. I stood in front of that kitchen sink, an ice princess on her frozen dais, standing inside an ice mountain of anger and grief and pain.

I went into the living room, and I walked over to the bookshelf. I picked up my Bible, and I opened it to the Book of Isaiah. I looked down at the verse that said *the stone that the builders rejected.* The prophet had spoken those words for the Jews. The Christians said the rejected stone was the Christ.

This day, I thought, the rejected stone was me. I was the child who had been sent away to school by inexplicably remote parents. I was the teenage daughter who had found herself lost in a heedless marriage. I was the wife who might have been sent to a state mental institution by a husband who had rejected her gifts. From now on, I would be the one to do everything that had to be done for myself and my sons. No one wanted me. And I would want no one.

At that moment, the divorce of my outer life from my cherished inner world with its brilliantly remembered vision of Divine Eye, became complete. Outwardly I would be what the world demanded that I be. And I would trust no one with my inner truths. Because in this earthly kingdom of the blind, the one-eyed woman was not king, queen, nor was she princess. She was lucky if she wasn't hanged, burned at the stake, or thrown out into the forests of the night. And that was cold fact, so cold it burned.

Once more rage flared up in me, and then it died and became ashes. I put my Bible back on the shelf, and I went into the kitchen to wash the dishes. For the first time in my life, I blessed the ordinary tiresome chores of housekeeping. I gave thanks for my home and my kids, and for the teaching that would shape a whole new life structure to fill up my shattered world.

By the end of that month, Stan had taken everything he owned. Even his small fishing boat was gone from the garage, picked up after I called him and told him that either he could come get that damned boat or I would sell it through *PennySaver.*

☆ ☆ ☆

Back then I saw Stan as a traitor. The one man I should have been able to trust had schemed to throw me into a state mental institution. I was horribly burned by what I regarded as Stan's absolute betrayal of trust.

Today I know that what I went through was by no means unique. And when I look back at the young Stan I see a terrified young man in his mid-twenties.

I suspect some mental health professional took it upon himself to tell Stan that his wife was mentally unstable. To Stan, that would have meant that his career was at risk and any chance for a normal home life was an impossibility. His wife and his marriage had become an unexploded bomb.

I also know, as I look back, that I must accept full responsibility for the mistake I made when I bought that wedding ring all by myself, without so much as informing Stan. He never proposed to me. He never told me he loved me. And I never thought of saying those three magic words, "I love you," to Stan. So at the age of seventeen, without even being aware of what I was doing, I manipulated Stan and myself into a misbegotten marriage.

That heedless decision not only shaped my life, it also impacted the lives of our two sons. It meant Philip and Arnold had to go through the agonizing heartbreak of their parents' divorce, of knowing that they would never again have their dad come into their bedroom each morning and tell them that it was time to get up and get ready for school. From that time on they would see their father only on weekends.

CHAPTER 37

Soon after I started my teaching career, I began taking voice lessons. I knew my professional life was going to be demanding and my kids would take up most of my home time. I told myself, I need to do one thing just for me, so that I'll know I'm an adult woman.

I met my voice teacher, Amelia, when I was a student at UNM. She and her husband had each studied voice in Italy back in the 1930's. Her husband had studied with the nephew of Maestro Antonio Cotogni, the famed teacher of Beniamino Gigli, and Amelia herself had studied with several teachers who had sung during the golden age of bel canto.

The first time Amelia heard my voice, she said to me, "You could have ten times the voice you have now. But if you don't learn how to sing properly, you'll soon lose your voice altogether."

I knew she was telling the truth. No one in the UNM music department had ever taken my voice seriously. For five years I had been tossed around from one short lived voice teacher to the next. Each one semester teacher had left me in worse vocal shape than the last. Notes that once had been easy for me were now impossible to sing.

When I began taking private lessons I said to Amelia, "I'll do whatever I need to do to get my singing voice in shape."

"Good," she said. "Let's get your voice warmed up, and then I'll have you sing a little bit from Traviata."

So that day I sang my first opera aria. Every note and every word of Verdi's "Ah, quell' amor" would become dear to me as the world of bel canto singing began to open up before me.

✲ ✲ ✲

At home I became more or less domestic. I started using the sewing machine my parents had given me as a Christmas present. I sewed kitchen curtains. I made T-shirts for my sons. When I watched television in the evenings, I hemmed skirts and dresses that I sewed for myself.

Every few weeks I would make bread. I'd take a Saturday afternoon and mix up bread dough in the mixer. Then I'd flop the dough out on a floured board and knead it until it felt just right. Not sticky, not rubbery, but soft and smooth, welcoming the touch of fingers and palms and the heel of the hand as the dough was flattened, then turned and flattened again.

When the bread had risen in the pans and then baked in the oven for almost an hour, the rich, yeasty aroma would find every nose in the house, on the front porch, or out in the back yard. My two kids and their friends would all come piling into the kitchen and slather slices of crusty bread with butter. Within an hour, less than two loaves out of the original six would be left, along with a generous scattering of breadcrumbs on table and stovetop and floor.

CHAPTER 38

One brisk fall day my father heard three of the men that worked for him talking in Spanish. A couple of the words the workers were saying came through loud and clear. *El viejo.* Literally, those words meant "the old one." And those young powerline workers were talking about my dad.

My dad stopped in his tracks, and then he went roaring into the shop area, saying at the top of his lungs to his startled employees, "Don't you call me that! Don't you call me *el viejo.* I ain't old! Don't you dare call me old."

"Aw, boss," said Anastacio, "We didn't mean anything by that. It's just like saying the old man. The boss. That's all it is."

"I don't care," said Daddy, in full rant. "You don't call me an old man. You don't call me *el viejo.*" He turned to go out of the garage, and then he turned back again and he said, "If any of you guys ever calls me an old man again, you'll all be fired!"

As Daddy stormed his way out of the shop area and headed for the power plant, he heard the men start to laugh. Later he told me, "I knew they were probably gonna go right on calling me *el viejo* behind my back." He broke into a grin. "But by golly, they'll never call me that to my face again."

As my dad turned around and bent over to put a plate in the dishwasher, I saw that his hair had turned completely white and was thinning on top. And his movements were more careful than they had ever been.

How could God create a world where the people you loved kept on getting older? Especially someone like my dad, who had always been so filled with kinetic energy that he left younger men spinning in his wake.

CHAPTER 39

In January of 1968, I became an ex-wife. It was brief and unceremonious. Stan and I met at the lawyer's office, where we signed the papers. The lawyer took us over to the courthouse, and we went into the judge's chambers. They were dark and wood paneled, with one small light on the judge's desk. The judge glanced up from some documents he was working on. "Have you got the papers?"

"Yes, your honor."

"Give them to me."

The lawyer handed over the papers, and the judge signed all the copies. And that was it. We were in, and I was out. In less than two hours I had morphed from being a wife into being a divorcée and a single mother.

I went back to my car with the copies of the divorce papers in my hand. I opened the car door. I sat down in the driver's seat and unfolded the papers. I stared down at the divorce decree with the judge's signature on it.

After awhile I started my car and drove to the babysitter's to pick up my two boys. On the way, I kept thinking there should have been mourners. Men clad in black suits and ties, women in black crepe dresses and widows' veils, all standing around an open grave with its polished mahogany coffin waiting to be lowered into the earth.

I was the only mourner for a sad marriage that should never have been born. And now after eleven years of a pain filled half life, my marriage was deceased. Ended without ceremony. No music by Bach. No eulogies for eleven married years that were now as dead as any corpse.

I parked my car in front of the babysitter's home, and I went in to get my sons and take them home and make their dinner.

CHAPTER 40

A few weeks later, I came down with the flu. I knew I would be home for the better part of a week. And I knew my job hung by the merest thread. So my fevered dozing was laced with anxiety.

On the third night, I woke up from a fitful sleep. And the next thing I knew, I was walking into my darkened kitchen. I knew I had to make a start on all those dishes, and I dreaded it.

I reached out to pick up a knife to wash. But to my dazed surprise, my hand went straight through the knife handle and on down through the counter of the drainboard. In my half asleep state, I stood there and I kept on trying to pick up the knife, with no success. Then I tried to pick up one of the dirty plates, and my hand went right through the plate.

In the flash of a second or less, I came wide awake. "I can't touch anything," I cried. "I can't lift anything! Archangel Michael, please help me!"

I found myself being picked up by a whirlwind of energy, and I went flying down the hall, feet first. As I went through the wall to my bedroom, I could see where all the studs and joists were located. And I felt a gritty sensation as my energy body passed through the plaster on my bedroom wall.

Then I was floating high over my bed, looking down at my body. I was so scared I was shaking all over. I kept on saying, "Archangel Michael, please help me!"

I could see my body through the back of my head, which was another shock. And I found myself spinning around until the positions of my arms and legs were exactly the same as on the physical body lying on the bed below me. And then I was back inside my sleeping physical body. I gave a deep sigh of relief as darkness flowed over me.

The next morning I said to the Archangel Michael, "Please don't let me fly out of my body anymore. It scares me, and I've got so many things to do." And I gave the plaintive cry of all young divorced mothers: "I don't have time."

The flu passed, and I went back to my teaching and my home life. And I managed to forget about my out-of-the-body experiences. I kept telling myself they were only dreams.

☆ ☆ ☆

In May of 1969, at the end of my second year of music teaching, the principal called me into her office after school. "Our funding has been cut for the coming year," she said. "I've told the superintendent we don't need a music teacher. So you'll be let go at the end of the year."

The principal turned away from me and got out some papers, and she said to me, "Sign here. And don't think you'll be getting any job recommendation from me."

I signed the papers, and then I looked at the embittered and burned out principal with whom I had been dealing for the past two years, and I thought to myself, Maybe I don't need a recommendation from you.

I walked out of her office, and I went straight over to the office of the assistant superintendent of the Bernalillo Public Schools. He was the man who had originally interviewed me for my job.

"I've just been informed that the post of music teacher is being cut," I said to the assistant superintendent.

He leaned back in his chair and looked over at me, and he gave a sigh. "That's right," he said. "It's the problem we always have with federal funding for education." He got to his feet, walked over to the window, and he stood there and looked out.

"The first year," he said, "The federal government comes into your school, and they tell you they're going to give you all this money to improve education, no strings attached. And that first year we built new classrooms for our kids."

He turned back away from the window. "The second year we had enough money for buying textbooks and hiring additional teachers, including a music teacher. Then the federal government tells us there are school systems out there that have misused the money they've been given, so we need to do more paperwork. And in order to do all that paper work, we have to take money out of classroom budgeting so we can hire extra secretaries.

"By the third year, we haven't got that much money left for education, but we have got a lot of book keeping that we never had before. And to pay for that we have to cut back on things like art and music teachers. In the end our kids wind up being no better off than they were before. And we're stuck with a lot of new federal regulations that just get in our way."

The assistant super looked over at me and he said, "I'm sorry you're leaving us. Is there anything I can do for you?"

I smiled at him and I said, "I would be grateful if I could have a letter of recommendation from you."

"Sure," he said. "When you start interviewing, just call my office and we'll send it right out."

I left his office feeling vindicated. I hoped that my leather faced principal would find out that I'd gotten myself a letter of recommendation from her boss. An assistant superintendent, no less. And when she did find out that I'd gone straight over her head to get myself that gilt-edged recommendation, I sincerely hoped she'd damned well choke on it.

CHAPTER 41

One summer morning, my retired parents and I went for a drive across the Rio Grande River, heading on out to a shabby tract home on a half acre of land. There we met a man who had built himself a real novelty. He had taken an old car, tiny and European, and he had pulled out the car's engine and installed a home-built electric motor. It was 1969, and that guy's car was running on electricity.

My dad had read about that man and his electric car in the *Albuquerque Journal*. For an electrical engineer, an electric car was catnip. So Dad did some serious research, and he found the man's telephone number. Then he called the man and made an appointment to go see that car for himself.

To me, that undersized sedan looked the way any old car would look after it had sat in someone's yard for a good long time. The front bumper was loose, and the nondescript gray paint was dusty and tired, with metal shining through the worn spots. But never mind all that. To the proud owner, and to my father, that drab little vehicle was a thing of beauty.

Mother and I sat and waited in the overheated back seat of my parents' car, while Daddy and the electric car owner went through the male vehicle dance. They walked all around the electric car, talking earnestly. Then the car's owner lifted the hood, and he and Daddy talked some more as they pointed at various unnameable components.

More than an hour passed as the two men peered and discussed, delving into the innards of that curiosity. When he straightened up, my father had a smile on his face and a glow in his eyes that only came when he was looking at something he loved. "He's talking about building one of those electric cars for himself," Mother said as she gave a prim and feminine sigh.

I scrootched up my face and I sighed, sinking a little further down into the overheated back seat. I knew it would be at another hour before Daddy would budge. For my father had been transformed into a man with a vision, a man with a dream born full-blown in a moment's time. Daddy was already making plans to build himself an electric car. At that moment life was sweet for my dad.

It wasn't until we were getting into the electric vehicle to go for a short drive that something seemed to go a bit wrong. Daddy started to open the passenger door of the electric car with his right hand. But then he dropped his hand to his side, still talking to the other man while he used his left hand to jiggle the door handle.

Mother looked at over me with worry in her eyes. "I don't know what's wrong." She shook her head. "Daddy has a numb spot on his shoulder that won't go away. We've been to the doctor, and they think it might be something like tennis elbow. They can't do much of anything for it."

I nodded but I wasn't really paying attention. Mother's life had always been one anxiety attack after another. She told me, "I always feel if I worry about something enough, it'll never happen. It's the things I don't catch that do us in."

But this, I thought, was certainly small ado about nothing. Older people always had their aches and pains, and Dad was well up in his sixties.

The old car creaked and squeaked as Mama and I and the two men got into that tiny electric vehicle. Then the doors were slammed extra hard so they would stay closed. And I forgot all about Mother's remark as we moved off down that street.

I was amazed at how quiet that electric car was. There was absolutely no noise from the motor at all, only small clicks that came through when the automatic gearshift went from low to second to high gear. That and the soft rumble of tires as they rolled over the asphalt were all that told our ears that we were moving.

☆ ☆ ☆

The day after that test drive, I started summer university classes to complete my certification as an elementary classroom teacher. Mother and Daddy had already arranged a one year house exchange with a college professor and his family. They would be living in my parents' home in Santa Fe, while my parents would live in the professor's apartment in Honolulu. So by the end of that summer, my parents had packed and left Santa Fe to go have themselves a long overdue Hawaiian honeymoon.

CHAPTER 42

That fall I landed myself a job as a first grade teacher at the Bel Vista Elementary School in Albuquerque.

At that time a new assistant principal, Mrs. Ruth Ramirez, had just started working there. Everyone at Bel Vista was excited about having Mrs. Ramirez at the school, for she was one of the shining lights in the administrator training program. And everyone knew that her uncle was an advisor to the president in Washington, DC. So Ruth Ramirez was destined to go straight up the ladder at Albuquerque Public Schools and beyond.

Mrs. Ramirez was a striking woman, tall and slim, with dark hair and eyes that had brown rimmed irises with brilliant gold centers. She had a brisk no-nonsense air about her. She also had a shining track record as a classroom teacher. It seemed like tired old Bel Vista Elementary was in for a revival.

One day I met Mrs. Ramirez just as she came out of the teacher's lounge. "Your handling of playground duty is below standard," she said to me. "Make sure you are out there on that playground the moment the bell rings."

Shocked, I said, "Of course."

When I went into the teacher's lounge, everyone was sitting in absolute silence. All the teachers had their heads down. We all ate quietly, and then we silently went back to our classrooms.

Over the next several weeks, our principal, a tall man with a bloodhound face and jowls that sagged, began staying in his office more and more, while Mrs. Ramirez prowled the halls. And over the succeeding months, the entire staff began to simmer with resentment. No one said anything, not even in private. Almost the entire school year went by with all the teaching staff keeping their heads down.

In March, the year end teacher's evaluations came up. Both principals came into my room on a Monday morning. The New Mexico March winds were blowing that day, and the kids were totally unable to concentrate with all the gravel that was blowing up against the metal walls of our mobile classroom. For the next hour, the two principals stood next to my classroom door, silently making notes on their clipboards.

I'd never had an evaluation like this. None of the kids had seen anything like it. Instead of settling down, they began getting more and more noisy, more and more restless in their seats. Finally the morning recess bell rang, and the children boiled out of the classroom and onto the windy playground.

As I came back into the classroom after making sure the kids were playing on their side of the playground, the two principals handed me their evaluation sheets. Then they pointed at a "Fuck" that one of the first graders had managed to scrawl on the chalkboard on his way out the door.

Mrs. Ramirez said to me, "We're recommending you be fired at the end of this school year." And without another word, both principals turned and walked out the door.

The rest of the day passed in a haze. I stayed in my classroom, and when the kids left to go home that afternoon, I sat down at my desk and I put my head in my hands.

☆ ☆ ☆

That evening, after my two sons were asleep, I went into my living room and sat down on the floor, facing the couch, with my Bible in my hands. I read a few words, but I don't remember what they were. Finally, I put my head down on the couch and gave a silent cry. "Please help me, God. I don't know what to do."

And I found myself in the midst of a great ocean, all alone, swimming in terrible black waves under a darkened sky. I kept trying to head to shore, but the waves kept slamming into me, one after the next, until I thought I was going to drown. I came up for what I was certain would be the last time, coughing and sputtering and choking. I lifted my face to try and take in some air, and then I felt a hand grasping me by the back of my collar.

I turned my head, and there was a man swimming in the ocean with me. He had a shining light all around him, and the most intense eyes, and he was holding me up, keeping me from drowning.

"Help me." My voice came out as a gasp.

The moment those words were out, I found myself with that man on a beach, looking out at the stormy ocean with its terrible whitecaps and the dark rain coming down. There was another man standing there, with a beard and long hair and piercing eyes. He was writing in the sand with his long wooden staff. The bearded man looked over at me and then lifted me up on his back, just as my father had when I was small. He started running over rough boulders and past the great waves that crashed with loud roars, hissing up on the sands of the beach, trying to get at me.

The running man didn't stop until we came to a beach overlooking a small bay. The sun was shining, and there was white sand all around. The water was serene and blue. And there the bearded man had me slide down off his back. I stood there on my wobbly feet with my knees shaking, and then I turned and saw the other man who had held me up and kept me from drowning. And I knew that man was the Christ. And Jesus said to me, "You'll be safe here."

And then the two men disappeared.

The next thing I remember was coming back to full consciousness, with my head lying on the couch. Without a word or a thought I got up and went to bed, and I slept without a dream all night long.

CHAPTER 43

The next day, I thought I would stay in my classroom and eat lunch by myself, but something made me get up and go into the teacher's lounge. As I sat down at the table, one of the teachers said to me, "You look really unhappy."

And it all came out of me. "My evaluation was terrible. Mr. Bloodhound and Mrs. Ramirez are threatening to have me fired."

Instead of doling out commiseration, the teachers all immediately said, "Go see Louise. She's the National Education Association representative for Bel Vista, and she'll help you. Her husband is one of the most respected principals in the whole of the Albuquerque public school system. Get Louise to help you."

So that afternoon after school I went to Louise's classroom, and I told her what had happened. She sat there, a lovely older woman with beautifully coiffed gray hair. Louise listened to me carefully, and then she said, "You don't know why you were hired, do you?"

I stared at her and I said, "What do you mean?"

"Close to the end of the last school year, the previous first grade teacher had to leave because her husband was being relocated to Georgia by the military. It was all very sudden. And we had a beautiful young teacher's aide who wanted to become a teacher. Mr. Bloodhound liked her very much. Perhaps, a little too much.

"Now," Louise said, "I don't think there was anything wrong going on between the two of them. But Mr. Bloodhound did put

Miss Aide in charge of the first grade class. And we all thought this was just until he could hire a new teacher.

"But last May he informed the teachers that Miss Aide would stay on to teach the first grade class for this school year as well. So we teachers held an after school meeting, and I went down to the National Education Association office. When I told them what was going on, the NEA filed a formal complaint, which was upheld. It is against state regulations to have anyone teaching in any classroom without a degree in education and without proper certification. It could not be allowed."

I looked at Louise with comprehension dawning in my eyes. "So Mr. Bloodhound was forced to hire a new teacher. And that was me."

"Yes, and Miss Aide quit her job. Now, none of this was her fault. She was just doing what she was told to do by her administrator. But she took the brunt of it."

"And what about Mrs. Ramirez?"

Louise sighed. "Her family is aligned with a group led by a man named Reies Tijerina."

I was shocked. "You mean those people who murdered that poor night watchman?"

"Well," said Louise, "Tijerina has got a lot of support among some members of the Spanish community. And some of them are prejudiced against Anglos, particularly ones with blond hair and fair skin like yours."

I sat there and looked at Louise. "What can I do about any of this?"

"Here's what I'm going to have you do. I'm giving you a set of sample lesson plans. You take these, and you write up all your lesson plans exactly the way I do mine. And then you get busy and completely redesign your classroom."

The next day I got to school before seven o'clock, and all that day and late that evening after school, I worked. I took down all the old bulletin boards, and I cleaned out all the cupboards and shelves. I completely rewrote all my lesson plans the way Louise showed me, and I followed those plans closely throughout each school day.

At the end of the week, I went into the teacher's lounge, and another blond teacher was sitting there in tears. "I've been told they're letting me go," she said. "They never told me a thing, and now this."

Another blond teacher and a dark haired, dark eyed Spanish teacher spoke up. "We work together all the time," the blond teacher said.

"That's right," said the Spanish teacher. "We do our lesson plans together, we exchange work stations for the kids, we do everything exactly alike. And look what we got on our evaluations."

On the Spanish teacher's evaluation, all the ratings were excellent. On the blond teacher's evaluation, all the ratings were from bad to worse. "How can this be?" the two teachers asked indignantly. "Exactly the same lesson plans, and this much of a spread in our ratings? This makes no sense at all."

That afternoon, after we had finished going over my lesson plans, Louise said to me, "We only have one more week before your final evaluation. What I'm going to do is have a friend of mine who works at North Area Administrative Office as an elementary classroom consultant to come to Bel Vista and observe your class."

✲ ✲ ✲

The following week, Susan Schliemeyer came to my mobile classroom at 9:00 a.m. All that morning and afternoon, she sat and observed me and the kids. And all that day, the wind blew so hard that airline pilots reported they saw tumbleweeds blowing past their planes on both sides, faster than their airplanes could fly.

For me and for my first graders, that entire day was like living in the middle of a battlefield, with blowing gravel and sand hitting the metal walls of our mobile classroom with a sharp noise that sounded like shrapnel. By the time the kids left for home, I was exhausted. Susan, who had not spoken a word all day long, said, "Let's have a cup of coffee. I have some in my thermos."

We sat down over coffee, and the first thing Susan said to me was, "I have never seen any teacher do such a fine job under such difficult conditions, and with such an immature group of first graders. This is as professional a job of teaching as I've ever seen. For your first year in an elementary classroom, this is extraordinary work."

For the first time in two weeks, I took a deep breath and gave a sigh. And I said, "Thank you."

After our conference Susan went back to the North Area Office. A few days later Bel Vista's principal, Mr. Bloodhound, was called into the North Area assistant superintendent's office. And a couple of days after that, I happened to run into Mr. Bloodhound as I was walking from my mobile classroom to the school office. He lowered his head and turned away from me, with his eyes fixed on the ground. And he said not a word.

CHAPTER 44

A few weeks later, I got a note in my teacher's box that said, "Ms. Bengtson, please call me." It was from Mr. Sanchez, the principal of Sierra Madre Elementary School in West Mesa.

That afternoon after school, I made the call. I heard a pleasant voice at the other end of the line. "Ms. Bengtson, did you get my messages?" he asked me. "I've been trying to get in touch with you for the past three weeks.

"No, sir," I replied in astonishment. "I haven't received any messages at all."

"Well," Mr. Sanchez said, "I just wanted to let you know that you've been transferred to Sierra Madre, where you will be teaching third grade. I'd like to talk with you on the first day of teacher orientation in August."

"Yes, sir," I said. "I'll be there."

That final week of school, there were eight of us Bel Vista teachers and one school counselor that all went out to dinner together. We'd all been threatened with being fired at one time or another, and so we called ourselves the Bel Vista Elementary Rejects. And we had a blast.

On the last day of school, I gave Louise a single rose and a note that said, "Thanks for everything." And I went home to my two sons, my voice lessons, and all my bills.

CHAPTER 45

It wasn't until my parents returned from Hawaii in June, after their twelve-month house trade, that the subject of Daddy's arm came up again.

Both Mama and Daddy were full of their second honeymoon, talking about living in the same building as Jack Lord, the star of the hit television series *Hawaii Five-O.* They had come home with pictures and stories and happiness that bloomed inside them both.

"It took me almost forty years to have a real honeymoon," Mother said. "And, oh my, Hawaii was beautiful."

Daddy's smile was pleased and proud. "We had a good time," he said. "We really saw a lot over there."

"Twelve months wasn't nearly long enough." My mother looked off into the distance. "Your father and I actually went house hunting in Honolulu."

I sat up straight. "You did what?"

"We went looking for a house to buy. We were just crazy to stay there. But the prices were way too high for us, and the fact is you can't own land in Hawaii."

"Yep, that's right," said my dad. "There are a few Hawaiian families that own almost all the land there. You lease the land, and then you buy or build your own home. So your Mother and I decided we'd just stay here in Santa Fe."

"Oh darn," I said. "I could've gotten a job teaching over there, and then we all could've lived in Hawaii."

"Well, the prices over there are spectacular." My mother shook her head. "Everything costs, especially housing."

I laughed and said, "It was just a thought."

When Daddy got up to go look around the outside of the house, Mother turned to me, her face serious. "I took your father to see the doctors in Honolulu. They have fine doctors over there, some of the best in the world. We saw a neurologist, and he diagnosed Daddy as having a condition related to Parkinson's."

A coldness settled in me, flowing down into my heart and my abdomen. "What kind of condition?"

"Well, they don't know exactly what it is. For want of anything better, the neurologist called it supra nuclear palsy, but that's a descriptive term." Mother looked at me with the courage that always came over her in the hard moments of life. "This is something that will never go away, but what it might do—well, they just don't know."

Coming in the front door, Daddy said, "The doctors in Honolulu gave me a complete CAT scan. And they didn't find a thing wrong with me. The old brain's okay."

I couldn't think of a thing to say. I thought of my father when I was a kid, climbing power poles and telephone poles with ease. Bossing his men, and the office help, and his family. Even making sure that the dishes in the dishwasher were placed just so. "It takes an engineering mind to know how to put dishes in a dishwasher so they get really clean," Daddy would say to me in all seriousness.

In his college years, back in the 1920s, my dad had acquired the nickname "Speed" because he did everything at top speed. Whenever Daddy came into the home-cum-office where we lived and worked, he was like a white tornado blowing through.

"Liz-beth," he would call out, "I need to get these things from the electric supply house in Santa Fe right now."

And for the next five minutes or so, Daddy would storm and holler, while everything and everybody flew straight up in the air. And then things would all settle down again once he'd headed out the door.

And now at sixty-eight, going on sixty-nine, Daddy already had an air of aging about him. An aura of fragility now framed his body energies.

CHAPTER 46

It was on a hot summer day in Albuquerque that I first discovered my top notes. I was singing Verdi's *Caro Nome,* and Amelia was playing the accompaniment. Her husband, Nicki, was in his room, lying there in his weakness and tiredness, but still keeping one ear on the singing coming from the living room.

"You've got to vomit your whole voice up into the mask," Amelia said to me. The mask was an inverted triangular area from the tip of the nose on up to the forehead. It was where the sinus cavities were located. "Just think vomiting, and let your voice go up into the mask."

So I sang, "Caro nome, che il mio cor…"

And every few bars, Amelia would say, "Vomit! Vomit!"

Stifling my giggles, I kept on vocally vomiting up and out, "Col pensier il mio desir…"

And on to the final flourishes, with Amelia's "Vomit! Vomit!" doing a steady crescendo. As we came to the last note, Amelia said to me, "Now, sing it up!"

And without thinking, I did just that, sending my voice spiraling up to a dizzying height, singing a final E above High C.

It was not a pretty note I sang. It came out a whistling squeak. But there it was, my very first high E, and it was on pitch. Never in my whole life had I ever sung that note before.

Amelia gave me the cutoff. I released the note, and the two of us looked at each other in mutual astonishment. Then my teacher smiled up at me and gave me her highest accolade. "Good," she said. "That high note needs work, but it's there."

Happiness poured over me. Then out of the back bedroom came Nicki's voice, saying in his rich Russian accent, "Womit! Womit!" And Amelia and I broke out in delirious laughter.

That day I could not go home after my lesson. I went to a coffee shop and had a cup of coffee and stared out the window, feeling a letdown. How could I leave the world of high E's and come down to going home, dealing with two active and rebellious junior high school age sons, doing the everlasting dishes, worrying about paying the bills, and—God have mercy on me—even balancing my checkbook.

The guilt of spending money on lessons three times a week, was overwhelming. Yet I knew I had to do this. It was all I had that said, "This is for me. I'm doing this for me and for my dreams."

Even when my voice was choked with guilt, or tight with worry and anxiety, or dulled by the white faced exhaustion of teaching twenty-five kids on stormy or windy days, I kept on singing. Mondays, Wednesdays and Fridays I would drive across town to Amelia's modest adobe style home for my lessons. And I kept slogging away, laboring and struggling to find my own voice.

Paradoxically, it was my good musical ear that got me into trouble. At home, I could do an effortless imitation of Joan Sutherland or Beverly Sills. I listened to the turn-of-the-twentieth-–century recordings of Amelita Galli-Curci and Luisa Tetrazzini, spinning out of my small collection of plate sized, black vinyl, 33-rpm recordings. And I could turn right around and do a pretty good imitation of those old golden-age singers.

So I was swinging wildly between this singing style and that, without any vocal legs under me to give me stability. One day I could sing coloratura phrases and high notes without any effort. The next, I would find myself struggling. And then the day after that, my voice would go south, and finally it would come back. It was all so erratic.

CHAPTER 47

I have two framed diplomas on the wall in my office, right above my desk. One is my undergraduate diploma that says, "The University of New Mexico has conferred the diploma of Bachelor of Music Education..." And the second one says, "The University of New Mexico has conferred the diploma of Master of Arts..."

On the day I turned sixty, I got those two diplomas out of my filing cabinet and went to a shop to buy frames for them. Then I came home and wrestled with screwing holders into the wall. I hung the diplomas so that they looked just right, in the perfect spot where I could see them whenever I glanced up from my computer screen.

I wanted to remind myself who I really was. I was a woman with two degrees and almost two hundred semester hours on my transcript from the University of New Mexico. I was a woman who had worked to support her two sons. I was a woman who had taken care of her dying mother.

Those diplomas started getting me out of bed in the mornings. They began lifting me up out of an endless round of hopelessness. I was not just a semi-invalid who would be forever financially dependent on her older son. I was a woman who had overcome obstacles in her life. It was time I remembered that. It was time for me to remember the years when I became a real teacher.

✲ ✲ ✲

It was late August of 1971 when I first drove up the long incline to West Mesa, a small and isolated community set in the endless lava fields to the west of Albuquerque. I gripped the steering wheel tightly to keep my hands from shaking as I turned into the school parking lot where ten or twelve cars were already parked. I gathered up my purse, my notebook, and an information packet I had received in the mail, and I walked into the school office.

A woman with a pleasant smile looked up from her desk. "Are you the new teacher?"

"Yes, I am."

"I'm Elena Montoya, Sierra Madre's secretary. The teachers are meeting in the school library. I'll take you there."

I took a deep breath as I followed the secretary down a long hallway lined with classroom doors. I was surrounded by that familiar school smell, made up of books and chalk dust and kid sweat that hung in the air, along with the acrid odor of the commercial disinfectant that wafted through the open doors of the kids' restrooms.

I glanced through open classroom doors, glimpsing bulletin boards that were already half finished. I realized that the other teachers had all been working on getting their classrooms set up for at least a day before I'd been told to arrive.

We came to the school library, and the secretary opened the door. Fifteen teachers sat on low chairs at kid size tables. I gave a small smile to the teachers as I quickly made my way to a back table and sat down. I told my hands to stop shaking as I opened my bag and took out a couple of ballpoint pens.

As I arranged my materials, one of the teachers looked over at me. She was a sweet-faced woman with soft brown hair and the air of authority that comes from years of teaching. She said, "Are you the new third grade teacher?"

"Yes," I said. "I am."

"Welcome to Sierra Madre." She smiled at me. "I think you're going to like it here."

Hope sparked in me. "I am?"

"Oh yes. You'll like Mr. Sanchez. He's a good principal. We all feel lucky to have him." Her eyes twinkled, "My name is Nora

Connolly. I teach third grade. My classroom is right across the hall from you, so if you need any help or have any questions, feel free to come see me, and we'll talk."

Inside my chest a weight started to lift. "I'm sure I'll be doing just that," I said as I smiled back at her.

The murmur of voices in the library stilled as the door opened and Mr. Sanchez, the principal of Sierra Madre, came in. He was a short man with a round face and an energetic stride. His eyes looked over the library full of teachers, stopping for a moment when he saw me. I sat up straight in the small chair, and I looked back at him, seeing the intelligence in his eyes. I knew my future as an professional educator depended on this man who had the look of someone with years of experience in teaching and administrative work.

Mr. Sanchez began by telling the group about his trip to Lake Tahoe. "My wife and I were in the casino, and I decided to play the slot machines. And I won!" Over the laughter of the teachers, he went on, "There was a big bunch of coins that came out, and it turned out I'd won enough money to pay for our vacation."

Throughout that long day of meetings, I took copious notes. And I spent much of the lunch break reading through handouts. I talked with several of the teachers, getting to know them, and gradually I found myself settling down.

After the day's meetings were over, I made a couple of trips out to my car and I lugged boxes of teacher stuff to the door of my classroom. I unlocked the door and walked into my classroom, and I looked around. The linoleum floor had been cleaned and waxed. Shelves, green chalkboards, and dark green metal cabinets took up most of the wall space. The kids' desks were all pushed together at the back of the room, and the teacher's desk had been shoved over to a corner of the room.

I put my boxes on the tables, and I began arranging desks and tables and chairs. I placed books from the school library in a small freestanding bookshelf at the back of the room. I stowed away stuff that I had scrounged for my class, like the carpet samples that were eighteen by twenty-four inches. Those would be used by my kids when they were done with their work and could take time out to sit on the floor in the small classroom library space, and read a book.

The intercom box at the front of the classroom coughed static, and Mr. Sanchez's voice said, "Ms. Bengtson, would you please come to my office."

"I'll be right there," I called up to the intercom.

I looked around at my classroom and at the mess all around me, with half finished bulletin boards and stacks of reading materials and textbooks that I had been assigned, and more stuff all over every flat surface in the room. I picked up the lesson plan notebook that every teacher had been issued, and I headed out the classroom door.

When I got to the principal's office, Mr. Sanchez was sitting behind his desk. He looked up as I walked through the door to his office, and he smiled at me. "Sit down and let's talk."

I gave him a nervous smile and sat down in front of his desk. Mr. Sanchez's first words astonished me. "I want you to know how happy we are to have you as one of our teachers here at Sierra Madre. I hope you'll find this to be a good experience for you."

"Thank you," I said, shaken by the kindness I saw in his eyes.

His round face settled into a smile. "I think you'll like our staff members. I notice you've made friends with Nora Connolly."

"Yes, I have. She seems very nice, and she's offered to help me."

"That's good, because Nora is a true master teacher. Whenever you need any help, you go to her. She'll give you a lot of good ideas for your class."

My eyes opened wide. Whenever any teacher or principal called someone a master teacher, that meant they were special. Mr. Sanchez went on, "I'd like you to have your first week's lesson plans on my desk by tomorrow afternoon."

"I'll have my lesson plans ready by then," I promised.

"Good," he said. As he got up from his chair, he added, "By the way, I had a call from the principals at Bel Vista."

Chilled, I opened my mouth to speak, but before I could say anything, Mr. Sanchez said, "I want you to know that I will judge you solely on your performance in your classroom here at Sierra Madre."

"Thank you, sir," I said. "I appreciate that."

Mr. Sanchez gave me a nod, and he walked out the door of the office.

I sat there for just one moment, feeling a profound sense of relief. And then I went back to my classroom to work some more.

CHAPTER 48

"Good morning, boys and girls. My name is Ms. Bengtson, and I am your third grade teacher. Please raise your hand when I call your name, so that I can see who you are. Can you do that for me?"

"Ye-e-es," said the children, like a well-behaved chorus.

"All right then. Dennis Alvarez?"

"Here." And the hand of a slender boy at the back of the room went up.

"Cindy Anderson."

"Here." A girl with straight blonde hair and wearing brand new blue jeans and a blue blouse raised her hand.

"Carmela Gutierrez."

"Here." Curly brown hair, intense brown eyes.

"Ricky Hirsch"

"Here." A young boy with dark brown skin, tightly curled hair and eyes full of mischief waiting to happen.

The roll call went on as hands around the room went up. Finally I asked, "Is there anyone here whose name was not called?"

Silence. My kids all had their eyes fastened right on me.

"All right then. The first thing I'm going to do is read with each one of you individually. This will take about three or four mornings. When you're not reading with me, you'll be working on your assignments. I'll also be handing out worksheets. These are just for starting you off to see how much you can remember from second grade. And then I would like to have each of you write about the best time you had during summer vacation (tried and true). Finally, after you've finished your written assignments, you can choose books for free reading."

And we were off and running.

The class had that first day quietness as the children all worked on making a good impression on teacher. I knew that wouldn't last too long, so I went through giving each child an individual reading inventory as quickly as I could. That would show me what each child's strengths and weaknesses were.

By the end of that first week I had completed the IRIs and set up the reading groups. But rather than giving the kids round robin reading sessions, which I felt was a complete waste of time, I taught them phonetics, the sounds that each letter and each letter combination represented. With mid-level and advanced readers, I worked on word structure, prefixes, suffixes, and the like, along with things like using the dictionary. The list was, of course, endless.

Each morning I would spend an hour reading with individual students. Then I would give each student a workbook assignment that was aimed at that student's particular skills level. Before lunch we would work on spelling. In the afternoons we'd have math, art, science, and social studies.

Three times a week, during the last twenty minutes before going home, we'd have a session of classroom music. I had read a report that showed third grade children who had learned to read music at a third grade level performed better in reading than their peers who could not read music. So I made sure to work with my kids on basic music reading.

It wasn't long before my class began to jell, as much as it ever would. It turned out this class was packed with kids who were a lively handful. Keeping them all on track all day long was an ongoing challenge.

The second grade teachers would all laugh at us third grade teachers when we ate lunch in the teacher's lounge, "We're sure glad you've got our last year's classes." And to the fourth grade teachers, they said, "Look out. You're up next year."

So I had plenty of reasons to have some after school talks with Nora Connelly. Especially one day when I turned around and realized that some of the boys in the classroom had dumped the entire contents of the classroom pencil sharpener into the coffee cup on my desk. I told Nora about this, and I asked, "What should I do? They're a bright bunch, but it's like they're angry with me."

"It seems to me you're being too structured," Nora said. "The kids you've got can't handle that kind of pressure. Try giving them more time to move from one task to the next. Give them time to breathe. And be more relaxed. When a teacher is quiet and smiles at her kids from time to time, the class is always a lot happier."

I took Nora's advice, and it worked. Not that my energetic bunch turned into saints, but they did behave themselves most of the time. And at the end of each day, I made sure to clean out that pencil sharpener.

CHAPTER 49

One night I dreamed that I was standing on a hill above a white sandy beach that circled a small inlet. The air was clear and pure, and the water all shades of blue. Small waves sparkled in the bay, and the skies were as clear and blue as the water.

I turned and I saw an angel standing next to me. In my dream, I knew this was Archangel Michael. He was built like a wrestler or a weight lifter, and he had on an immense, sky blue robe. I wanted to laugh, because in addition to that oversized bathrobe he was wearing, he also had blonde hair, pageboy length, and piercing blue eyes.

Archangel Michael smiled down at me. He gestured toward the tranquil bay and said, "Look."

I turned to look, and I saw a small white whale, an albino whale, swimming in the circular bay. "She wants to swim in the deep ocean," I said. "She wants to migrate with the other whales."

"Look at me," said Michael.

I turned and looked up at him as he gazed at me in deep seriousness. "You will not be out in the greater world until you are much older," he said. "For now, you must keep to this shelter so that you and yours can grow in safety."

I looked out at the small white whale, and I saw how eager she was and how much she grieved as all the other whales began their journey to the south. She swam around and around the bay, faster and faster, slapping her tail on the water in frustration.

"Your time will come," said the Archangel Michael. "And you will be up here with us soon enough. Until then let your watchword be patience."

CHAPTER 50

One morning after I'd brought my kids into the classroom, I turned around from my desk, and I saw a cage on Ricky's desk. And Ricky and the other boys in the class all began talking at once.

I held up my hand and I said, "One at a time, please. Ricky, what's in the cage on your desk?"

Ricky said intensely, "Teacher, Joey and I were at the golf course club, and we were out by the swimming pool with some other kids, and we saw this king snake swimming in the pool, and we caught it, and my mom said we could keep it in a cage, and we brought it to school this morning, and please, teacher, please, can we keep the snake here in the classroom? We'll take him home every weekend. Promise!"

Feeling cold chills down my back, I said, "Turn the cage around, please Ricky, and let's see your snake."

Ricky scrunched up his face imploringly as he turned the cage so I could see an eight-inch king snake moving around inside the heavily screened cage.

And the boys all burst out, "Oh, please teacher, can we please keep the snake here at school? Please?"

"He won't be any trouble. Honest, he won't."

"Yeah, teacher, we'll take good care of him. You won't even have to do anything."

"We'll take care of him. Really, truly, we will."

"Oh, please, teacher, please?"

I looked at each one of those boys and I said, "I'm going to say some very important things to you right now, and I want you all to listen up, very carefully. I am a person who is afraid of snakes. Really afraid."

"He won't hurt you, teacher, honest he won't."

"He's not poisonous or nothing like that."

"Yeah, we won't let him hurt you."

I held up my hand again and waited for complete silence. "I will let you keep the snake in the classroom under the following conditions. First, there will be no horseplay with the snake. No taking him out of his cage without permission. No dropping him down the back of some girl's dress. And absolutely no quarreling or fighting over who gets to hold him. Do you all understand me?"

The wide eyed boys all nodded their heads with vigor.

"And you must ask my permission before you ever take the snake out of his cage. Only if you have all your work done, and I've checked it, do you get to have him out of his cage. Otherwise, he stays in his cage. Have you all got that?"

"Yeah, we've got it." More nods. Breathless silence.

"Now, if there is one time, just one, that any one of you breaks any of these rules, the snake will go home that very same afternoon, and he will not be allowed back in the classroom. Ever.

"So it's up to you to behave really well, and observe all the rules. You do that, and I will allow you to keep the snake in the classroom until the end of the school year."

All the boys and a few of the girls burst out clapping and cheering. I looked at them with my sternest teacher face and raised my hand to quiet them.

"And everything—everything!—depends on you getting your work done and behaving well in the classroom."

"Okay, teacher."

"We can do that."

"We'll be good."

"We promise, teacher."

"All right then. We'll leave the snake in his cage until we've come in from afternoon recess. And then a few of you can get him out and take him to the free reading area in the back of the classroom. And be sure to be very gentle with the snake. Have you got that?"

Big nods. "Yeah, teacher."

"We've got it."

Ricky held up his hand. "Teacher, I know how to handle snakes," he said. "You don't grab them or try to hold onto them. You hold them in your two palms with your hands open, and you let the snake keep moving. You can't squeeze a snake, 'cause if you do that you could hurt him, and the snake could even die."

"Okay," I said to the class. "Ricky's in charge of the snake. So now let's put the cage up on the back shelf, and we'll start our day's work."

For the next six weeks of school, I had a well behaved bunch of third graders in that classroom. They worked hard all day long, and for about a half hour every afternoon, the snake was brought out of his cage and gently passed around.

One day Ricky came up to me, holding the king snake in his hands. "Teacher, you don't have to be afraid of the snake. You can even touch him if you want to. You can just touch him with one finger. He's not slimy like a frog is. His skin feels sort of like velvet."

After a few minutes of Ricky's gentle persuasion, I reached out with my right index finger, and I touched the moving king snake. "You're right," I said to Ricky. "His skin does feel velvety."

Ricky smiled up at me. "You don't have to be afraid of snakes, teacher. Most of them won't hurt you."

I smiled back at Ricky, and I said, "You know what? You're right. I think that from now on, I won't be nearly as afraid of snakes as I have been."

Sometimes children can be our best teachers.

CHAPTER 51

After four years of voice lessons, Amelia looked at me one day in despair. "I don't know that we'll ever be able to turn you into a true coloratura," she said. "I think you might make a pretty good light lyric soprano."

My temper and my stubbornness made my jaw clench and my lips tighten. I looked right back at my teacher and I said, "I'm going to sing coloratura."

Amelia drew in her breath in astonishment. "Well," she said. "All right then. Let's try the first act aria from *Traviata.*"

Angrier than I had ever been with my teacher, I focused every bit of will and concentration on the notes, the words, the phrasing, the expression. And I sailed right on through the whole aria, from the opening recitative to the very end, where I came out with a true E-flat above High C. And that high note actually sounded like a real note.

After the note died away, Amelia stared up at me in astonishment. "Well, that was good! Why don't you sing like that all the time?"

I had no answer for that except to admit, shamefaced, "This time I was mad at you."

Amelia looked up at me in surprise, and then she laughed. "Sometimes I sing best when I'm good and mad," she said. "It can help."

Not too long after that Amelia said, "I think you ought to have a recital. You and Forrest can sing the duet from *Rigoletto,* and we'll work on some of the songs from the Lily Pons album."

So then I worked for hours on evenings and weekends, learning and memorizing my music. Memorization was always a painful chore for me. I was always afraid of forgetting the words. The music I always had down, but memorizing words was a long and sweaty process.

CHAPTER 52

On the day before my recital, Philip asked me if his friend Albert could come to our house and stay the night. I'm sure I gave one of those absentminded parent answers, like, "Uhmm."

And that evening Albert showed up. Philip had decided he wanted to camp out in the garage, so the two boys put sleeping bags out in the garage. Soon I began hearing talk and music floating through the garage door. But I was not paying too much attention because I was getting everything organized for my recital the next day.

I ran over my music, and I checked to make sure I had the right shoes, jewelry, and cosmetics all laid out. Then I carefully pressed my forest green velvet recital gown. I did a quick check on the two boys, and then I went to bed. I fell asleep running through the music in my mind.

Sometime after midnight, I was awakened by Philip turning on the overhead light in my bedroom. I mumbled and tried to pull my pillow over my head, and then I heard the words, "Mom, I'm in trouble."

I sat up, blinking, and I put on my glasses and looked up at my son. "What kind of trouble?"

Philip flinched as he said, "Well, Mom, Albert and I went out tonight, and—Mom, there's a policeman in our living room."

My heart dropped into my lower pelvis. What had Philip gotten himself into? I pulled on my ratty old bathrobe and walked out into the living room where a young, slender policeman was waiting. His dark eyes had that cop look, the look of toughness, of having seen too much, and he gave me a quick hard look. But when he spoke, his voice was gentle. "I'm sorry to have to tell you this, ma'am, but your son is facing some serious charges."

I sat down on the couch. "What happened?"

"Your son Philip, and his friend Albert Gonzales—"

"Mom," interrupted Phil, "Albert and I went out to go to his place. The neighbors next door to Albert's house… Their oldest girl was having a pajama party, and we thought we'd scare the girls. But the man's wife was sleeping in that room, and he called the cops on us."

"The father of the girl has decided to bring charges against your son," said the policeman, sounding even more gentle. "Ma'am, I'm sorry to bring you this news, but these are serious charges. Your son is in real trouble."

I found myself looking down at the paperwork the policeman handed me, and I stared at the blurry words. My hands shook as I signed the papers. Finally the policeman left, and Philip came and sat down next to me on the couch.

I bent over, completely doubled up from pain and shock, and I said, "Phil, I can't stand this."

"I'm sorry, Mom," said my son. "We didn't mean to do anything wrong. Albert and I, we thought we'd have fun teasing the girls."

I sat up and I looked at my son. "We're going over to talk with those parents right now," I told Philip. And the fear in his eyes turned into frozen terror.

Philip and I drove to the neighbor's home in silence. We pulled up in front of a tract home and got out of the car. The front porch light was on, and when I pressed the doorbell, a very angry man came to the door. I said, "Mr. Sanderson, I'm Philip's mother. I was wondering if we could talk for a moment."

The man stared at me for a long moment, and then he opened the door, and Philip and I walked into the small living room. As we sat down on the couch, his Japanese wife came in from the back of the house.

I said, "Mr. Sanderson, I want to tell you how terribly sorry I am that my son was involved in an incident like this. I apologize to you from the bottom of my heart, and I'm sure my son does too."

And then, because I couldn't help it, I started to cry silently. I just sat there as tears slowly wandered their way down my cheeks.

The Japanese wife looked over at her husband and she said, "Oh, the poor mother. She suffer so much."

But her husband was still angry. He said, "Let me tell you what happened this evening, and you'll know why I called the police. Albert and Philip climbed over the wall in our side yard, and they started tapping on the bedroom window. My wife was sleeping in there, and she woke up, and she was terrified.

"So I got out my thirty-thirty rifle, and I walked up to that window just as your son tapped on it. I broke the window and shoved the barrel of the rifle right through the window-pane. And then I put one hand right through the hole in the window, and I grabbed your son around the neck, and I told Phil that he'd better stay right where he was, or I would shoot him."

Sitting beside me on the couch, Philip shivered. "I didn't move, Mom," he said. "I stayed there until Mr. Sanderson came out with his rifle. And then he made me come inside the house. And then he called the police."

"Where was Albert?" I asked.

"Gone," replied the husband with a grim voice. "He'd high-tailed it out of there, but that won't help him. I told the cops about him, and they've already been to his parents' house and talked with them."

"You cannot be so mean to this mother," said the Japanese wife in her accented English. "You must do the right thing."

The man began to look as though he might be relenting, and I said, "Mr. Sanderson, what my son did was terribly wrong. There's no excuse for what happened tonight. I do hope the girls are all right."

"The girls were not in that bedroom," said the wife. "This night they sleep in my room, and I am in my daughter's room. That why I was there when tapping and tapping start at the window, and that scare me a lot."

Her husband looked at me nervously. "I had that rifle pointed right at your son. If I'd pulled that trigger, your son would be dead."

I felt as thought I might faint. But I couldn't. Not here. Not now.

The Japanese wife looked over at me, and then she sat straight up in her chair and she said to her husband, "Don't you dare say such things to the poor mother. Look at her. See how much she suffer."

And finally the man looked at his over at wife, then back at me, and he relented. "I'll tell you what," he said. "If Philip gives me his promise never to do anything like that again, I will write a letter to the juvenile authorities. And I'll make sure that they understand that your son is basically a good kid that got himself into trouble."

I sat trembling on the couch as I felt relief pour through me. "Thank you, Mr. Sanderson. And you decide whatever you want my son to do for you in order to make some kind of reparation for what has happened tonight. Anything you want him to do, he'll be here and he'll do it."

Mr. Sanderson looked pleased by that. "Well," he said, "I've got a retaining wall that I'm building in the back yard. Phil can come over after school and work with me, laying bricks and maybe doing some yard work for the next several weeks."

I looked over at Philip and I said firmly, "He'll be here every day, right after school."

On the way home, I told Philip, "I'm going to have to call your dad tomorrow and tell him about this."

"I know," came the low, miserable voice.

And not another word was spoken.

The next morning I called Stan and told him about what had happened. I read the paperwork to him and told him Philip would have to be taken down to talk to the juvenile authorities.

And Stan said immediately, "I'll make an appointment, and I'll go down there with Philip, and I'll talk with them."

CHAPTER 53

The evening after the policeman's midnight call, I dressed in a forest green velvet evening gown, and I went before a small audience at the Unity Church of Albuquerque and I sang.

My recital was like a wedding. I couldn't possibly have changed the date or called it off. My parents had come down from Santa Fe, and I'd notified all the people I knew. The tenor Forrest Tucker would be singing duets with me.

I hadn't said a word to anyone, least of all to my parents, about Philip's being in trouble with the law. And that evening, both my sons sat in well-behaved silence, both of them wearing their good suits and the new ties that I'd struggled to get them to wear.

When I walked out onstage, I was thrilled to see my Shakespeare professor, Kathryn Simons, and my fellow teacher and lifesaving friend, Louise. Both women were sitting out in the audience, each wearing a lovely dress.

Amelia played the introduction to my first song by Stefano Donaudy, and I sang. And lo and behold, there was my voice. Not an imitation of some other artist's voice, but my own voice.

I sang two Italian songs by Donaudy, and then I sang Mozart's "Un Moto di Gioija," Grieg's "Pretty Margaret " and "Les Roses d'Ispahan" by Gabriel Faure. I sang the first act aria from *Traviata.*

Forrest and I sang duets from *Traviata* and *Rigoletto*. And my dad recorded it all on his enormous Sony reel-to-reel tape recorder.

☆ ☆ ☆

The following week, Stan took Philip to see the juvenile counselor. After it was over, Stan called me and said, "That counselor bawled the living hell out of Phil. He told him that if he ever got himself in any trouble like that again, the judge would throw the book at him. And then he let Phil go. So Philip knows the score. From now on, he either stays on the straight and narrow, or he's in deep shit."

For the next several weeks, Philip went over to the Sanderson home every evening after school. And there my son learned how to lay a neat brick wall.

Several years later, when Phil was in the navy, he came home on leave, and he went to visit Mr. Sanderson. The two of them sat out in the back-yard, and they reminisced about Phil's one and only brush with the law. Phil told me, "Mr. Sanderson and I shared a few laughs about that night."

But at the time, raising a teenaged Philip meant that at least once a year I was thrown into a state of acute terror.

☆ ☆ ☆

Arnold, on the other hand, was always the quiet one, the dreamer. When the original *Star Trek* began airing, Arnold turned into Mr. Spock. I remember driving my two sons home one day when a nine-year-old Arnold leaned over, looked at the odometer and said, "Mother, by my calculations, we are now one-point-zero-three-six miles from home."

The weird thing was that when we got home and did the math, it turned out that Arnold was right. And in high school Arnold always made excellent grades in math and science.

✡ ✡ ✡

A few days after the concert, I took my parents' tape recorder out to school, and at lunchtime the teachers listened to some of the pieces I had sung at the recital. By coincidence, Louise was there that day. She had retired from classroom teaching, and she was now working part time evaluating children for the resource rooms.

As Louise listened to my tape she told me, "This is a beautiful recording, but it doesn't capture the sweetness of your voice."

And I thought to myself, At last I'm really singing. And I felt that happiness that came to me when I knew that I was doing something really right.

As we ate lunch, Louise told me what had happened to the two principals at Bel Vista. "Mr. Bloodhound has been retired. It was time. He was moved to another school, and by the end of his first year there, the parents were up in arms and they went before the school board. At the end of that year, he was more or less forcibly told to go home. I think everyone was relieved when that happened."

"Whatever happened to Mrs. Ramirez?" I asked.

"She's in the process of destroying her own reputation. She's so autocratic in her treatment of her teachers that the people at North Area office are unhappy with her." Louise looked over at me. "It's a real pity," she said, "Because she is so intelligent."

I nodded. "Yes, she is. But I can't say I'm surprised to hear this."

"No," said Louise. "But it's always sad when someone with so much promise doesn't quite make the bar in the field of education. It's a challenging thing, being a school administrator, and we need all the good people we can get. A tragedy, really."

I looked at Louise for a long moment, and then I slowly nodded my head and said, "It is sad, isn't it."

CHAPTER 54

For a long time, it didn't seem that Daddy's condition, whatever it was, was going to make that much difference. He still went outdoors to make sure that men doing yard work around the house did their jobs right. He did a lot of charting, following the stock market through those discouraging recession years, and he looked after his two aging cars with love and devotion.

Then Daddy began to develop dizzy spells. One time he was outdoors overseeing yard work when suddenly he spun around and fell flat on his back. Mother was terrified, and the doctors changed his medication once again.

However, the supranuclear palsy kept right on with its glacial progression. By the time my sons were in high school, my father had lost any ability to use his right arm. His muscles had frozen into hard knots that could not be relaxed, and the pain had to be controlled with medication.

My son Arnold spent his high school summers in Santa Fe, helping Mother take care of his grandfather. And I would drive up on weekends with Philip, and we would all help care for their granddad until we had to go back to Albuquerque.

One morning I was helping Daddy dry his back off after his shower. He gave me a flash of his old stubborn look as he said, "I'm gonna beat this thing, you know. I'm gonna get better pretty soon."

But he didn't get any better. Over the next two years, he became increasingly inactive. The doctors finally operated on his right arm, cutting the nerves to relieve the pain, and from that time on, Daddy's right arm flopped at his side. He took to wearing the arm in a sling, as though the arm had been broken.

☼ ☼ ☼

One day Amelia said to me, "I'm going to start composing an opera. I haven't done any composition for a long time, and now I have an idea for a children's opera. I am going to call it *Aza, A Russian Rapunzel.* And I want you to help me write some of the lyrics for my opera."

"Of course I'll help!" I said. "When do we start?"

"Right away," said Amelia. "We'll start at the beginning, where this noble and very handsome prince is out hunting. And then he sees this beautiful young woman imprisoned in a tower, and he falls in love with her."

So I went home and I began writing, struggling to put the words together that would be just right for the story and for the music that Amelia was writing.

And this is a bit of the lyrics I wrote for the opening aria of the prince:

> Ah, now the sun arising tints all the woodland gold.
> The noble stag stands crowned with light.
> Majestic, brave and bold.

A wonderful young soprano, Lindsay Albertson sang the role of Aza, and she did a beautiful job. *Aza, a Russian Rapunzel* was performed at the University of New Mexico recital hall, and it wound up winning a national award from the American Women Composers Guild. After winning that award, Amelia gave me a beautiful silver cup, which I still keep on the shelf of my secretary. It says, "Aza, A Russian Rapunzel, 1978." It also has Amelia's and my names engraved on it.

CHAPTER 55

On the morning of my fortieth birthday, I walked into the school office. The school secretary looked up at me, and she said, "Your parents just called. They asked me to tell you to call them back."

I looked at Elena for an anxious moment. Then I picked up the office phone and I dialed. When my parents answered the phone, my mother's voice cheerfully said, "Happy birthday!"

Dad said, "We tried to call you at home earlier, but you'd already left."

The warmth in my heart turned into a smile. "I did leave early this morning," I said. "I've got some things to do in the classroom. I'm glad you called."

"We just wanted to wish you a happy fortieth birthday," he said.

And Mother added, "How are you feeling?"

I laughed and said, "I feel as though I should have a black armband decorated with an arrow going through a broken heart. Other than that, forty is fine."

I hung up the phone, and I turned and said to Elena, "Reaching forty makes me realize I can never go back."

"That's the truth," Elena said to me. "We never can go back."

I walked out of the office and down the hall. I was forty, and my sons had left home. Arnold was going through college on a work-study program. Philip had joined the navy when he graduated from high school. My years of raising two sons had become vivid flashes of indelible remembrances.

I had always thought of all the things I would be able to do when my sons were raised. But I had never realized how empty my life would seem once both my sons were all grown up and gone from home. I went into my classroom, and I stood there for a moment and looked around, realizing how much my life had changed, altered by the deep flowing currents of time.

✲ ✲ ✲

That year another third grade teacher and I began exchanging classes for one hour every Tuesday and Thursday afternoon. Marian Glass would teach my class social studies, while I taught her kids science and music.

I managed to get all the parents for both Marian's class and mine to buy their kids flutophones, which were heavy-duty plastic recorders, real musical instruments that the kids could easily learn to play. In addition to singing and playing rhythm instruments and all the other activities that make up a music class, I taught both my kids and Marian's students to play flutophones and read music.

By the end of the year, Mr. Sanchez was so pleased with this informal program, he said to me, "I'm going to suggest that we use our two band and orchestral teachers to do some work in general music with all of Sierra Madre's kids."

All the parents, all the teachers, both music teachers, and even the superintendent of North Area were enthusiastic about Mr. Sanchez's idea. But when it got up the ladder to Central Office, it died. The people in the Music Department, and various other bureaucracies, poleaxed our idea, saying it did not fit their requirements.

Some of the worst enemies of kids having what they really need in the arts can be politicians and midlevel administrators and bureaucrats. The worst of those folks can be deadly to anything in the arts. Too many kids, throughout the years, have been deprived of too much because of such ignorant attitudes.

CHAPTER 56

One day Amelia said to me, "I have another idea. Why don't we see if we can go and sing opera in the public schools?"

I looked at her in astonishment. "That's something that nobody in Albuquerque has ever done," I said. "I think it would be a great idea. Let me see what I can do about getting us a grant for this project."

So I went home and contacted a friend of mine who was the principal of Algodones Elementary School back when I was teaching music in Bernalillo. Bernie now worked for the Albuquerque Public Schools in the administration. When I called him, Bernie said, "Let me see what I can do." And Bernie wound up getting our little opera company a thousand dollar grant to give twelve performances.

When Amelia heard this, she said, "That's wonderful! We need to start working on short operas, about twenty minutes long, that we can perform for the students."

And so we began rehearsing *El Majo y la Maja,* a Spanish tonadilla, or short opera. It was about thirty minutes in length, especially after we added a couple of arias to it, including "Malaguena" for our tenor, Forrest, and "Al pensar en el dueño de mis amores" for me. To the delight of the Spanish-speaking elementary students, we sang the entire tonadilla in Spanish.

Lindsay and Forrest and I also sang Mozart's *Impresario* in several elementary schools. We had costumes and wigs and makeup, and we sang one performance after another in elementary school lunchrooms, with Amelia accompanying us with her usual flair.

I remember driving back to Sierra Madre after one *Impresario* performance. I hadn't had time to change, so I still had on my white wig, my eighteenth-century gown, and all that stage makeup, complete with a beauty mark on my left cheek.

I pulled up at a stoplight at the turnoff for Paradise Hills. There was a road crew working, and a young man in a hardhat was waving the cars on. When I pulled up in my car, he started to wave his flag at me. Then he almost dropped the flag. He stared at me with an open mouth as I made the left turn to go up the hill to Sierra Madre Elementary School.

When I got to the school, it was lunchtime. Instead of eating lunch, I went straight into the teacher's restroom, and I did a lightning fast change into my school clothes. And then I went out and brought my kids in from lunch recess, and I started teaching them their math lesson for the day.

Later that year, some of Amelia's voice students performed Ned Rorem's opera *Three Sisters Who Are Not Sisters*. This was presented to our students at Sierra Madre, and Mr. Sanchez liked it so much that he wanted us to do more opera performances for the school. But we would never have that opportunity.

CHAPTER 57

My mother had always been a light sleeper. Now her energy level was down, and she was living her life in a state of flaccid dreaminess. Finally, Daddy took Mother to the doctor. Tests showed that she had an abnormally high production of blood platelets.

My parents called and told me about this, and I went up to Santa Fe to visit them. That afternoon, while Daddy was taking a nap, Mother said to me, "The doctors say that I will probably develop leukemia within the next three years." Her tone was steady and her eyes were clear. "When they told me that, I said that's all right. Seventy-three years is enough time for me."

"Mama! Mama!" Daddy was suffering pain from the muscle contractions in his arm.

"I'll just go and see about Daddy." Mother got up from the dining table and went into the bedroom.

I sat at the table, staring out the window, unable to process what Mother had just told me. Even if the leukemia happens, I said to myself, it probably won't be that soon. Maybe it will be quite a while. Maybe even a decade. But my life and my future seemed dim and floating, like a dream.

From then on I began playing time games. I was a gambler computing the odds. I knew my parents, who had been there like tall trees when I was five years old, had to be somehow immortal.

Or if not immortal, then maybe they would still be here for me, just a little longer. Just a little more.

✲ ✲ ✲

The last two years of my father's life were a nightmare. Daddy was completely bedridden. He lay in his bed, day after day. He couldn't sleep for more than an hour. Then he would wake up and start calling, "Mama. Mama."

And my mother would be at his side, taking care of him, day and night.

One day Daddy told me, "You know, you always were a good kid. Never gave us any problems. I hardly ever had to scold you, and when I did, your Mother sure got mad at me. But you were always a good kid," he said. "Never any problems."

I didn't know what to say. As my eyes began to fill with tears, I turned my head and left the bedroom. I knew Daddy was trying to say good-bye to me, but I couldn't bear to accept that. Not yet. Sometime in the future, weeks or months away, but never now.

But the slow stages of leaving were inexorable. Later that evening, Daddy told Mama, "I can see my mother at night when I start to go to sleep. I had forgotten how beautiful she was." Already the next world was becoming more real to my father than the world he was preparing to leave.

✲ ✲ ✲

In May of 1979, I went to Mr. Sanchez's office, and I told him that I was going to have to leave teaching. I knew that my teaching was suffering because of my father's illness and his impending death, and I knew that I could not handle that slow, agonizing departure and deal with a classroom full of kids.

Mr. Sanchez said to me, "If you ever need a job, you call me, and whatever school I'm at, if there's an opening available, the job is yours."

That evening, I went home and I cried.

CHAPTER 58

One Saturday in January of 1980, Arnold and I were visiting my parents. We were doing whatever we could to help Mother now that Daddy was completely immobilized. Right after breakfast, I heard Mother call to me from the bedroom. "Whitney, come in here."

Arnold and I walked into the bedroom, and Mother looked up at me from where she was standing. She was holding Daddy's hand, and she said, "I think your father is dying."

As she bent over, I looked into my father's blue eyes, dim and distant. Even as Mother and Arnold and I watched, my dad's blue eyes faded into a pale emptiness, strange and blank.

For a moment, it seemed subtle to me, something that could hardly be seen. But then his whole face seemed to settle into a vacant stare. I gazed down at that face and at the thin and rigid body, and I saw only a shell.

The next thing I remember was sitting by my father's body while Mother went into the kitchen to call the doctor and our minister. My left hand was resting on Daddy's shoulder. I felt the skin and muscles slowly begin to cool.

As I sat there beside my father's body, I sensed the vast mysteries of God, the mysteries of eternity, the departure of that inner life that is the realm of the soul. Those mysteries that had gently brought closure to my father's earthly life were greater than my wishes, my dreams, or my desires. I could never have slowed the coming of my father's death, nor could I have speeded it up, even though I had wanted to do both, often at the same time.

The weeks and months leading up to my father's death had been agonizing. And I realized that the time after his death would be filled with grief. But that one moment had a quietness. There was a calmness to it. I think that's because angels were there, and their light and tranquility shone down over the passing of a good man. It was a moment when the veil between the human and the divine dissolved into luminance.

I sat there beside my father's body, suspended in time and space, seeing my world through a lens where all of time was at once distanced and yet telescoped into the closeness of an instant.

My father was a stubborn, hardworking man, a collection of cussedness and contradictions, of sensitivity and humor, of courage and perseverance. When I was only five years old, he had moved his family to Pecos and taken us into a whole new life in that post World War II world, a time that had long since vanished.

I remembered my father putting me back up on my horse after I'd fallen off. Always get back on your horse right away, he'd said to me then. And that was what I had always done. No matter what the world threw at me, I always got back up on my horse again, just like Daddy had told me.

Even in the face of mortal danger to all his life's work, his good reputation, and his manliness, my dad and my mother maintained a steady course, with a courage that was laced with Irish temper and tough Swedish stubbornness, as our family's battle against legalized corruption and injustice went on, year after year.

Sitting there beside my father's cooling body, I half smiled as I remembered a summer's day in 1972 when my dad and I got into his car to drive to Kaune's grocery store. As Daddy started up his antique Dodge station wagon, he said, "Be sure and put your feet on either side of the hole in the floor of the car."

I looked down, and I saw a hole big enough for me to easily put my foot through. As Daddy started up the old station wagon, I stared down at the hole in the car floor. "Daddy," I said, "Why don't you get yourself a new car. Or at least fix the hole in the floor."

“Aw, this old car’s okay, just the way it is,” he said. “It drives just fine. The engine runs as smooth as can be.”

And it did too. The station wagon’s engine hummed in perfect harmony with itself. “Just you keep your feet away from that hole in the floor,” said my dad. “You’ll be fine.”

He backed the car out of the drive, and we drove over washboard dirt roads and then headed on down the paved thoroughfare, the pavement a blur between my feet. Daddy looked over, and he saw me looking down at the hole in the floorboard. “You know,” he said to me, “This is a good old car. Nowadays they don’t make cars like they used to.” He took the turnoff toward Kaune’s, his callused hands wrapped stiffly around the steering wheel as he drove with the special care of the old. “You remember that black Dodge sedan we had when you were little?”

“I sure do,” I said. Who could forget the black Dodge, as faithful as an old horse, always uncomplaining, lugging all those power poles up the Pecos Canyon, ending its days sitting in the weedy plant yard, with Daddy intending to fix it up any day now, just as soon as he could locate the parts for it.

“That was a good car.” My dad shook his head, remembering. “Back in the 1930s, they made car bodies out of reinforced steel. Nowadays, they make those little foreign cars out of aluminum and plastic, and then they stick a sewing machine engine in the trunk. But that old Dodge was a good car. They don’t make ’em like that anymore.” We both were silent for a moment, out of respect for our old black Dodge sedan.

In the whole world, there was never anyone else like my father. Not in all of Creation. Just like Daddy’s old and holey fedora hat, just like Daddy’s antique diesel engines and generators in the old power plant, just like Daddy’s good old Dodge car, it was a case of “No sir, they don’t make ’em like that anymore.”

CHAPTER 59

Six months before Daddy's passing, Mother had told me she wanted a soprano to sing "Ye now are sorrowful" from Brahms's *German Requiem* for Daddy's memorial service. I had talked to Lindsay, the brilliant young soprano who studied with Amelia, and she had told me that she would sing. But when Mother asked me to call her, Lindsay said regretfully, "I'm sorry, but I'm not available on that day."

I hung up the phone, and I turned to my mother and said, "Mother, Lindsay can't sing for Daddy's service."

My mother's face fell. She looked at me with eyes so sad and disappointed, I couldn't bear to see her look that way. So I said, "It's okay, Mama. I'll sing the Brahms for you."

Mother looked up at me with hope and concern in her eyes. "Honey, are you sure you can do it?"

I looked at my mother sitting there on the couch, so small and tired. "I'll dig up my copy of the *Requiem*, and I'll start working on it right now."

For the next five days, I labored over the Brahms *Requiem*, sitting at Mother's Chippendale upright piano, going over words and music, singing *sotto voce* as I walked around my parents' living room with its soft green carpeting and its flagstone fireplace, and the front window that framed the view of the Santa Fe mountains.

Every morning I warmed up and practiced, working my voice. All day long I said the lyrics out loud. I thought the phrases through.

I studied the expressive markings. And every day when I practiced, I worked each vowel and each note into my singing voice.

I didn't dare to shed a single tear. I knew that if I started crying, I wouldn't be able to stop. That much crying would wreck my singing voice, so I didn't think or feel at all. I just kept on working the Brahms into the center of me.

✲ ✲ ✲

The day of Daddy's memorial service came, all clear and sunny. As my mother went into the church sanctuary to take her seat, I walked upstairs to the choir rehearsal room, and I put on mother's choir robe.

Just as I came down the stairs, our pastor, Jim Brown, called me into his office and said, "Look behind you."

I turned around and there stood my son Philip, in full naval uniform. I went to him, and I threw my arms around him. We held each other tightly, and I started to cry. But I had singing to do, so I quickly stopped the tears. I kissed my son and ushered him out the back door so he could go into the sanctuary where he would sit with Mother and Arnold.

I blotted my eyes, I took a deep breath, and I walked into the choir loft. And my father's memorial service began.

That day I sang for my father in the sanctuary of the First Presbyterian Church of Santa Fe. It was where the child Whitney sat in the balcony, right next to her father. Where the teenage Whitney sang in the church choir. Where a young Whitney had fallen in love with a handsome high school senior named Richard DeLaney with all the delirious madness and speechless shyness of that first unattainable adolescent crush. The same sanctuary where the eighteen year old Whitney was married to a man she could never truly learn to love. The sanctuary where her two sons had been baptized.

On that clear January day in 1980, Susie Loriaux, our church organist for over twenty-five years and my mother's friend, played the opening measures of the Brahms solo on the pipe organ that my parents had given donations to help the church buy. And on that January day, I sang for my mother and for my father, "Ye now are sorrowful."

Every word that I sang sounded infinitely soft and far away. "Howbeit, ye shall again behold me, and your heart shall be joyful. And your joy no man taketh from you."

I felt the security of my breath sustaining each musical phrase. "Look upon me. Ye know that for a little while, labor and sorrow were mine. But at the end, I have found comfort."

And the final phrases were shaped in my mind and on my breath, as words and notes floated out into the church sanctuary. "Ye shall again behold me… Shall behold me…"

✲ ✲ ✲

The day after Daddy's memorial service, Philip and Arnold and I drove to Albuquerque, to their father's house on Moonflower Circle. Philip and Arnold got out of the car and unloaded their suitcases.

I drove on home, got out of the car, and went inside my large mobile home, and I looked all around me. My sons were gone. Both of them were grown up and moved out. They were on their own. Now nobody but me lived in this mobile home.

I tamped down emptiness and looked at a couple of dishes still standing in the sink. I had forgotten about them when I went up to Santa Fe to stay with Mother for those last few weeks.

I walked down the hallway and looked through the bedroom doors. Philip's bedroom was clean and bare. It had always been a mess for the ages when he'd been living at home. One day when he was still in high school, I'd gone into Phil's bedroom to clean, and when I lifted up the mattress to change the sheets I found a desiccated hamburger, complete with ketchup, squeezed between two flattened and mummified pieces of bread. It looked like it had been there for months if not years. I walked back into the bedroom where Arnold Paul had slept. The bed had a quilt on it, along with an old pillow, but no blankets or sheets.

All the rooms in this mobile home are empty, I thought, coming back into the kitchen. I sat down at the table and leaned forward and I put my face in my hands.

I had left my job of teaching in June of 1979, just six months ago. Now I wondered if I had been insane to do that. Mother certainly thought I was. Her anger over my leaving teaching still simmered. But I hadn't been able to teach and to deal with my father's dying. One or the other, but not both. During Daddy's last year, my emotional outbursts had threatened to take over my life, even in the classroom.

And now I was directionless. All my adult life, I had always done for others. When I was married, I had tried to become a good wife, according to the 1950s *Ladies Home Journal* visions of what a good wife was. Although, I thought wryly, my version of *Journal*-wifery with its endless, isolated housework had been less than sterling.

After the divorce, I had become a mother with an endlessly messy kitchen and two kids who were my bane and my joy. And every year I had taught twenty-five kids reading, writing, math, and everything else that they needed to learn.

I would never again lead students into my third grade classroom. No more reading groups. No more supervising kids on the playground. No sons at home. And no father in Santa Fe to call and talk with. Never again.

Where could I go from here? What point was there to my life with the anchors of kids and career and Daddy all gone, leaving large dark vacant spaces. The kitchen darkened as the sun lowered over the West Mesa. I got up from the table, and I went into Arnold's bedroom and lay down on his bed. And there I curled myself up into a fetal position as the pain of Daddy's being gone finally hit me.

✡ ✡ ✡

The dictionary defines the word "chthonic" as being "of the gods of the underworld, the world of the dead, the netherworld." Chthonic brings up the call of the darkness, those deep curtained areas of our minds where all our fears and all our most profound dreams lie hidden.

Those curtains are pulled back when we deal with death in any of its forms. Whether the deceased is young or old and fully ready to leave this world, whether the dying itself is a falling asleep, or whether it is an end to excruciating agony, the impact on the mind of the observer, upon the very center of the mourner, goes beyond words and reason.

The phenomenon of death taps into centers that are like the tangle of cables that were nested behind the control panels in my father's power plant. Those thick, black-covered cables were charged with thousands of volts of electricity. Had I ever disobeyed my father's strict instructions and walked behind that board and touched one those cables, it would only have taken one tiny frayed area of insulation to send an enormous charge of electricity through my body. My father told me if that happened, no one could save me from death by electrocution.

At five-and-a-half years old, I had absorbed those momentous words with focused attention. Even at that age, I could tell when my father was giving me a profound and important truth. He was speaking with the voice of God Almighty. And I never even thought of doing anything other than obeying him.

Looking directly at my father's dying had exposed me to a current of energy with enough of a charge to leap sizzling through the air. His death changed not only my mind but my body. My brain waves had been permanently changed, and my body chemistry and my life had been forever altered.

Now I saw my inner soul as a stranger that had silently taken up abode. There was a force stronger than I, bending me in agonizing rhythmic patterns of grief that went beyond emotion, beyond time, beyond everything in my life. I had become indescribable to myself. I no longer knew who I was.

Never again would I fit comfortably into the memories and the patterns of thought, habit, and feeling that had cocooned me since childhood. Now I was forty-one years of age and, for the first time in my life, I had no father.

My dad had been the center of our family's planetary system. He was the Saturnian Capricorn around whom our lives and our identities had revolved. "El hombre de la luz," the people of Pecos had called him. The man of the light. My father was all of that and more. He was an irresistible gravitational force, with family and linemen and workers all circling in orbit around him.

Now my father was gone. My sons were launched out into the world on their own life journeys. My mother was a widow. And I was a single ex-schoolteacher. I kept thinking that this would be a good time for me to die.

God, however, refused to oblige my request. I wondered why. Surely I was useless now. I kept pulling my knees up against my chest as I lay in that bed, curling my body as tightly as I could around those empty pain-spaces. I couldn't find a tear to shed. Dark days melted into darker nights as I lay there in unsleeping silence all night, trying every morning to find the strength to stand up and go into the bathroom and take a shower.

Then one night I felt myself float up out of my body, rising up into a bubble of space and time. I was hovering over a pool of water that was absolutely pure, absolutely clear, and perfectly circular in shape. The bottom of the pool was shaped like a funnel, sloping down into a darkened center that seemed to go on down forever. As I watched, springs of colored waters began to flow up from that deep, dark, liquid center, rising up to the top of the clear water and then flowing out in concentric circles of colors, blue and gold and red and purple, like the iridescent colors that gleam on the surface of an oil-filmed puddle.

Carl Jung would say this is a mandala, I thought dreamily as I hovered, an observing eye, looking down at the pool with its encircling, flowing, flower-like colors. I watched those colors until peace flowed into me. And finally, I slept.

CHAPTER 60

Eleven months later, in December of 1980, Mother called me and said, "Please come stay with me. The doctors have diagnosed me with acute lymphoblastic leukemia." She paused and then she said, "They tell me I have six weeks to three months to live."

I couldn't speak. My chest felt like it was clamped in a vise. Tears started running down my face and dripping off my chin. I took a couple of breaths, and then I managed to strangle out the words, "Don't go anywhere." I took another deep breath and I said, "Please don't go anywhere."

What I was really saying was, "Please, don't die."

For a moment Mother and I were silent. How could this happen so soon after Daddy's death? He had passed away last January, and this was only December. How could lightning strike twice so quickly?

"Could you come up to Santa Fe and take care of me?" Mother asked. "I'm in the hospital, and I'm not hurting any, but the doctors are going to check me tomorrow to see if I have any tumors. That's the one thing I'm really scared of."

I bent over double, my right hand clamped around the edge of the breakfast bar as new pain washed through me. She's already in the hospital, I thought. She's calling me from the hospital. I knew I was going to have to move to Santa Fe and live with Mother. I was going to have to pack dog and clothes, along with as much stuff as I could get into my small hatchback. And I would have to take off for Santa Fe, leaving my mobile home abandoned on its dirt lot. This was finality. Everything that I had, everything I'd ever worked for lay splintered in small shards.

I flashed back over the past four months, seeing new patterns in what I had thought were random incidents and behaviors. The previous June I had felt compelled to collect every cardboard box I could find, for no reason that I could see, and bring them home from the Dumpster behind Safeway. When I got the boxes home I began packing all my clothes.

It was the strangest feeling to be compelled to do something that made absolutely no sense at all. I kept crying out to my guides, "Why am I doing this? What's going on?" And underneath it all, the unspoken question, "Am I going completely crazy?"

By early November my refrigerator had broken down. I kept trying to go to a store where I could buy a new one, but I couldn't do it. I couldn't even pick up a *PennySaver* to look for a second-hand fridge. And I could not get close enough to that refrigerator to clean it out, even though I kept getting whiffs of things that smelled pretty high. I couldn't even go grocery shopping. I could only buy food for one day at a time, no more.

And I kept compulsively taking stacks of books and recordings to the library. I took all my kids' clothes out of their closets, along with a lot of my own clothing, and gave them all to the Salvation Army.

"My kids are both gone. They've left home forever," I thought. "They'll never miss their old clothes."

So now the inside of my mobile home looked like a cross between a storage garage and an explosion in a box factory. And it smelled of rancid, rotting food.

I told Mother I loved her, and I would be up there the very moment I could be.

"I'll be in the hospital for at least a week," Mother said. "Oh, and the doctor wants you to call him right away."

"I'll do that tomorrow," I promised and I hung up the phone.

I looked around and I thought, "My God, I'm all packed and ready to move. Except for that darned refrigerator, everything's ready to go."

The next morning I called Mother's doctor. He said, "We need you to make an appointment with the blood bank in Albuquerque. They'll draw some blood to make sure your blood type is compatible with your mother's. Just in case she might need a transfusion." So I went in and had a big needle stuck in my arm.

The following Friday, I drove the sixty miles to Santa Fe with Polly, Philip's elderly black mutt-dog, panting in the back of the Honda, lying on top of the bags and boxes that held all my few remaining possessions.

I don't remember going into my parents' home and starting to unpack. Nor do I remember anything about bringing Mother home from the hospital. But I know I must have done that. And I know I called a friend and offered to pay him to go in and clean out the mobile home and move all my furniture up to Santa Fe and, above all, throw out that wreck of a refrigerator. And I started taking care of Mother full time. For the next three years I kept on praying that the two of us would be able to live on her modest income.

✲ ✲ ✲

One afternoon there was a local news show on Mother's small television set that sat on her dresser. The anchorman was talking about the fact that everyone needs to have at least six hugs a day. Otherwise, they would get a condition known as skin hunger. I told Mother, "We can't have you getting skin hunger. So from now on, I am going to be sure and give you six hugs a day." And I hugged her right then.

From that time on, whenever I forgot a hug, Mother would remind me with her mouth turned up in a prim little smile and her eyes twinkling, "I haven't had my fifth hug yet."

And right away, I'd give her another hug.

CHAPTER 61

In November of 1982, Mother's oncologist, Dr. Stephenson said to me, "We're going to take your mother off the treatment. I don't believe in having any patient of mine living her life being a zombie in remission."

"I don't want my mother to die," I said. "I don't know if I could live with that kind of decision."

Dr. Stephenson answered me, "This is not your decision. It is my medical judgment that your mother should not continue to live as she is. There is zero quality of life for her, and she is never going to get any better." Then the doctor added the dread words I had heard so often over the past two years. "Once she's off the chemo, your mother will have six weeks to three months to live."

That evening as Mother lay in her bed, in a somnolent sleep, I went into my room, and I sat down at a small table that faced a white wall. I opened my Bible, and I lit four white candles. And I bowed my head and sent out a wordless silent cry for help.

A movie screen began to take shape on the white wall in front of me. I sat there, transfixed, watching the brilliant colors on that screen flowing and coalescing as they took shape.

And then, without knowing how it happened, I found myself standing on a vessel that was being rowed by Egyptian oarsmen. Just ahead of us was an immense galley, its sides adorned with woven garlands of flowers. A pair of thick, heavy hawsers connected our smaller vessel to that great river galley.

The steersman on the galley was calling out a chant for the rowers, as enormous drums sounded their deep-throated cadences. Long oars on both vessels lifted and fell, perfectly synchronized with the chanting and the beat of the drums, all of the oars rising up and then dipping down into the dark waters of the Nile.

Amidships on that great galley was a sarcophagus on a flower decked dais. Within that sarcophagus was the linen wrapped body of my uncle, the man who had raised me from the time my parents had died in a plague that had swept through Egypt. My uncle had given me the only home I could recall, and he had been my only surviving family member.

I looked around at the small crowd of people, all standing quietly on the smaller craft. They were friends, subordinates, and members of my uncle's household, all here to honor a good man on his final earthly journey. Looking up at the larger galley, I saw the dark outlines of soldiers who had been under my uncle's command. There were four rows of kilted men, two rows on either side of my uncle's sarcophagus, all of them standing erect, all facing that flower decked sarcophagus. As the rowers picked up speed, the flares on the torches that ringed the decks of the two boats were blown back in streamers by the breezes of the river as the two vessels moved through the night waters of the slow and powerful Nile River.

Standing in one small area of our smaller vessel were five or six women. They gazed into bronze mirrors as they daubed their faces with red paint to represent tears and blood. Occasionally, one of them would let out a cry that a few of the other women would pick up. For a moment or two, they would sob and moan. Then they would fall silent as we moved through the quiet darkness and the torchlit waters of the night.

On and on the two great vessels traveled, moving through the water with sounds that would ever bring back the memory of that endless journey. The dip-splash of oars, the muffled booming of great drums, the sharp intermittent cries of the mourners. And the soft smell of flowers blending with the smoke given off by the rich incense that glowed in holders.

As the night grew deeper, the professional mourners began crying out more and more, walking up and down, giving their shocking cries, staring straight into each person's eyes, stripping away all defenses. I flinched as one of them passed by, trying to keep myself from being pushed to the front of the gathered mourners, hoping to remain unseen.

Reed flutes began to wail, and singers on the galley ahead of our vessel began singing the songs that told of my uncle's life. They sang of his heroism, which was real, and of his great physical stature, which was pure fiction, for my uncle had been a short man with a bald head and a little round potbelly.

The musicians played and sang not only for the assembled mourners but for the listening gods as well, those spirits who walked the land of Ancient Egypt, those great beings that all knew were hovering in the air above the dark waters of the Nile, listening to the singing of Uncle's achievements, his honors, and his many conquests in battle. For he had been a warrior from early adolescence.

The boats moved on as the brilliant stars spun endlessly above the Nile. The music became faster, the drums more insistent. The shrieks and wails of the mourners shredded the young man's nerves, threatening to break down the walls of his silent composure. And I was that young man.

A priest walked through the mourners, who gave way as he passed. He came closer and closer to me, and I began to shake my head as my lips formed a silent "No."

The priest stopped before me, and he raised his hands, which held a brilliantly colored sash. He placed the sash around my neck and then turned away from me and walked toward the bow of the boat. I tried to dig in my feet, to stand firm, but my legs had turned into the waters of the Nile.

One man to my right and another to my left took me gently by the arms, and they walked with me as my legs and feet moved beneath me, slow and unwilling. I kept on shaking my head, moving my lips, trying to form words, but I could not utter a sound.

The priest and my two escorts brought me to one of the two huge posts that held the hawsers connecting our boat with the great sarcophagus-bearing galley just ahead. The young priest turned to me. With compassion in his eyes, he said loudly, so that all could hear, "You must cast off the lines."

Immediately the mourners and the assembled company let out a great cry. I fell to the deck, crying out, "I cannot."

The priest stood before me, compassionate and firm. "You must."

Finally, as the mourners wailed even louder, I gathered myself and came to my knees. I tried to lift one heavy line off its huge post, but it was impossible to move. I stood up and I bent my knees. Grabbing the hawser with both hands, I pulled up with all my strength. The heavy line came up a little ways. Sweat broke out on my body as I took a deep breath, then pulled up again, and yet again, until my back popped and my muscles strained and protested.

Then, without any warning, the hawser slipped off its post and splashed into the waters below. The mourners wailed and sobbed, now tearing at their hair and clawing their faces. All the men and women on the boat were now tearing at the draperies of linen that they wore over their finest clothes.

Everyone poured out flasks of scented oil that ran down over their huge wigs and soaked into the linen draperies. Then they reached into large clay jars to take out handfuls of dust that they scattered over their wigs, faces, and shoulders, until they all looked like faded mummies.

The priest's helpers led me to the port side of the boat. I stood before the second hawser, my head shaking back and forth as the sounds of grief and anger and shock and pain that I had been holding inside myself began coming out as short, barking groans.

I clamped my teeth against my lower lip until the blood began to run, yet still those traitorous sounds came out of me, beginning to separate me from the spirit of him who could not be gone, who could not have left my life.

The second hawser was stiff and cold from the soaking it had been taking from the splashing of Nile waters against the front of the boat. Again and again I pulled at that heavy rope, yet it refused to budge.

Finally, I squatted down while the priest called out to the gods. I took a deep breath and groaned aloud with the strain as the hawser began to slide up the post. The strength within me must have come from the gods, for I know I was not capable of moving that hawser, yet move it did, slowly and reluctantly releasing that last earthly tie to one I had loved for all of my young life.

I gasped in pain as the rope came free of its mooring, knocking against the deck as it slid away and over the side of the vessel, splashing down into the river currents. I fell to my hands and knees, scrambling, trying to grab that hawser, to return it to its post, but to no avail.

As the mourners on both vessels began a cacophonous screaming, all of them ululating their high and mournful cries, as flutes wailed their eerie tones, I collapsed on the deck. All my defenses shattered, I began screaming and crying, calling out to my uncle to come back to me as the galley ahead began to pull away.

The oarsmen in the great galley picked up the tempo of their rowing, and we followed, moving faster and faster as the darkness of the night began to recede. At last, galley and boat both entered an immense semi-enclosed lake.

Silence fell as the galley swung to face the east, where the black curtain of the sky was lightening. Our smaller vessel pulled up, well astern of the huge galley. And we waited.

The sun came up with the swiftness of a desert dawn, its golden light reflecting off the lake waters as a brilliant streamer of light. Once more the deep drums began to beat as the rowers on the galley began rowing straight into that light reflection. Tears streamed from my eyes, and I blinked, trying to keep the galley in my sight. But as the sun's brilliance became more and more intense, the galley bearing my uncle's sarcophagus disappeared completely into that Light, and it was gone.

The drums abruptly stopped. All the mourners on our small vessel stood, frozen and still.

And just as unexpectedly as it had begun, my vision faded. I was alone in the small Santa Fe bedroom with its spare furnishings and white walls, wondering at what I had just seen and what it all meant.

I knew the soul who had been my uncle in that lifetime was now my mother. I knew I had been a young priest back then, no more than nineteen, and that I had stayed a priest all my life. I knew that once I had recovered from my uncle's death, I had spent my life ministering as a counselor to those in mourning for their loved ones.

And that was all I remembered as I came back to full present-day consciousness. I never found out if that young priest married, or if he had any children. I never even got his name. I only know that he gave his uncle love and honor at those final ceremonies that marked the end of a hard life of service to Egypt.

And now I was doing the same service for my seventy-three year old mother who lay in her bedroom, sunk in an unbroken sleep. Once again, the responsibility for overseeing that solemn period when life would leave the body and move on into the realms of light was mine.

For a long and silent time, I sat before the small table with its white cloth and its Bible and its candles, not thinking, not feeling. And I found myself accepting the responsibility for the task ahead of me.

The first thing I asked myself as I arose from that altar was, "Was this vision for real?"

The answer that came was my sense of kinesthetic feeling. I had been in the middle of a group of three-dimensional human beings, warm and breathing and living. I had felt the sensations of being in that young man's body, his frame, his musculature, his fitness, and his firm stride. I had felt myself inside that male body that shivered in the chilled river air. I had felt the weight of myself and sensed the weight of things and people around me.

Within that three-dimensional Egyptian world, an unfolding of events had taken place without any psychic push or mental direction from me. Things were as they were in my vision, they unfolded in an orderly way, and they came to a clear and unambiguous ending.

CHAPTER 62

The long days and lonely nights passed. I sat alone at the table at every meal, dreading the future. Then one day I decided, just on impulse, that I would try setting a second place at the dining table. That second place setting would be for the Lord Christ.

I got down plates and cups from Mother's best china shelf, and I got out some good silverware, and I set my place at the table. Then I laid out another plate right across from mine. Shaking my head and smiling, I put servings of chicken and potatoes and peas on the two plates, one for the Christ and one for me.

Sitting at the table I thought to myself, I sure am glad nobody's watching me do this.

When I finished eating, I put my plate and silverware in the dishwasher. I put the leftovers from the second plate in the refrigerator. Waste not, want not, as my grandmother always said. And then I spent the afternoon doing small chores with a smile on my face.

I kept on setting two places at the table for the next several weeks. Fortunately, no human visitors showed up at mealtimes. And Mother was too ill to come out of her bedroom, so I gradually lost my feelings of embarrassed self-consciousness.

✲ ✲ ✲

In June of that year, my older son Arnold completed his coursework for his bachelor's degree in mechanical engineering. Well, almost.

One hot day I drove down to Albuquerque to pick Arnold up, along with all his stuff. After getting everything packed in the back of the hatchback, we went by the classroom building where he'd been taking a course in writing. Arnold went in to take a look at his final grades that the professor had posted on the classroom door.

I waited in the car until Arnold came back. When he opened the car door and sat down, he was in shock.

I looked at him in surprise and said, "What's wrong?"

Arnold said, "I got a D-minus in writing. This means I'm not going to graduate this semester."

The two of us just sat there for a few moments. This meant that my son's plans for going out to California and finding a job were on indefinite hold. Finally I started the car, and we headed toward the freeway.

After a long silence, I said, "You know, Arnold, this may be a blessing in deep disguise. Why don't you stay with Mother and me for the summer. You can help me take care of Mother. And you can take your writing course over again in summer school. You can drive Mother's car to Albuquerque and back, and I'll give you some tutoring, so you can get your grade up to at least a 'C'. That way you'll have your degree by the end of August."

And that's what we did. It was only much later that I realized that my silent prayers for not being left alone with Mother in her final days had been answered.

CHAPTER 63

Three months before Mother's passing, she looked up from her bed and she said to me, "I see your father every morning at dawn, just as I start to wake up. He's wearing his brown double-breasted suit with the vest, the one he used to wear when he was teaching at the University of Denver.

"I look up at him, and I say to him, 'Daddy, what are you doing here?' And he smiles down at me and he puts his finger to his lips and he says to me, 'Shhh! Don't tell.'"

Mother's eyes were anxious as she looked up at me. "Does this mean I'm crazy?"

I looked down at the frail woman lying in her bed. "No, Mother. You're not crazy."

Mother gazed off into a far distance as she spoke in a soft voice. "Some mornings I see my mother standing at the foot of my bed, looking down at me. And there's this beautiful woman with her. She's tiny and she looks so energetic. She's dressed in a cotton dress with an ankle-–length skirt, and she has on a poke bonnet, like the kind farmwives wore back in the nineteenth century."

Mother looked up at me. "I wonder if that woman is my Grandmother Hosie. She died when my mother was only thirteen, and that was a long time before I was born."

✡ ✡ ✡

What grace my Mother had. She was not afraid to die. Not until the very end, until that morning when she could no longer speak, no longer move her lips or swallow, did I see fear in her eyes. Yet even then my mother's fear was not a deep-rooted fear of death. It was the fear of the singer waiting in the wings. It was the fright of the young girl standing on a diving board, looking at the deep water and thinking to herself, Can I do it? Can I make this leap?

On that November day as I looked down at my mother in the soft rose light of her last earthly dawn, I had to say to her, "Mama, you know this can't last much longer. So whenever you like, you go on up and stay with Daddy. You'll be safe with Daddy."

I was astounded when Mother opened her eyes long enough to whisper the word, "Safe?"

"That's right, Mama. You'll be safe with Daddy."

After completing Mother's morning routine, I left her bedroom, and went to go shower and dress. And when I came back, Mother was gone. I stood, looking down for a minute. Then I went to her dresser and picked up a Bible, bound in white, and I placed it in her hands.

I stood there at the foot of her bed, once more looking down at that stilled and pallid face. I took a shaky breath, and I began to sing The Lord's Prayer. On that clear November morning, my mother had taken leave of her earthly life. I sang to lift her musical soul up into the Light with song and with prayer.

I went out of Mother's bedroom and walked across to Arnold's room. He was just up, studying one of his books. "Arnold," I said, "Mama has just passed away. Do you want to come and see her?"

Arnold's eyes widened. He stood up from the work table, looking stricken, and he gave one quick, silent nod.

We walked into Mother's bedroom, and we stood silently at the foot of her bed, and then we went out of the room.

And immediately the world intervened. There were people to be notified. Doctors to pronounce Mother. The people from the mortuary.

It all happened so quickly. In little more than an hour and a half, the sheet-draped body was carried out to a black van. The big black rear hatch was closed, and the van drove silently out of the driveway and headed off down the dirt road.

Arnold and I went back into the house, into emptiness and vacancy of spirit.

A few months later, Arnold moved out to Los Angeles where he began a career as a technical writer for a company that designed and manufactured parts for airplanes.

CHAPTER 64

In December of 1984, my guides began urging me to travel. "You need to go to Hawaii. This will be a hard winter, and there will be a flu epidemic. If you stay here in Santa Fe, you will become very ill, and it will take you a long time to recover."

So I called my son Philip. "I'm planning on going to Hawaii right after Christmas," I said. "I'd like to spend a couple of days in San Diego with you before I go."

"Sure. Mom. We'll find a place to put you. It may be an air mattress on the living room floor, but it'll be here for you."

Then I called and made a plane reservation. Then I went in my bedroom and opened the closet door and started looking through my wardrobe to see what to pack.

✲ ✲ ✲

When I got to Philip's home in San Diego, I saw the unhappiness in my son's eyes. I knew his marriage was not a good one. But all I could do was to give him a silent hug.

One morning I was reading the *San Diego Union-Tribune* over breakfast, and I saw an announcement that thrilled me. "Oh, this is wonderful," I said. "Joan Sutherland is singing with the San Diego Opera." I looked over at my two sons. "I would like so much to hear Joan Sutherland sing in person, just once in my life." So

Arnold and Philip and I got our tickets, and the three of us went to hear the singer who had been my inspiration during my student years at the University of New Mexico.

Even in that final period of her career, Joan Sutherland had a splendid vocal instrument. I was astounded at the difference between listening to her recordings and hearing her voice live. There was a richness of tone that hung in the air of that auditorium that did not come through on the recordings.

I left the theater transported, in a state of bliss from listening to the shimmer, the glow, and the high notes striking sparks. What would it have been like, I wondered, to hear Sutherland sing that first Lucia, way back in 1959. Or to hear her young voice singing Handel's *Let the Bright Seraphim.* Even now, I can hear Joan Sutherland's live voice in my mind, singing Verdi's arias.

The very next day, I got on a huge, nearly empty airliner and I flew to Hawaii.

CHAPTER 65

It was a slow year for tourism in Hawaii. On Oahu all the streets were deserted, the shops were empty, and Waikiki Beach was sparsely populated with only a few determined bikini clad sunbathers stretched out on the sand. I began doing some half hearted sightseeing, walking along deserted boulevards with empty shops and wandering through Punchbowl Cemetery without meeting a single soul.

One morning I got up early and I took a taxi to Pearl Harbor. I wanted to beat the crowds, which I was certain would be there, even during a slow season. But not one person besides me showed up. After waiting for almost half an hour, the two sailors manning the launch said, "We'll take you out to the memorial."

So I got on board, and I took my seat. The only sound was the puttering of the motor, and even that began to fade into dimness as the small boat moved over the still waters of Pearl Harbor. I looked up at the immense flag, Old Glory, floating in the gentle breeze, flying at half mast over the silent elegance of the structure that glowed white in the sunlight, and I began to feel the weight of old grief hanging in the air all around me.

When we got to the memorial, one of the sailors carefully handed me out of the launch. I remember standing alone in the entrance, then walking inside and looking around at walls lined with brass placards listing the names of men who had died on that December day when I was only three days away from my third birthday.

I was startled when the motor of the navy launch started up and the boat pulled out and left me standing there all alone inside the memorial. The sound of the launch faded, and I found myself enveloped in silence. Even my breathing and my heartbeat seemed to make too much noise.

Moving as quietly as I could, I went over to the elongated portholes. I looked up at the soft blue sky and then down at the water. After a moment I began to see the outline of one of the Arizona's smokestacks and the slow bubbling of oil rising up out of her fuel tanks, forming iridescent rainbow patterns on the surface of the water.

I walked over to the brass plaques that lined the walls, where I read one name after another. I remembered what Mother had said to me about seeing the memorial. "Those names were a blow to my heart. I remembered Pearl Harbor so well. And it all came back to me."

Here and now, time was being measured out in milliseconds. The hush was overpowering as I stood there, gazing at the simplicity of portholes and brass plaques.

Here, in this place, ships had been blown up, sunk, destroyed. So many young men killed. So many trapped in the darkness under the burning waters, wondering what had happened as their air began to run out. Here America had literally been forced into the greatest war in history and then propelled into world leadership.

At last I heard the navy launch coming to get me. I walked to the entrance, and I turned around for one last look. For a few precious moments, it had been my privilege to stand all alone in this hallowed place. And as the launch pulled up, I took one final look around, knowing that I would never again see the Pearl Harbor Memorial in just this way, in solitude and in stillness.

CHAPTER 66

The next day I flew to the Big Island of Hawaii. I got off the airplane, and the first thing I noticed was the scent of flowers that hung in the air. As I sat in the taxi that took me to my hotel, I saw flowers of every description.

That evening I walked from the hotel down to the local shops where I got myself some flip flops and a real, honest-to-goodness shocking pink muumuu. I bought one of those flower tiaras that Hawaiians love to wear, and the shop owner placed a lei around my neck.

Happiness was complete when I found a bookstore with books on Hawaiian traditions and history. I carried two heavy bags of books back to my hotel room, where I sat on my bed, wrapped in my flowery pink muumuu, a lei of tiny purple and white orchids around my neck, my head crowned with flowers. And Max Freedom Long's books on kahunas were strewn all around me.

I read about kahuna traditions and healers as I watched a two-day-long festival of hula dancers on television. I felt like I was being drenched in Hawaiian culture, saturated in new ideas, marinated in colorful hula costumes and dances.

✲ ✲ ✲

A few days later, I rented a car and drove up to the top of Kilauea. And there was absolutely no one there. Even the tourist center was closed, with not a soul in sight.

I parked my car in the deserted parking lot, and I began walking on some of the paths around the volcano, until I lost my way. I saw ohia berries, gleaming red against barren earth, and I visualized myself picking a few of those berries. I saw myself in my mind's eye, scattering the redness of the berries on the gray lava of the frozen caldera that lay before me.

A feeling of absolute serenity came over me. All around me was a clear and pure and invisible shield of protection. It was as though I could do no wrong, as though only good would come to me as long as I was in Hawaii.

Then, without knowing how I got there, I found myself wandering through a field of black lava tubes that towered up as high as houses. I walked up to one long tube, and I stepped inside that cylindrical tunnel that had once been formed by the flow of Pele's lava. Not even a bird's song sounded as I walked toward the light at the other end of the long lava-formed tunnel.

I came out of that great cylinder, and I stopped for a moment and looked out over the still vista of the power of the sacred fires of the earth. This was Pele's home, and her majesty was everywhere around me.

When I finally got back to the deserted parking lot, I looked down over that silent scene. Everywhere I had gone in Hawaii, there had been a stillness, like a blessing. What was it that was happening to me in this place?

☆ ☆ ☆

A few days later I was at a beach, sitting with books and yellow writing tablets all around me. Philip had called me the day before, and he'd said to me, "Mom, my marriage is over."

All I could say was, "Oh, honey, I'm so sorry."

Now I was writing to my guides, asking about Philip, asking what would happen to my son.

The guides wrote back to me, "Philip will have three women in his life. This first wife has been a heavy trial to him. There will be a second woman who will come into his life, and she will test him still further. Both relationships were foreseen up here before this soul you know as your son went down into the earth. And both were observed to be temporary.

"The third woman Philip will meet will be his true soul mate. You will recognize her when you see her. The two of them will overcome much, and they will create a good life together."

And at that moment I saw the image of a woman with long, curly brown hair that cascaded down her back. I could not see a face, but I saw that long beautiful hair.

✲ ✲ ✲

I stayed until April on the Big Island, sightseeing, and quietly reading and writing. I read about Hawaii's long history, and I read about the fascinating monarchs of Hawaii, including Queen Liliuokalani. There was a woman whose life could be turned into an opera, I thought.

I read about Pele, the goddess of fire, the goddess of the great volcanoes that had created Hawaii. I read about Pele's power, her ability to assume different shapes and identities, Pele as a sexy young woman in a hot red dress, contrasting with the blessings that the goddess gave to those who helped her when she wore the guise of a helpless old woman.

The quiet days passed. I drove all around the Big Island, seeing the coffee plantations, churches and chapels, ancient altars, beaches with black sand.

✲ ✲ ✲

On my final evening in Hawaii, I went to a great beachside hotel to have my last dinner on the Big Island. Before I went into the restaurant, I sat quietly on a large lava flow, watching a mother mongoose and her pups, a flock of tiny Riki-Tikki-Tavi's, all chittering and scampering over the lava, all engaged in curiosity and play. There was no one else but me, sitting there, watching the beauty of the young ones.

I realized that the whole of Hawaii had become one great temple for me. A place of welcome, of serenity, of the closeness of all the spirits that governed the ocean, the winds, the volcanoes, and the islands.

The sun began to set, and the air became cool. I went into the restaurant, and I ate an excellent seafood dinner, while I listened to musicians sing and play Hawaiian music, the most beautiful popular music ever invented. I chatted with the waitress, a middle-aged woman with dark Hawaiian skin and a stern look on her face. I told her I would be leaving Hawaii the next day. "I'll miss Hawaii," I said. "This is one place where I would like to stay forever."

Immediately the sternness vanished from the waitress's face to be replaced by a warm smile. "You wait right here," she told me firmly. "Don't you leave till I come back."

I laughed a little. "All right. I'll just listen to the music."

"Good," she said as she bustled off.

A few moments later, the waitress was back with a beautiful lei, all multicolored, fragrant blossoms. "Here," she said to me as she put the lei over my head and settled its fragrant flowers around me. "Now you will come back to Hawaii."

And she gently gave me a hug and kissed me on both cheeks as she said, "Aloha."

There were tears in my eyes as I said to the waitress, "Aloha. I will come back to Hawaii."

The tiny waitress with the face of a Hawaiian noblewoman gave me another sweet smile and nod. Then her face became stern once more as she hurried off to take care of her many tables.

I had been given a departing blessing from Pele herself, or from one of her many ambassadors.

CHAPTER 67

After I flew back to the mainland, I stayed with Arnold at his apartment in Los Angeles. One morning, after Arnold had left for work, I went into the kitchen to make myself a cup of tea. I filled an old pan with tap water and put it on the small stove next to the kitchen sink, and then I turned the gas flame up on high.

As I waited for the water to come to a boil, I washed out a chipped white cup that had its handle broken off. I put a chamomile teabag in the cup, and I placed the cup in the sink. As the water came to a full rolling boil, I lifted the pan off the burner. And with my right hand holding the cup, I began pouring the bubbling boiling water into the white cup.

Suddenly, the pan broke loose from the handle with a snap. The pan flipped over, and boiling water splashed all over the white cup and all over my right hand. I could feel the soft sensation of live bubbles of steam on the back of my hand.

I went into shock. But my left hand put the pan back down on the burner, and then turned on the cold water from the faucet. I stuck my hand under the faucet, letting the cold water keep me from feeling the burning sensation that was already beginning to run all through my hand.

"What do I do now?" I thought.

My left hand, of its own volition, reached up to the cabinet over the sink. Opening the door, I stretched up on my toes, and I grabbed a large gray plastic pitcher down from the highest shelf.

I put the big pitcher under my right hand so that the tap water began filling the pitcher, and then I plunged my right hand down into that cool tap water.

I picked up the pitcher of cold water, with my right hand thrust down into the water, and I carried the pitcher out to a chair in the small living room. I sat down on the shabby armchair, and again I thought, "What now?"

I began doing the kahuna breathing that I had read about in Max Freedom Long's books, the books that I had bought on the Big Island. I began to breathe slowly and carefully, taking a breath in to the count of four, holding my breath for the count of four, letting my breath out to a count of four, and holding my breath for another count of four.

I repeated this "four-square" breath over and over again. I felt my head becoming light and woozy, and still I kept on breathing that breath.

As I sat there breathing, I saw Light building. First a shell of Light, then a large balloon of Light that kept on expanding all around me, filling up the room. Finally I beheld an enormous Pacific Ocean of Light that filled up everything, everywhere.

I let my breath out in a big sigh, and I sent all that Light straight up, a huge fountain of Light that contacted the brilliant Star of Light that I could see right over my head. I gave thanks to the Star of Light, and I chanted out loud, over and over again, "Thank You that my right hand is now healed. Now whole. Now healthy in every way."

Closing my eyes, I saw a vision of my right hand in perfect shape, looking like a beautiful whole hand, healed and wonderful. I breathed Light down into my left hand, and then I put my left hand down into the pitcherful of cold water. Holding my left hand over my right hand, I saw a stream of Light beginning to flow from my heart, down my left arm, flowing into the palm of my left hand. Again and again, I took in my breath and then slowly exhaled as the Light streamed from the palm of my left hand and flowed all around and all over my scalded right hand.

Over and over again, I silently repeated my prayer of thanks that my hand was now healed.

After a little while, the water in the pitcher got warmer, and my right hand began to feel uncomfortable, so I got up and went out into the kitchen and turned on the cold water tap. I ran more cold water over my right hand, filling the gray plastic pitcher until it overflowed. Then I returned to the chair in the living room, and again I sat down. I breathed more Light into my left hand. The Light flowed from my left hand into my right hand as I visualized my right hand healing rapidly.

I kept on breathing and praying and chanting and visualizing. After about twenty minutes, something in me seemed to click. I got up from the chair and went into the kitchen. I put my right hand under fresh water from the cold water tap as I prayed and visualized. Then I turned off the kitchen faucet.

Holding my right hand up, I looked at it carefully, turning it back and forth, first the palm, and then the back of my hand. There was no pain. And I couldn't see any burn or redness on the hand.

I walked out into the living room, and I held my hand up in the sunlight coming in through the small window. "There's no redness on my hand." I spoke out loud, startling myself.

I walked to the front door, and I went outside and sat down on the front step, feeling lightheaded and dizzy. I held my hand up in the sunlight, and it looked perfectly normal.

I couldn't believe what I was seeing. I put my hand right up in front of my face, so close that my nose almost touched it, and I went over my right hand and fingers millimeter by millimeter, looking for some evidence of a burn. But there was no burn. There was nothing at all.

Finally, I looked closely at the webbing between my right thumb and forefinger. And there I saw two tiny blisters, the size of pinheads, on the delicate skin. And that was all there was.

A few minutes later, I got up to go for a walk to clear my spinning head. As I walked I kept looking down at my burn-free, pain-free right hand. Even the pinhead blisters were gone. There was no sign that I had ever had a burn at all. No pain, no redness, no blistering, no burning sensation. Just nothing. Nothing at all.

I walked down the sidewalk in a trance of disbelief. I kept looking at my hand, unable to believe what I saw. Or rather what I wasn't seeing.

A few people on the street began looking at me in a peculiar way. I suddenly realized I was holding my right hand up to stare at it, and I was staggering like a drunk. Back and forth my feet wove, making my perambulation a thing of curiosity for bystanders.

By the time I had circled the block and gotten back to the apartment, I was laughing out loud. I sat out on the front step for what must have been an hour, staring at my hand, letting the miracle of healing soak into my consciousness. Fortunately, all the neighbors were at work, or I might have had to answer some interesting questions.

As the day and then the week wore on, my hand showed no signs at all of ever having been burned by a whole panful of boiling water. I had a perfectly healthy right hand, and that just couldn't be true. But there it was.

✲ ✲ ✲

A few days later, I flew to Albuquerque and I took the shuttle from the Albuquerque airport on up to Santa Fe. As the shuttle reached the top of La Bajada hill, I saw the familiar Sangre de Cristo mountains. But I did not feel the sense of coming home that I had always felt whenever I saw the Santa Fe mountains come into view. It dawned on me that I had no family left in Santa Fe. There was no one in all of New Mexico for me to make a phone call to and say to them, I'm home.

A sense of knife-blade loss cut through the air between me and the small adobe buildings clustered at the foot of the horse's head mountain. I realized that all the roots that had anchored the soles of my feet to New Mexico earth were now shriveling up.

But that just couldn't be true. I was tired from my trip. That was all.

CHAPTER 68

On the day of my forty-seventh birthday, I got up well before dawn. I got dressed, and I drove to Pecos. The sun was rising as I came down the hill and drove on past the Casanova building, driving slowly by the Wyner home with its river rock walls and the Forest Service Station with its white homes and its offices and its green lawns and great trees.

I drove past what had once been our horse pasture, where Mairsy Doats and Pronto had grazed on the grama grass that grew in dry gray-green clumps. Heads down, they had swished their tails endlessly to keep the summer horseflies off their backs.

I drove on out of town, past the Pecos Monument, and I turned onto the Las Vegas highway. And then I turned onto a side road and drove past the adobe houses of Rowe. A mile or two later, I came to an unnamed dirt road. I turned onto that road, and my Datsun ground its way up to the top of the Glorieta Mesa.

I took the two track turnoff that went out to the cliff edge of the mesa. And there I parked Mother's Datsun in the center of a clump of piñon, juniper, and scrub cedar trees.

I picked up my writing notebook and some pens, and I got out and walked to the edge of the mesa. For one moment I looked out over the river valley. Then I sat down, and I started to write.

Back in 1976 I had a home and a career as a third grade teacher with the Albuquerque Public School system. Arnold was a senior in high school, and Philip was a sophomore. My father was slowly becoming disabled, and Mother was taking care of him.

By the spring of 1978, Arnold was in college, and Philip had graduated and joined the navy. In June of 1979, I left teaching. My father died six months later in January of 1980.

My mother and I were given a year to grieve for Daddy. Then I had to set my grieving to one side to take care of Mother until she left this earth.

I gazed out over the mesa view of the Pecos Valley, lost in memories. Looking back, I realized that my entire adult life had been spent doing for others. Teaching. Raising kids. Taking care of my mother. During those years I had grown into a woman who was capable of taking care of everyone around her. But I could not even remember what it was like to take care of myself.

A snapping sound, sharp as a rifle shot, echoed through the clear air of the mesa, startling me and making me jump. Turning my head, I saw a twelve-foot juniper tree, a ragged and dusty evergreen, trembling and shaking. One broken branch flopped down over the edge of the mesa cliff. Only bark and splinters attached the shattered branch to the juniper tree as it swayed back and forth in the still air.

I looked up, and I saw a huge eagle with a creamy underbelly. His twelve-foot wings flared out against the pale winter sky. I could see tiny notches edging the pinions of those huge wings and the outspread tail feathers. And tucked against the underside of the eagle's belly were two great talons.

I listened to the "whup-whup" of the eagle's wings as they beat up and down, sounding their counterpoint to the timeless silence of the mesa. Powerful wing strokes carried the eagle away from the mesa's edge. Then, like a master pilot, Eagle tilted his wings so that he lost a few feet of altitude.

Eagle stabilized himself so that he and I were exactly at eye level, me seated next to the sheer thousand foot drop of the mesa cliff, and Eagle less than fifty feet away from me, hovering in the air in profile. And there he floated with his wing feathers shivering and trembling, attuned to every small current of the gentle moving air. Great tail pinions balanced each small trembling movement of the outspread wings.

Only the crystalline winter air kept Eagle from being dashed to the rocky ground more than a thousand feet below. I had a sense of being out of my body, even disembodied from my own breath, which kept jerking in and out in quick, shallow gasps.

I stared at the great bird as he hung profiled in front of me, gathering in the pale winter sunlight so that streams of golden iridescence flashed over his brown feathers. This must be a golden eagle, I thought. Nothing else could have that coloring, no other bird could be that large. But I had never heard of golden eagles living on the Glorieta Mesa. How could such a large bird survive up here, especially during the winter months?

With an effort of will, I pulled myself back into my body and silenced my gasps. My spirit quietened as I accepted being in the presence of pure wildness. I sat there, frozen into stillness, not blinking, not even breathing. One small movement might startle that beautiful wild creature, and he would be gone. The glare from Eagle's dark eye lanced through me like sun-fire. His fierce orders unfolded in my awareness. Take courage! Lift yourself up!

Over many thousands of years, Indians from the Pueblos of the Pecos Valley must have climbed this mesa on foot, climbing up to this sacred space of the gods to hold their ceremonies. I wondered if they had come to dance up here, high on the mesa, to dance in the company of great golden eagles like this one.

I had a flash of remembrance, of the long-ago Eagle Dancer, Tony White Cloud, dancing at the Pecos Pueblo, way back in 1947. I remembered the eagle dancer's body silhouetted against the large campfire. Nearby were the crumbling walls of the old adobe church, a black shape against the dark starry sky. I remembered the dancer's moccasins thudding down on the adobe earth as the drummer struck his drum.

I remembered watching the eagle dancer's arms outstretched with black and white eagle feathers trembling in the firelight; I remembered the eagle dancer dancing under the diamond brilliance of the Milky Way stars; I remembered him dancing for all the ancient ones who lay buried in shallow graves in the hard and rocky ground of the ancient Pecos Pueblo.

Suddenly, Golden Eagle banked and turned away from me, away from the mesa, soaring off into the distance, leaving only his piercing cry behind him.

CHAPTER 69

The following summer, I went to Austria to attend a six-week seminar for opera singers.

My guilt was overwhelming. I knew I was overspending. But I could not stop myself. I had to go. I had to find out if I could have a career as a singer. I had to find out if I was good enough.

I flew into Graz on a warm clear day. I took a taxi to the students' quarters at the *studentenheim,* and I checked in. Then I went to my tiny room and started unpacking my suitcase.

Just as I was hanging my jeans in the miniature closet, I heard my mother's voice coming through the ethers, loud and clear. "What do you think you're doing in this horrible place! There are Nazis here! We fought a war with those butchers, and now they're all around you! You just turn yourself around, young lady, and you get yourself right back home to the good old USA!"

What kind of insanity is this, I thought. These are the eighties. World War II is ancient history. These days the dangers are the terrorists that are running around Europe. And we've also got radioactive breezes blowing in from the fresh meltdown in Chernobyl, which I guess is right over the hill from Graz. So what is there to worry about? All that can happen is I'll be blown up by terrorists. Or else I'll turn green and start glowing in the dark.

"I'll fix you so you can't sing one note if you stay in this dreadful place," my mother threatened.

And one day later, I had one of the worst cases of bronchitis that I had ever had. When it came time for me to sing my audition piece before the voice faculty, I had to croak my way through Rossini's aria, "Una Voce Poco Fa."

By then I was good and mad at my mother. Sainted or not, in heaven or not, she was interfering in my life. Hadn't I done enough for her? Taking care of her, day and night, for three solid years? And here she was, just as full of Irish pushiness as ever she had been. Why couldn't Mother just fly away to Heaven, like any good Presbyterian lady should. And stay there!

There was a simmering silence from the heavenly realms after I'd handed Mother that thought. But I didn't care. Here I was in Austria, with opera singers all around me, and I was going to make the most of it. As for my mother, I snapped at the ethers, my mother can go straight to Hartford, Herrington, and Hampshire. That's right, I told my mother. Just see if I grieve for you anymore.

Defiantly, I began working with Barbara, my voice teacher at AIMS. We started work on Mozart's "Ach Ich Fühl's," Pamina's aria from *The Magic Flute.*

And right away I got a lecture on stage deportment. "What's with the eyebrows?" Barbara said one afternoon. "They wiggle up and down with every note. Stop that."

So I watched myself in a small mirror as I vocalized, trying keep my eyebrows under control. And I worked and I memorized, just as I had done for so many years.

One day the woman who ran the seminar called me into her office. I had signed up to audition for the agents who were coming to hear the singers. "We're not putting you on the audition list," she told me. "You're in your forties, and you're too old to start a singing career. You can go home and maybe sing for a few small local companies."

I walked out of that office, devastated. All those years of dreams and hopes and hard work were left behind me, shards of glass on that office floor.

When she heard about what had happened, Barbara told me, "Don't worry about her. There's plenty you can do with your voice."

But I only began to regain my confidence when I sang for a famous German baritone. As I sang the Mad Scene from *Lucia di Lammermoor,* he got very excited. He started walking around the studio where we were working, giving me directions, lifting his eyebrows as I sang the final high E-flat.

At the end of the voice session, the German baritone looked at me in astonishment and said, "Where did you learn to sing?"

I answered, "I study with a teacher in Albuquerque, New Mexico."

The famous baritone just stood there, looking at me, and he shook his head.

✡ ✡ ✡

A few weeks later, another one of the AIMS voice teachers and an accompanist and I were riding on the *strassenbahn,* one of the local streetcars. A little gray-haired grandmother sitting behind us spent a good ten minutes or more spouting German to the instructor.

As we got off the streetcar, my friend and I asked the instructor, "What was that lady talking about?"

He gave a sigh. "Oh, the usual Nazi propaganda," he said. "World War Two was started by Jews wanting to make money, Hitler was a sweetheart, and none of the concentration camps ever existed."

Oh heavens, I thought. Mother was right on the money. There really are Nazis here in Austria. It was a chilling thought.

✡ ✡ ✡

Life would get even chillier when I returned to Santa Fe and realized that I was rapidly running out of money. All my worst nightmares were coming true. I was all alone, I was almost flat broke, and I had no idea where my life was heading. The workings of all my internal gyroscopes came screeching to a halt as the remains of my fragile world came crashing down all around me. I was totally directionless.

✲ ✲ ✲

Fear—terror, really—is an odd thing. It feels like floating. Like there are no connections to the cold life of Earth. Like the world with all its pain is being held at bay. The underlying dark dread, the anxieties, the fears all rising up from the darkness below have, for the moment, no reality.

The day I left Santa Fe was a warm and pleasant day, but I was bitterly cold inside. I had given Mother's two cocker spaniels away to what I hoped were good homes for them. My belongings had almost all been sold or else given to the Salvation Army. All that I had left was what I had in the back of my inherited Datsun hatchback. My favorite books. A dozen or so LPs of opera singers. My clothes. My Apple Macintosh with its noisy printer.

I wasn't sure if anyone in Santa Fe knew that I was leaving. But what did it matter. No one was there for me. No parents. No family. My New Mexico roots had shrunk until they were as dead as dried twigs. I drove through Albuquerque, but I did not stop there. I headed west, on to Gallup, where I stopped briefly for gas and lunch.

I reached the city of Phoenix after dark. I knew I could not stop at a motel. I didn't have a credit card on me. I had paid it off and cut it up before I left Santa Fe. Now I had only enough money left to buy gas and eat. I drove on through the city, and I left it behind.

I kept on driving until I was so groggy I was afraid I might not be able to drive safely. So I pulled well off the freeway and parked the car under a few desert trees, the kind that look almost dead until you are close enough to see tiny leaves peeping from twigs and branches. I didn't move from behind the steering wheel. I just put my head back on the headrest and I fell asleep, praying that I was invisible. That nothing and no one would disturb me.

When I awoke, the sun was well up. I started the car, and I pulled back onto the freeway. The only stop I made was to fill the gas tank and grab a bite to eat.

That day I drove endless miles of Arizona and California desert highways, through Needles and Barstow, coming down into the hills and valleys east of Los Angeles. How dreary that dry scenery looked compared to the pine-covered mountains of Santa Fe and Pecos.

At last I came to a small apartment house on a noisy semi-residential street. I turned into the driveway and drove around to the back of Arnold's apartment. I parked my Datsun behind his Honda hatchback, and I got out of my car. Arnold's back door was unlocked. I opened it and I walked into the kitchen, and I went into the front room where a startled Arnold looked up from his Mac.

It was New Year's Day of 1987. Utterly defeated, I looked at my twenty-nine-year-old son and I said, "I'm so sorry. I've lost all my parents' money. I don't have anywhere else to go."

Arnold's face paled as he began to absorb what I had said. But he said nothing to me. Not one word of blame or anger. But that didn't help me. I knew I was failing my son. From this moment on, I would be nothing but a liability to my son Arnold.

Over the next few weeks, I was overcome with rage and pain and shame and guilt. I should have been able to do better, I thought. Why was it I could manage so much, but I could not manage my own money? How could I have been so irresponsible? Of course, the Reagan economic crash hadn't helped matters any.

I started having migraines, one after the next. I spent day after day in bed with a towel over my face to shut out the light that was like knives striking my eyes. And my back kept spasming until I could hardly walk.

I prayed, but no answers came. Instead, a foreboding blackness, unending and threatening, clouded my mind. The guidance I had always counted on was no longer there. I had been deserted, even by God.

Lying there with the pain of the migraines slamming through my head, I remembered something the astrologer Alan Oken had once said. "Venus is the closest planet to the Sun, which is the physical representation of the light of God. Venus is also the planet of love and of money. So if you want to know where you stand with God, just take a good look at your relationships and your bank account."

By that measure, I was definitely not one of God's favored children. I was dead broke, and I was utterly dependent on another person, which was where I had been all my life except for the eleven years when I was a teacher.

I spiraled down into an unending, self-hating depression. I was not mature. I was not able to cope. I had tried my best, but it was not good enough. I was not good enough. I couldn't even support myself. I was worthless.

Why should I be in this world at all? I was doing no one any good, I said to myself. I would be much better off dead than living like this. And Arnold would certainly be better off without having his mother draped around his neck like a half dead albatross. In the dark of night, I went spiraling down, sucked into an ever deeper black night of the soul.

CHAPTER 70

A year later, I was back on my feet, physically if not emotionally. In spite of all my self inflicted unworthiness, I was still alive and able to get myself dressed on most mornings. The black space that floated right in front of me had become a variable, overwhelming on some days, manageable on others.

One day I was eating lunch in a restaurant that specialized in pancakes. I struck up a conversation with the hostess, a petite and slender young woman. It was a slow time of day, so she came over on her break and sat down at my table, and we talked.

Her name was Sarah, and her face was the face of an elfin spirit, with a long fall of curly brown hair. Her blue eyes shone as we talked. Sarah told me she was an actor and that she did extra work on movie and television sets.

That broke through my shyness. I told Sarah that I had started writing a play, and I said, "I'm keeping it simple. It's one actor playing Mozart, and then there's me and an accompanist. Maybe I can take the show to college campuses. Something like that."

Sarah's eyes widened as she looked at me. "Oh no, honey," she said. "You can't do all that as a monologue for just one actor. You've got to give more actors a chance to work. You've got to write dialogue."

My mouth fell open. Then in my grass-green naiveté, I said, "Well, okay. Maybe I can write some dialogue. That's just a couple of people talking to each other. How hard can it be?"

Sarah smiled and reached across the table and patted my hand. "If you're going to be writing for actors," she said, "You're going to have to find a way to watch actors work." She gave me an infectious grin. "I tell you what, I'll give you the phone number for my agent for extra work. That way you can get on the sets, and you can watch the actors up close. Plus, you'll be making a little bit of money. About twenty-five or thirty dollars a day. And they'll feed you lunch and maybe dinner if it's a long day. But if you want healthy snacks, you'd better take them with you."

I wasn't at all sure about going in front of the cameras, but then I figured why not. I didn't have a thing to lose. And I sure didn't have any money coming in, and even a teensy bit of income was better than nothing.

The next thing I knew, I had a call come in one evening. My brand new agent said, "I have an assignment for you."

I grabbed a scratchpad and pen and wrote really fast.

"You'll be at the Veterans of Foreign Wars building in downtown Los Angeles. This is a TV movie, and it's a courtroom scene. You will be sitting in that courtroom all day, so bring at least two outfits that are right for the scene."

I had spent several days scrounging through thrift shops, putting together a small wardrobe of clothes to wear on the sets. And that evening, I packed my one and only suitcase so full of second-hand clothes I could barely haul it around.

The following morning I got up when it was still dark outside, and I took a quick shower. I fixed my hair, and I put on makeup, which I hated. I almost never wore foundation or eye shadow or penciled eyebrows.

Then I lugged my suitcase and my sack of healthy lunch and snacks out to my car, and I left before Arnold got up. By seven o'clock sharp, I was in line with about twenty-five or thirty extras to get signed in for the day's work.

After checking in, all us extras were all herded into what looked like a Masonic Lodge room, with fold down wooden chairs on both sides of the room, and some metal chairs and card tables set up around the open floor.

A young man in his twenties, with a bill cap on his head, came in and said in a loud voice, "All right, people. Listen up. You're going to be here for a couple of hours before we call you, so make yourselves comfortable. We'll be filming in the room right next door to this one, so do not talk. We'll call you when we need you." He turned abruptly and left the room.

That was my first introduction to Hollywood manners. I turned to the man sitting next to me, and I whispered, "Who was that?"

The blasé gentleman gave me a bored look and said, "He's the AD."

"The what?"

The man gave me another patronizing glance and said, "The assistant director."

"Oh." Something else I didn't know anything about.

As the door closed behind the young assistant director, the roomful of people began clustering in small groups. Some played silent card games. One woman got out knitting needles and brightly colored yarn and began busily knitting a sweater. A few people ate food from some lunch bags they'd brought with them. Others closed their eyes and napped.

I was thankful I had brought a book with me. As the room settled into what looked like a routine, I began to read about Mozart.

It was almost eleven o'clock when the AD came in and disturbed the charming hush with a loud announcement. "All right, people. We'll need ten of you for the jury, and the rest of you in spectator's seats. I want you all to line up by twos and follow me."

We all walked into the room next door where the filming was taking place, and we sat down. I looked around in amazement. There was a judge's bench at one end of the room, flanked by a jury box. And sitting at one of the lawyer's tables was Raquel Welch, who turned around and gave the extras one long look.

All around the back of the room were several large cameras. And there were huge lights everywhere. And off to one side was a sound man sitting and twiddling dials.

Right in front of the judge's bench was an actor dressed in a lawyer's suit. As I looked over at him, the actor turned his back on the judge and flipped up the back of his suit jacket and gave the judge a moon. Everyone in the courtroom broke into laughter, including the judge.

Then the director took a moment to speak with us. "You're spectators," he said to us. "Local townspeople who are supporting the mother of a high school teenager. She has sued a teacher who has been telling her daughter and the other children in the classroom that the history of Hitler's concentration camps was a lie."

"So remember, folks," added the busy AD, "We want lots of good energies from you."

I wondered what on earth kind of good energies that AD was talking about. After some thought, I decided I needed to look very serious and pay close attention to everything the actors said and did.

Great banks of lights went on, bathing us all in color-bleaching brightness. And the director said, "Action."

As the actors began speaking their lines, I sat there in the middle of twenty-some extras, doing my level best to generate good energies. Finally the director said, "Cut." And immediately the lights were doused, and we moved around a little in our seats to relax.

After more takes we broke for lunch, and after lunch more courtroom scenes were filmed, clear on up through dinnertime. The actors and the crew got pizza, I noticed, while the extras got nothing at all. I nibbled a bit on the remains of some sandwiches that I'd brought in my sack lunch.

By the time we were released and given our pink slips by the AD, it was almost ten o'clock at night, and I was dizzy with exhaustion and low blood sugar. I drove home in the dark, and I told my son, "This has been one of the most peculiar days I've ever lived through."

CHAPTER 71

One day, when I had a day off at home, I began to see a vision of immense golden Light pyramids descending all around the Kremlin in Moscow, each pyramid greater than the last, each one settling down upon the smaller pyramid beneath it until smaller pyramids were enfolded within larger pyramids like nested Chinese dolls. And as each pyramid descended, rays of Light would spill down over the immense buildings of the Kremlin.

Then I saw, located directly below the Kremlin, vast caverns with enormous crystal stalactites and stalagmites. As the pyramids and the Light spilled down from above, answering bursts of Light came up from the caverns beneath, until the entire Kremlin complex was bathed in crystals, pyramids, and Light.

Then an immense Niagara of Light came rushing toward the Kremlin from all around the world. Within that Light was every prayer for peace that had been ever been spoken, felt, or prayed for by any person from any religion around the world since the end of World War II, more than forty years before.

All of that Light, from above and below, and from all around the world converged on those great stone buildings until that huge complex collapsed into a pile of stones on the ground. The great cavern beneath the Kremlin opened up as the Light kept cascading down. Then with a roar, the Kremlin fell down into the huge cavern, and it was gone.

Stunned, I asked my guides, “What was that all about?”

And they replied, "This is the power of prayer operating to change world history."

I looked over at the empty space that the Kremlin had occupied, and I could not comprehend what they were talking about. I looked up at the angels. "I don't understand."

"Watch and wait," was all the guides would say to me.

I thought about that vision until it gradually receded into the background. And as one busy day succeeded the next, I forgot about it. It was not that I did not recognize the importance of what I was seeing. I did understand that these were powerful visions about what was happening down here on earth. But I had no framework in which to place those visions.

And beyond that, I didn't know what I was supposed to do with all this information that I kept getting. I wrote a lot of it down on yellow legal pads. But those tended to get buried under books, music, miscellaneous files, and just plain stuff. Eventually, one or another of those ratty-looking stacks would be boxed up or thrown away, and the writings on visions that had somehow landed at the bottom of one or another of those piles would get tossed out.

I was just as relieved as not when I cleaned house on those scribbled notepads. Whenever I read them, the power in those hastily noted words resonated in me too deeply for comfort.

But when I say I forgot about them, I didn't. Not really. I just pushed them to one side, thinking that someday I would get around to cleaning out my head, along with my files.

✡ ✡ ✡

A few weeks after my first introduction to Hollywood and show business, I got a call for *Jake and the Fatman.* And the day after that, I found myself in Hermosa Beach holding six blue and white balloons on strings, standing up to my ankles in white sand.

Right in back of me were two young actors in their early twenties. To our right was some kind of cement structure with a door in the middle of it. And off to the left was a camera behind a short length of chain link fence.

When the director called, "Action," the two young actors and I started walking toward the door of the cement structure. We were looking for my husband and their father, who was going to be coming out the door of what was supposed to be a prison. When I saw the actor that played my husband, I said to the two young balloon carrying extras with me, "Oh, there he is."

A few weeks later, I was at home, watching *Jake and the Fatman*, and for the first time I saw myself on national television. And I heard myself say that one improvised line that I had absolutely no business speaking. I was so inexperienced I hadn't realized that the microphone was picking up everything I said.

By the time the episode was re-run, somebody had realized there was a line in there that had never been written into the script, and my big scene had definitely been cut.

Throughout the next year, I would get a call from my agent once or twice a week. And the following morning I would put on more makeup than I ever wore, assemble my ragtag working clothes, and head on out to some godforsaken place for another day's work.

Extra work, I found, was an awful lot like people say the army is. Hurry up and wait. Most of the days and evenings were sheer boredom for me, broken by the few moments that the other extras and I spent walking back and forth, providing background as the actors spoke their lines.

I soon learned to catnap on the sets. In fact, I often slept more than I worked. I snoozed my way through a second gig on *Jake and the Fatman*. I snored through days of working on television movies. And along with myriad other extras, I caught a few z's on sitcoms that were filmed before more-or-less live audiences.

One day I was on the set of *Caddyshack II*, starring Jackie Mason. The company was filming in the City of Industry, which I thought was a lousy name for a town. But it was a beautiful, balmy day, and we were filming on a great golf course. I walked over to wardrobe to check in, and I saw Robert Stack talking good-humoredly with the wardrobe lady. I also saw Dyan Cannon off to one side, standing alone.

The high point of the day was a moment between shots when the comedian Jackie Mason carried on a rapid-fire exchange with an older, white-haired actor. “Come on,” Jackie was saying to the actor, “You ain’t a Jew. Are you a Jew? You’re no Jew.”

“Sure, I’m a Jew,” said the white-haired actor, reaching for the zipper of his fly. “And I’ve got the circumcision to prove it. Wanta see?” And the actor began unzipping his pants.

Everybody, including Jackie Mason, fell apart. I was the only one in that large group of experienced actors, crew, and extras who had an open mouth, wide eyes, and a bright red face.

CHAPTER 72

After a year of doing extra work, I quit working on the sets. By then I had spent way too many hours vegetating in too many dim and darkened waiting areas. I had begun to feel like my brain cells were starting to flake off. So in 1989, I started working at the Los Angeles Theater Center taking care of child actors and their mothers.

One day I came home from the theater, and the first thing I did was turn on the television set. Then I started to walk out of the room and head into the kitchen to fix myself something to eat. Just as I walked through the door, the television set warmed up. The sound was turned up way too loud, and there were shouting, screaming voices racketing off the walls of our apartment. Muttering to myself, I went back to turn down the sound on the television.

As I walked back through the bedroom door, I saw people on the screen, dancing around on top of a huge cement embankment of some kind. And then a voice came through saying something about the Berlin Wall.

I couldn't understand it. Was this a movie of some kind? But it couldn't be, because Peter Jennings was on camera, talking about the fall of Communism in East Germany. Then I began to realize that those were real people dancing on that television screen. Real German people, real Berliners, all of them dancing, drinking, celebrating the fall of that grimmest of barriers between the eastern European Communist bloc, and the western European democracies.

All through my childhood and my teenage years, I had read terrifying stories of people trying to crash through, get around, and dig under that wall, just to get themselves to freedom. And mostly, they had failed. And they had paid the price. Now I watched as that terrible wall was attacked with chisels, hammers, even pen knives. Whatever people had in their hands.

That's it, I thought. That's what my vision was showing me. I stood there and I watched for what must have been the better part of an hour.

As the days and weeks passed, that peaceful revolution swept through Eastern Europe and on into Russia, and the once mighty Soviet Empire collapsed. The power of the Kremlin, center of the Communist government, and its campaign for world domination had crumbled into dust. And it had all happened just as I had seen in my vision.

For weeks, I walked around in amazement. I had seen this coming. But I was frustrated because I didn't know what to do with all the information I kept getting. I couldn't even talk about it with anyone.

CHAPTER 73

One warm September day, I walked through the great front doors of the Los Angeles Theater Center, into the enormous theater lobby that was lined with white marble walls and marble flooring.

Inside, there was a ticket center, tables for refreshments, and a huge open space where theater attendees could stand around during intermissions, drinking expensive cups of strong coffee.

A grand flight of stairs led up to the mezzanine. And way up above the lobby and the mezzanine, sunlight spilled down from an enormous skylight.

I walked through the all but deserted lobby, into a narrow hall that led to a large, slow, creaky freight elevator that took me down to the women's dressing rooms.

I was taking care of child actors in Arthur Miller's play *The Crucible,* starring David Selby. It was my job to attend rehearsals and to stay backstage with the children and their mothers during performances.

Like all backstage areas, the communal womens dressing rooms were functional and barren, with cement floors and florescent lighting. Narrow shelves were bolted to the walls. Above the shelves were huge mirrors. One tattered and broken down easy chair, refugee from a discarded stage set, took up a dusty corner.

Next to the ladies room was a small room for the hairdressers. In this production of *Crucible* everyone did their own hair and makeup, so nobody ever used the hairdresser's room.

As always, I had come in early. As I waited in the dressing room, I read a book on Mozart until, one by one, the actors began coming in. Soon the echoing underground space was filled with the sounds of talk and laughter, interrupted by noisy toilets flushing in the women's room across the hall. Then Beatrice Manley came into the dressing room.

Beatrice was an older woman with a beautiful face and gray hair, and she played the role of Rebecca Nurse. As always, Beatrice was walking with the aid of her canes. But today her face was creased, and her eyes were filled with tears. Breathing in heavy gasps, she said, "I cannot make that three block walk from the garage where we have to park now. I don't know what I'm going to do. I may have to leave the show."

Beatrice groaned aloud as she sat down on a folding chair. "Right now I'm in so much pain, I don't know if I can go on."

All the actors fell silent. If Beatrice couldn't go on that meant her understudy would have to go on for her. And since the understudy had another role in the play, several actors would have to shuffle roles at the last minute.

Being professionals, of course they would do just that. But all of them stood stock still, looking at each other in shocked silence. And then they all turned to look at Beatrice.

I stood up, and I said to Beatrice, "If you would like, I may be able to help you. I do crystal healings, and I think it might help the pain if you would allow me to do a healing for you."

Beatrice grabbed my wrist and held it tightly. "Can you do that for me?"

I looked into her frightened, pain filled eyes, and I said, "Of course. Let's go into the hairdresser's room where there's a cot you can lie on while I work on you."

All the other actors stared at me as if I had grown a second head. But I paid no attention to their looks as I helped Beatrice to her feet.

With both hands clinging to my right arm, Beatrice hobbled slowly and painfully into the hairdresser's room. Moaning softly, she lay down on the small cot in the corner. A few tears leaked down the creases next to her eyes.

I went back into the silent womens dressing room to get my purse. Without saying a word, I took my big healing crystal out of my purse, and I went back to Beatrice.

"Do I have your permission to do this healing?" I smiled down at Beatrice lying on the cot as I said, "I always ask for permission, just to be sure."

Without a sound, Beatrice nodded her head.

"All right," I said, "I'll ask Divine Light Intelligence to allow this healing to be beneficial for you in every way."

Then, holding my large healing crystal in both hands, I paused for one quiet moment. And when the inner Light came, I began taking deep breaths, building the image of Light.

As the Light around Beatrice and me became more and more brilliant, I took a final breath and I held it for a moment, and then I let it out in a deep sigh. "Thank you," I whispered, as I stood quietly, feeling the connection to the Light.

Standing at Beatrice's head, I breathed the Light down into the crown of my head, and on down into my heart, and then I let the Light flow on down my arms into the palms of my hands. I breathed the Light from my hands into the healing crystal. Gently I touched the crown of Beatrice's head with the point of the large healing crystal, and I inhaled still more Light. I breathed out slowly, seeing that Light flowing from my hands into the crystal, then arcing over from the point of the crystal into Beatrice's crown chakra.

I breathed two or three Light breaths to fill the crown chakra, then moved the healing crystal down to Beatrice's third eye. And I continued on down, filling each of her chakras with Light.

Then I held the image of the Light around Beatrice as I moved my healing crystal down and all around her, moving from head to toe. And I saw Beatrice in that Light, being healed, becoming healthy, whole, and strong.

After about twenty minutes, I took a deep breath and I stepped back. Beatrice lay quietly on the cot with a peaceful look on her face. "That's it," I said to her in a soft, gentle voice. "Your healing is complete. You lie here and rest for a few moments, and when you feel like you're ready to get up, I'll help you walk back to the dressing room."

Beatrice murmured something inaudible as I left her resting and went back into the dressing room.

The understudy said, "How is Beatrice? Will she be able to go on?"

"She's resting for a few moments," I told her. "We'll see how she feels when she gets up."

The actors all looked at each other, then back at me. "Which costumes should we put on?"

I shook my head. "I honestly don't know. Let's wait a few minutes and see."

"We'll start our makeup and our hair," said one of the actors.

I put the crystal back into my purse, and after a few moments, I went into the hairdresser's room where I found Beatrice sitting up on the side of the cot. She had a dazed look in her eyes.

"How are you feeling?" I said to her.

"I think I feel better," Beatrice said in a soft surprised voice. "I'd like to get up now."

I supported Beatrice as she stood up, and she leaned heavily on me as we walked back into the dressing room.

"How are you?" asked her understudy anxiously. "Do you think you can go on?'

Beatrice straightened her body, and her eyes came into clear focus. "I'm fine." Her voice was firm. "I'm going on."

Everyone in the women's dressing room began to breathe sighs of relief. "Let us know what we can do for you."

"I'll be all right," said Beatrice. She walked to her place in front of the large mirrors that lined the dressing room and sat down to put on her makeup.

A short time later, all the actors went up onstage. And I went up to the balcony and sat down to watch the first act of *Crucible.*

I saw Beatrice Manley come onstage, walking with her canes. Her body was straight, and as she said her first lines, her voice was clear and firm. All through that first act, Beatrice carried herself with the dignity and the presence of Rebecca Nurse, the character of conscience in Arthur Miller's play.

Just before the end of the first act, I left to go back down to the dressing room. A few minutes later, the actors came in, all of them jubilant with the way the performance was going.

When Beatrice got off the big, slow freight elevator and walked into the dressing room, she was smiling. Her eyes were bright as she went to her chair and sat down. “I don’t feel any pain at all,” she said to the other actors. “I know I’ll be able to get through this performance.”

That day, Beatrice and all the rest of that amazing cast gave two brilliant performances. Beatrice Manley successfully finished out the run. And the Los Angeles Theater Center production of *Crucible* went on to win several prestigious awards.

CHAPTER 74

A few months after my near death experience, I was sitting on the grass at Brand Park, looking intently at a red rose that I was holding in my hand. I was trying to see if I could remember the exact shape of that rose, and then close my eyes and visualize the rose in my mind. I gazed deeply into the heart of the rose, and I tried to memorize the shape of one small rose petal. Then I closed my eyes and I tried to see that rose petal in my mind's eye. But all I saw was a sort of reddish blur, like a rosey red halo.

I opened my eyes and looked at the petal again, long and hard, and then I closed my eyes and concentrated once more, trying to call up the shape of the petal. More blur. I tried again, and then again, but each time the blur got blurrier.

I kept on trying to visualize the shape of that petal for an hour or more, until I finally gave it up. I'm just not a visual person, I thought. I do much better with sounds and auditory learning.

Late that night I was sitting quietly in my room. I turned off the lamp on the table next to my chair, and I closed my eyes. And I tried to visualize that rose petal one more time. I didn't even see a blur. I gave a deep sigh and I opened my eyes.

And I saw what looked like a whole lot of fireflies, shining like tiny lanterns, about three or four feet in front of me. Those glowing lights were all colors, red, green, purple, bright pink, blue, yellow and orange. They flew around like fireflies circling inside a bottle.

I saw more and more of those brilliant lights flying around in an ever tightening spiral. They began zipping faster and faster until they all blended and morphed into a solid three dimensional figure.

I blinked a few times before I recognized the figure of the Egyptian god Horus. What's he doing here, I thought. Maybe Isis, yes, but Horus?

I stared at that Being and its glowing colors, standing before me. The dark sleek feathers of a falcon's head rested on that three dimensional human body. The body of Horus. I saw a heavy gold collar that encircled his neck and gold armbands on his upper arms. He wore an Egyptian kilt, and on his feet were finely worked leather sandals. His upper body was well muscled, and he had tight abdominal muscles. He looked like he had oil rubbed all over his skin. There was a glow to the entire figure, yet that Light did not light up my dark bedroom. That living being with the falcon head of Horus was a light within itself.

I sat there, looking at that figure in a state of wonderment for what seemed like a long time. Then Horus cocked his head slightly, and it struck me that I was looking at a front view of this three-dimensional Egyptian god. This was unlike the ancient Egyptian paintings and carvings of gods, which were always in profile.

As the figure of Horus slowly faded, I looked down at my hands, and I saw multicolored fireflies swirling in my cupped palms. Those lights shone in pastel shades of the bright colors that I had seen in the Horus figure.

Looking back, I have no idea why Horus revealed himself to me, or why he showed up in my bedroom. I only remember the brilliance of the colors, and the fierceness of the god's falcon eyes.

I do know that there are parallel dimensions enfolding our universe and our world. Physicists only recognize eleven of those dimensions, but surely there are infinite numbers of them. And many of those dimensions are inhabited by intelligent beings. Like Horus and the rest of the Egyptian gods and goddesses.

What I have learned over a lifetime of visionary experiences is that there are those moments when the veils between us and those great dimensions thin out, so that we can behold gods, angels, and loved ones who have passed on. And occasionally they show us things that are inexplicable.

CHAPTER 75

One warm spring afternoon a documentary crew was preparing to film in a large conference room at the top of a twenty story office building. I was standing next to a bank of panoramic picture windows that looked down on shabby commercial buildings that had long since fallen on hard times. I gazed down at the streets where homeless people, drug dealers, and too many hard faced young ones walked the endless gray sidewalks.

For a flash of a moment, I remembered standing at a gravesite in the oldest cemetery in Santa Fe. Some of the gravestones in the older parts of that cemetery dated back before the Civil War. Many of them had barely legible names and some had the pitiful dates of children incised under dimmed and weathered figures of lambs and weeping marble angels.

I was standing at the foot of one of the newer graves, sweating in the sun's heat as I looked down at a simple bronze plaque that held my parents' names and dates. The letters and numbers on the plaque were dimmed by a covering of dry New Mexico dust.

It was fourteen years gone since I had last visited Mother and Daddy's grave. The last time I'd come was shortly before I left Santa Fe in 1987 to make that long and desolate drive to Los Angeles. Back then there were great conifers and green grass, and all the graves were kept trimmed and neat by the members of the Santa Fe Garden Club. But an endless drought had killed all the grass, and dusty evergreens now stood watch over neglected graves in what had become a cemetery of dust.

I knelt and poured a bottle of water over my parents' plaque. Then I dug some Kleenex out of my purse and used it to clean off their names and dates. I laid a red rose on their grave. And I stood there and I remembered.

This was not my parents' original gravesite. Back in 1985, when I had come home from the opera singer's seminar in Graz, Austria, I had visited the original grave, only to find a sodden hole in the ground, roughly covered over with grass.

Not knowing what had happened, I panicked. I went home and made calls, and finally our neighbor, Callie Renfrew, who was president of the Santa Fe Garden Club, told me, "There was this ninety-seven year old lady who knew she was dying, and when she came and saw your parents' grave, she told us that was her grave. She had purchased it many years ago, she said, so that she could rest right next to her husband. And she had all the paperwork to prove it."

"That's impossible," I protested. "Mother bought that grave from the old lady's sister. I don't know what happened to the paperwork. I've looked for it, but I can't find it. It's nowhere in her files."

"Oh my dear, it's all such a mess," Callie said. "The Garden Club has been responsible for the upkeep of that old cemetery for years and years, and it's all been done by volunteers. The lady who kept the cemetery records died not too long ago, and it turned out she'd never put anything down on paper. She just kept the information in her head, and when she died, it all went with her."

I choked back a hot word or two. "Isn't that just like Santa Fe," I said. "So where are my parents' ashes now?"

"We placed them in an empty gravesite close by. It's in a much nicer location. As far as we know, there is no one else that owns the plot where your parents are now lying."

"Good Lord, I hope not," I breathed.

"The ashes were moved with full respect," Callie told me. "I was there, and I personally made certain everything was done properly. Under the circumstances." She paused and said, "Your parents' ashes were treated with the greatest respect."

After a moment's silence, I thanked Callie for her concern and hung up the phone, and I went back out to the cemetery to search for my parents' new grave. When I finally located the grass covered grave with my parents' names on the plaque, I shook my head and I looked up at the blue Santa Fe sky. And then I felt Mother standing just behind my right shoulder.

"Well now," Mother said to me, "I think this new grave looks much nicer than the old one. That old grave was located right by a dirt driveway, and almost half the cars that came into the cemetery drove right over it." Mother looked around and said in a satisfied tone, "This is a much nicer location."

"Do you know what a fright you gave me?" I said to Mother. "I thought your grave had been desecrated. And all you were worried about was moving your final earthly resting place to a nicer spot, like you were rearranging the couch in the living room? Mother! What were you thinking?"

But Mother was already gone. She was probably busy moving the furniture in her and Daddy's home up in heaven. I threw up my hands. There was never any use in arguing with my mother.

The busy sounds of the film crew preparing to shoot the documentary cut through my memories and brought me back into the bank conference room. I turned around and I looked at all the activity.

The conference room itself was bare of everything but a few long tables and several dozen back spraining folding metal chairs. This was where our IANDS group met once a month. The acronym stood for International Association for Near Death Studies, which was a worldwide organization of about a thousand people.

There were right around twenty people at this Los Angeles IANDS meeting, including Nancy, the woman who was supposed to be giving the presentation. Nancy was in shock. There had been a glitch in communications, and she had been given no warning about a film company being there. It was one thing for her to do a presentation before a small group of people. It was quite another to be faced with a film crew, complete with soundman, cameraman, and a very young director. That entire crew looked like they were barely out of their teens, like they shouldn't even be out of film school.

"All right people," the young director said, "Those of you who will be sharing your stories, please sit on the chairs next to the wall. Those who would prefer not to be in the documentary, please sit on the other side.

As people walked to their chairs, I stood beside the windows. I couldn't move. All my long held fears rose up in me, simmering hot, keeping me from moving or speaking. I remembered my mother saying to me, "We don't talk about certain things. People will not understand. It's better to keep quiet. You don't want people thinking you're crazy."

I remembered a professor of psychology saying, "Anyone who believes in the existence of an immortal human soul is either deluded or mentally unstable."

I remembered Stan saying, "I've told your parents you should be put in the mental hospital at Las Vegas."

Now from the very center of my soul, rebellion rose up in me. I was tired of all those people who, as the American philosopher William James said, "believe in no god, and they worship him."

I was tired of living in the pall of fears cast like a black magical spell by the mental health industry, by all those behavioral psychologists who were more than ready to sacrifice the lives of visionaries and NDE'rs of all ages on the altar of their own limited and intolerant materialist reductionist views.

I thought to myself that it was time for me to break my lifelong silences. I walked to one of the chairs facing the camera. I sat down, and a young sound man with a lapel mic in his hand came over to me.

The dark-haired director was saying to us, "This is a documentary that will be included on the DVD of a Twentieth Century Fox feature film entitled *Stay*. Remember folks," the director added, "We're on your side."

"When will the feature film be released?" I asked.

"Sometime next year."

"How long will the documentary be?"

Most of us were thinking twenty, maybe thirty minutes in length. Maybe even longer. Everyone was visibly disappointed when the director said, "This will be a mini-doc. About ten minutes in length."

"Will it come out in theaters?"

"The feature film is being shot for markets in the Far East. Hong Kong. Taiwan. Japan."

"Oh, great," I said. "We'll all have fan clubs in Tokyo and Beijing."

A shaky laugh rippled around the room, then died out as we settled onto the hard metal chairs. A bank of fluorescent lights was switched on, flooding us all with a cold white light. And three hours of filming began.

Reuben Beckham said, "When I recognized that I was someplace in this horrendously black, black place, I tried to yell out, but there was no sound, and as I felt this terror, what I did was, I said, 'God help me. I don't belong here.'"

Peter said, "I've had lucid dreams. This was far more real than any lucid dream."

Nancy had tears in her eyes as she told us, "I was loved. For no reason. I had been so parched." All of us knew that feeling. The love that came from the Light. Being cared about in a way that nothing and no one on earth could give us. And knowing that we would feel homesick for that Light for the rest of our lives.

I said, "I saw a huge flower. And I found myself going into the blackest black. I could see this tiny dot of light. And I heard my mother say, 'Honey, would you like to come up here to be with us?'"

Another woman said, "When I came back from where I had been, I was tired all the time. I asked my guides why I was so exhausted, and they said, 'You have come back from a long way off. Think of this as a great big case of jet lag.'"

After the filming was over, I went home feeling as I always did when I had been in front of the camera. Daffy. A little delirious. With lots of adrenaline pumping through me.

But I didn't expect to hear anything more about the documentary. For one thing, I seriously doubted I would be included in the final cut. Film editing being what it was, I fully expected my story to land on the cutting room floor. And even if I was in the documentary, I'd probably never see it or hear about it, because it was going to be released in the Far East. I hoped the people in Taiwan would get some good out of it.

Months passed, and I got a call from a leader of our IANDS group. "I just wanted you to know the documentary is out," he said to me. "The title of the documentary is *Departing Visions.* And you're featured in it."

"I am?" I said in startled disbelief.

"You and three others, including Reuben. You can get it at Blockbuster."

I put the phone down, and for a moment I just sat there at my desk. Then I got my purse, and I went to Blockbuster. When I got to the store, I found the south wall had a large section of shelves that displayed DVDs of the feature film *Stay.*

I bought a copy, and I brought it home. I sat down and watched the six-and-a-half minute documentary. I thought, people are watching me as I speak about my near death experience. I felt shivers running down my back, especially when I went online and found out that six million copies of the DVD had been sold.

I wondered how all this was going to impact my life. But there were no changes to my life over the succeeding days and weeks. No one who saw me walking down the street had so much as a flicker of recognition in their eyes. No one stared at me when I went shopping for onions and fish at Whole Foods. No one said to me, "I know you. Aren't you in the movies or something?"

Yet I found my lifelong frozen silences starting to melt away, one slow drop at a time, like mountain ice melting under the sun of a Rocky Mountain spring. I began to talk about what it was like to die. I talked about being lifted up out of my body. I talked about being in the center of that Light.

We are valued, I said, and everything we do down here matters. Each one of us is a son or a daughter of God, and we are of infinite value to the Divine. Like the fall of the sparrow, everything we say and do and think matters to God. Every moment of our lives, we are loved and cherished by a Divine Light that shines around each one of us. We all come from Divine Light, and we all return to Divine Light.

I know that when I die, I will go to a wonderful place that I can't even begin to describe. There is no earthly language that can tell what it's really like up there. But I have been there, and I know